Identity in Question

Identity in Question
Anthony Elliott and Paul du Gay

Los Angeles • London • New Delhi • Singapore • Washington DC

First published 2009

SAGE Publications Ltd
1 Oliver's Yard
55 City Road
London EC1Y 1SP

SAGE Publications Inc.
2455 Teller Road
Thousand Oaks, California 91320

SAGE Publications India Pvt Ltd
B 1/I 1 Mohan Cooperative Industrial Area
Mathura Road, New Delhi 110 044
India

SAGE Publications Asia-Pacific Pte Ltd
33 Pekin Street #02-01
Far East Square
Singapore 048763

Library of Congress Control Number: 2008923976

British Library Cataloguing in Publication data

A catalogue record for this book is available from the British Library

ISBN 978–1–4129–2242–5
ISBN 978–1–4129–2243–2 (pbk)

Typeset by C&M Digitals (P) Ltd., Chennai, India
Printed in India at Replika Press Pvt Ltd
Printed on paper from sustainable resources

Contents

Acknowledgements

Identity in Question derives from a conference of the same title held at St. Hugh's College, Oxford, UK on 28-29 June 2005. The Conference was jointly organized by the Centre for Critical Theory (CCT) at the University of the West of England, Bristol and the Center for Citizenship, Identities and Governance (CCIG) at The Open University. We owe considerable thanks to Fiona Watt and Elizabeth Williams at CCT, and Denise Janes at CCIG for their excellent administrative support and help throughout the conference.

We are grateful to the staff at St. Hugh's College for the many ways in which they support the conference and made our work possible over two fabulous summer days. We would also like to thank those academics that gave of their time to join the work of the conference, but for one reason or another are not represented in this collection. In this context, we acknowledge in particular the contributions of Richard Sennett, Lynne Segal, Anthony Moran and Alison Assiter.

We are greatly indebted to Daniel Chaffee, who assisted us with all aspects of the final editing process at Flinders University, Australia. His meticulous attention to detail, interpersonal skills and good humour proved vital in pulling all the chapters together, and in fact his many suggestions have added considerably to the book.

Thanks to our editor at Sage, Julia Hall, who commissioned the text and supported it's progress in so many ways, and to Mila Steele who has helped to guide it to completion. Thanks also to Katie Forythe and Rachel Hendrick at Sage for their sterling work in getting the whole thing fit for purpose! Finally, Anthony would like to thank Nicola Geraghty, along with Caoimbe, Oscar and Niamh. Paul would like to thank Jessica, Ella and Natalya.

Anthony Elliott, Adelaide
Paul du Gay, Oxford

Notes on Editors and Contributors

Lisa Baraitser is Lecturer in Psychosocial Studies at Birkbeck, University of London, and an integrative psychotherapist in independent practice. She writes on the maternal in the fields of psychoanalysis, social theory, feminism and philosophy. She is author of *Maternal Encounters: The Ethics of Interruption* (Routledge).

Zygmunt Bauman is Emeritus Professor of Sociology at the universities of Leeds and Warsaw. His recent books include *Liquid Times* (2007) and *The Art of Life* (2008).

Ulrich Beck is Professor of Sociology at Ludwig-Maximilian University in Munich and at the London School of Economics and Political Science. His recent books include *Cosmopolitan Vision* (2006) and *Power in the Global Age* (2006).

Elizabeth Beck-Gernsheim is Professor of Sociology at the University of Erlangen. She is the author, with Ulrich, Beck, of *The Normal Chaos of Love* (1995).

Drucilla Cornell is Professor of Law, Women's Studies and Political Science at Rutgers University, USA. She is also a Professor at the University of Cape Town, and holds a National Research Foundation Chair in Customary Law, Indigenous Values and the Dignity Jurisprudence. Her most recent book is *Moral Images of Freedom* (2007).

Paul du Gay is Professor of Organizational Behaviour at Warwick University and Adjunct Professor of Organization Studies at Copenhagen Business School. His recent publications include *Organizing Identity* (Sage, 2007) and *Conduct: Sociology and Social Words* (eds. with Liz McFall and Simon Carter, MUP, 2008).

Anthony Elliott is Professor of Sociology at Flinders University, where he has served as Associate Deputy Vice-Chancellor (Research). He is also Visiting Research Chair of Sociology at the Open University. His most recent books are *Concepts of the Self* (2nd edn, Polity Press, 2007) and

Making The Cut: How Cosmetic Surgical Culture is Transforming Our Lives (Reaktion Books, 2008).

Jessica Evans is Senior Lecturer in Sociology and Cultural Studies at The Open University, UK. Among her publications are *Identity in Question* (2000, co-edited with Paul du Gay and Peter Redman) and 'Against Decorum! Jo Spence, a voice on the margins' (2005), in *Jo Spence: Beyond the Perfect Image*, (Barcelona, Museu d'Art Contemporani de Barcelona).

Stephen Frosh is Professor of Psychology in the School of Psychosocial Studies at Birkbeck College, University of London. His most recent books are *Hate and the 'Jewish Science': Anti-Semitism, Nazism and Psychoanalysis* (Palgrave) and the second edition of *For and Against Psychoanalysis* (Routledge).

Charles Lemert is John C. Andrus Professor of Sociology at Wesleyan University, USA. His publications include *Durkheim's Ghosts: Cultural Logics and Social Things* (Cambridge University Press, 2006) and *Thinking the Unthinkable* (Paradigm Press, 2007).

Angela McRobbie is Professor of Communications at Goldsmiths College, University of London.

Jeffrey Prager is Professor of Sociology at UCLA, USA. He is the author of *Presenting the Past* (1998).

Janet Sayers is Professor of Psychoanalytic Psychology at the University of Kent, UK. Her latest book is *Freud's Art* (2007). She is currently completing a biography, provisionally called *Picasso's Freud: The story of Adrian Stokes*.

Editors' Introduction

Anthony Elliott and Paul du Gay

Whilst undoubtedly one of the most central issues in contemporary social science and social theory, the notion of identity has undergone dramatic changes in recent years. The aim of this book is to provide a detailed analysis of those changes, by confronting the impact of – amongst other social forces – globalization, postmodernism, post-structuralism, psychoanalysis and post-feminism upon our identities in an age of widespread social uncertainty and insecurity. The discussions in this volume of how the contemporary age transforms our understanding of identity range across the major traditions of social theory prominent today. The result is a decisive intervention into debates concerning identity, individualism and individualization.

This Introduction seeks to sketch out, in a necessarily provisional manner, the theoretical backdrop for the contributions contained in this book. We begin by situating identity within a broader set of debates over postmodernism and postmodern culture, which until relatively recently have been an essential ingredient of many studies of identity. We then turn to look at some recent alternative accounts which emphasize ideologies of individualism, as well as the emergence of individualization processes, in the constitution of identities today. In the final section, the contribution of psychoanalysis to the analysis of identity is considered and reviewed.

Identity after postmodernism

One of the central theoretical legacies of the final decades of the twentieth century was the current of postmodernism, which has had a tremendous impact in cultural and media studies as well as having significantly influenced social science conceptions of identity. As one of the key buzzwords of recent social thought, there is no need here to retell the narrative of the rise of the postmodern (see Smart, 1993; Bauman, 1997) – although it is, we suggest, worth pausing to reflect briefly on its implications for the analysis of identity. The term 'postmodern identity' is undoubtedly one of the most widely used in much recent social theory, ranging as it does across transformations in subjectivity from information culture to iPods, the crisis of masculinity to mobile phones. Nonetheless, some terminological precision is needed in this context. It is important to distinguish, first of all, the more structural, socio-logical term 'postmodernity' from the aesthetic, more cultural term 'post-modernism'. Whilst postmodernism denotes an aesthetic style or form of culture which takes off in the West, roughly speaking, following the decline of modernism, especially in the fields of popular culture, literature, architecture and the plastic arts, postmodernity means something more specific about changes in everyday life, social relations and the lived textures of identity. Postmodernity, at least in terms of identity, involves the deconstruction and reconstruction of the self as fluid, fragmented, discontinuous, decentred, dispersed, culturally eclectic, hybrid-like. Postmodern identity means life lived in the wake of the collapse of modernist grand narratives of reasons, truth, progress and universal freedom, with a profound recognition that the Enlightenment search for solid foundations and certitude was, ultimately, self-destructive. A streetwise, sceptical culture, postmodernity involves a radically ironic turn (see Rorty, 1989). Rejecting the Enlightenment dream of solid, foundational forms of life and knowledge, individuals in conditions of postmodernity live their lives as a kind of artful fiction. Identity, in the post-traditional world of the postmodern, becomes principally *performative* – depthless, playful, ironic, just a plurality of selves, scripts, discourses and desires (see Elliott, 2004).

For some theorists of the postmodern, these profound social and cultural changes signal the end of modernity altogether. The postmodern, in this view, is the historical unfolding of an epoch *beyond* modernity. However, for other theorists of the postmodern condition, including Zygmunt Bauman, who contributes to this volume, postmodernity should not be conceptually bracketed off from modernity in this fashion. Postmodernity, as Bauman's work makes clear, is not some overarching totality in the same sense as modernity. Rather, the postmodern is perhaps best conceived as a form of reflection or state of mind that rounds back upon the modern itself. In Bauman's influential formulation, 'postmodernity is *modernity minus illusions*' (Bauman, 1990). What this means, essentially, is that fabrications of postmodern identity do not mark a point beyond modernist forms of life and identity, but rather function as reflective engagements and reworkings of some of the core presuppositions that frame personal and social life.

The debate over the postmodern, which focused largely on the eclipse of modernity, raged during the late 1980s and 1990s. During this period, social and cultural analysts of identity drew from the modernity/postmodernity debate to consider afresh major transformations in personal and social life. In social theory and cultural studies in particular, much valuable work was done on the intersections between subjectivity and personal identity on the one hand, and new forms of popular and media culture on the other. In general, this was a period of consolidation for the development of identity studies in the humanities and social sciences. That said, the 1990s, or at least the latter half of them, were a time of mounting criticism of the notion of post-modernity, and by association the critique of postmodern identities. For one thing, the unduly negative side of postmodernity became increasingly palpable and frustrating to many critics. The postmodern culture of 'anything goes' may have seemed liberating and intoxicating to some, but for others it was merely another narrative about 'endings', with little of value to say about the novelty of identity-transformations in the current age. For another, it was increasingly evident to any casual observer of politics and society that modernity was far from over, and that modernist solids, traditions and customary ways of organizing identities continued to inform our social practices.

In Chapter 1, 'Identity in a Globalizing World', the doyen of postmodern sociologists Zygmunt Bauman situates identity in the aftermath of post-modernity. Moving beyond the modernity/postmodernity division, Bauman reflects on the increasingly fractured, fluid, mobile and liquid dimensions of identity strategies available to women and men in these early years of the twenty-first century. As the do-it-yourself biographers of our own identities, people today for Bauman are increasingly caught up in (and subject to) the globality of networks and with that their dependencies – all of which renders identity inconsequential, episodic and brittle. Emphasizing the decentred character of the self in the wider circuit of globalization, Bauman writes of 'the atomization and privatization of life struggles, self-propelling and self-pertuating'.

Identity as an individualized project

The period when postmodernism was pre-eminent in critical social theory displayed one quite curious feature. Postmodernism seemed to mix trans-formations in identity and culture in equal measure. If there was pulsating desire and frenetic depthlessness to postmodern identity, there was also cultural dispersal, discord and disillusionment. In this, postmodernism made a fetish out of difference, thereby underwriting the plural, multiple and frag-mented texture of human experience in an age of intensive computerization and hi-tech. Yet it was ironic that postmodern thought should be so mad with desire for difference, given that its own tendency was to actually total-ize the eclipse of identity. For authors working in a broadly postmodern tra-dition, and certainly for those influenced in some significant way by the premises of post-structuralist social theory, identity appeared largely as an upshot or construct of the linguistic or symbolic systems which help con-stitute it. Identity in social theory had, arguably, always been about repre-sentations and signs; but with postmodernism, even the interior life of the subject became coterminous with the supremacy of the signifier. A variety of concepts were introduced to capture this symbolic determination of the subject, from Foucault's notion of 'technologies of the self' to Baudrillard's account of 'simulacra', or the virtualization of identity. These accounts, in quite different ways, sought to specify the ways that the decentred world of postmodernity extended to the core of experience and everyday life, locking identity into new structures of seduction, securitization, mediatization and virtualization. The political conundrums (and, in time, dead-ends) of postmodernism were that culture in the form of decentred and differential identity seemed increasingly out of step with our rapidly globalizing world – particularly the globalizing forces of media, communications and culture. It seemed difficult, to say the least, to track signs of cultural difference and identity diversity in a world increasingly dominated by the News Corporation, CNN and Yahoo.

As a consequence, new theories of identity emerged. There were, for example, a variety of new theories of individualization – for which identity in the broad sense was conceived as more than a mere 'imposition' from the outside, or 'society'. According to this account, identity is viewed not as an outcome of external linguistic or symbolic systems, but as an open-ended and reflexive process of self-formation. In recent years, social theorists such as Ulrich Beck and Anthony Giddens have developed powerful accounts of such a view. For the Giddens of *Modernity and Self-Identity*, identity today becomes increasing reflexive: self-identity is cast as a self-defining process that depends upon the monitoring of, and reflection upon, psychological and social information about possible trajectories of life. Any such information gleaned about self and world is not simply incidental to experience and everyday life; it is actually constitutive of what people do, who they think they are, and how they 'live' their identities. 'The reflexivity of modern social life', writes Giddens, 'consists in the fact that social practices are constantly examined and reformed in the light of incoming information about those very practices, thus constitutively altering their character'.

Somewhat similar arguments are developed by Beck, as outlined in his contribution to this volume in Chapter 2 – 'Losing the Traditional: Individualization and "Precarious Freedoms"'. Traditional practices, the anchor of premodern societies as well as all early phases of modernization, take on a radically different status in conditions of what Beck calls 'reflexive modernization'. Reflexive or accelerated modernization for Beck means that traditions become less secure or taken for granted, and that consequently the production of identity is something that becomes more and more open to choice, scrutiny, debate and revision. This is an identity process that Beck calls 'individualization'. To live in a detraditionalized world is to live in a society where life is no longer lived as fate or destiny. According to Beck, new demands, opportunities and controls are being placed on people today, such that it is questionable whether collective or system units of meaning and action are socially significant. The rise of reflexive modernization, according to Beck, is the living of lives increasingly decision-dependent and in need of justification, re-elaboration, reworking and, above all, reinvention. As a consequence, problems of self/society cohesion – the integration of individualized individuals into the network of broader social relations – necessarily arise in novel forms at both the micro and macro levels.

The new social theories of individualization have been subject to a barrage of criticisms. Some critics argue that Giddens and Beck's account of DIY self-actualization exhibits a distinctly individualist bent, in a social theory that reduces struggles over power and politics to mere individual negotiations of personal change. Other critics have argued that the thesis of reflexive monitoring of the self clashes with more critical understandings – psychoanalytic, post-structural and post-feminist – of subjectivity in terms of repressed desire, difference or sexual power. In Chapter 3, 'The Global New Individualist Debate', Anthony Elliott and Charles Lemert review these criticisms of the thesis of reflexive individualization, as well as social theories of manipulated individualism (roughly speaking, the Frankfurt School from Adorno to Habermas) and isolated privatism (covering the work of various North American cultural critics). Drawing from recent research conducted by the authors on the changing social and emotional contexts of individualism across Europe, North America and Australasia, Elliott and Lemert contend that there is an emergent 'new individualism' sweeping the globe – one centered on continual self-actualization and instant self-reinvention. Today this is nowhere more evident than in the pressure consumerism puts on us to 'transform' and 'improve' every aspect of ourselves: not just our homes and gardens but our careers, our food, our clothes, our sex lives, our faces, minds and bodies. This reinvention trend occurs all around us, not only in the rise of plastic surgery and the instant identity makeovers of reality TV, but also in compulsive consumerism, speed dating and therapy culture. In a world that places a premium on instant gratification, the desire for immediate results has never been as pervasive or acute. We have become accustomed to emailing others across the planet in seconds, buying flashy consumer goods with the click of a mouse, and drifting in and out of relations with others without long-term commitments. Is it any wonder, Elliott and Lemert ask, that we now have different expectations about life's possibilities and the potential for change?

What are the broader social forces sustaining this new individualism? Elliott and Lemert suggest three key institutional features impinging on people's emotional experiences of globalization: consumerism, neo-liberalism and privatization. In conditions of advanced globalization, people's language for expressing individualism is more and more fixed into the syntax of possession, ownership, control and market value. There is, they suggest, a pathological, blinkered fixation on *instant change* – whether of the body, selfhood or society. This desire for an instant reinvention of the self links to much broader institutional transformations of the world order. For the culture of globalization, as sociologist Richard Sennett has noted, is governed by the logic of acute short-termism. Authors such as Sennett see the flexibility demanded of workers by multinational corporations as demonstrating the reality of globalization, promoting a dominant conception of individuals as dispensable and disposable. But, according to Elliott and Lemert, Sennett fails to critically probe just how far down the global ethos of short-termism penetrates the emotional landscape of the self. For it is precisely the emergence of an ambient fear of disposability – of not measuring up to the craze for reinvention in our personal and intimate life, family and work – that fuels the emergence of 'the new individualism'. This is a form of individualism based on a new cultural imperative for people to be more efficient, faster, leaner, inventive and self-actualizing than they were previously – not sporadically, but day-in day-out. Such an imperative lends to social life a radically experimental quality, with the thrills and spills of the new individualism to the fore. But the emotional costs are also high. Such emotional tribulations are not simply private problems however, as the new individualism is first and foremost a consequence of our world of intensive globalization. In smashing apart traditional national boundaries, globalization, ironically, offers people a kind of 'absolute freedom' to do whatever they like. The irony is that the world of 'everything goes' has become crippling, as the anxiety of choice floats unhinged from both practical and ethical considerations as to what is worth pursuing. For those enticed and seduced by the new individualism, the danger of self-reinvention is a form of change so rapid and so complete that identity becomes disposable. Instead of finding ourselves, we lose ourselves.

In 'Heeding Piedade's Song: Feminism and Sublime Affinity'(Chapter 4), Drucilla Cornell, seeks to highlight the affective dimensions of imaginative re-identification within feminism and the wider social world. She argues that, if feminism is ultimately to concern itself with women as subjects, then there is a deep sense in which feminists should not seek in advance concepts that would limit the imagination in its portrayal of the richness and complexity of that subjectivity. In pursuing her ethical claim that in their struggles to build transnational alliances feminists must at times forsake the drive to rationally 'know' each other, Cornell argues for the importance of the play of the imagination in sublime reflection. Simply put, she represents sublime reflection as a way of enabling feminism to explode what she describes as 'the sedimented meanings we associate with the name woman, and even with the name women'. Through a reading of Toni Morrison's novel *Paradise*, Cornell shows how aesthetic ideas seek to express that which can never be conceptualized, including the ideas of reason themselves. She argues that in Morrison's novel, 'paradise' evokes a number of aesthetic ideas that 'force us towards new insights and visions that defy total comprehension'. Paradise in its most profound sense is itself an aesthetic idea, its promising being more than any notion of it can contain. But it is just such a promise, Cornell suggests, that Morrison evokes as a possible new covenant, a new way of relating to nature and a different, ethically altered humanity.

Identity studies and the new psychoanalysis

Perhaps nowhere has identity been so radically placed in question than in recent theoretical versions of psychoanalysis. For many decades, interest in psychoanalysis throughout the social sciences and humanities amounted to little more than a cross between Freud and Lacan. This was not altogether wholly negative. Arguably, such a conceptual approach to the criss-crossings of desire and discourse did produce some genuinely insightful studies of identity, particularly the analysis of 'identity politics' (see, among others, Frosh, 1991; Hall, 1996). From sociology to cultural studies, psychoanalysis was employed to probe the emotional maps that actors both inherit and refashion to orientate themselves to other individuals and the wider world. In this sense, psychoanalysis functioned to provide a theoretical vocabulary for grasping how social actors, both preconsciously and unconsciously, define themselves and come to identify with others across time and space. In all of this, critical social theory sought to underscore the disruptive powers of the repressed unconscious in the reproduction and transformation of our interpersonal, cultural, sexual, ethnic and racial identifications.

In recent social theory, however, greater analytical attention has been given to the imagined or constructed dimensions of identity constitution. As a result of theoretical developments in post-Lacanian as well as post-Kleinian and related object-relational theories, a contemporary preoccupation with both the representational and affective dimensions of human imagination has moved centre stage in critical social theory.

In Chapter 5, 'Top Girls? Young Women and the Post-Feminist Sexual Contract', Angela McRobbie focuses upon the reconfigurations of femininity which are being stabilised around precisely the sort of work on the self that is characteristic of the 'new individualism'. In particular, for McRobbie, it is young women who find themselves being 'hyper-actively' positioned in relation to a plethora of economic, social and cultural changes of which they are now represented as the privileged subjects. McRobbie seeks to interrogate the claims of this new, post-feminist, 'female individualization', and to investigate what gender values underpin its constituent discourses and practices.

Through a thorough analysis and critique of the sort of 'can do' girlhood envisioned in the British 'New' Labour government's modernising projects, particularly in relation to employment policy, McRobbie shows how the duality of sexual difference is re-confirmed anew, and gender norms are reconsolidated and re-stabilised, within a predominantly commercialized and individualized framework of change, empowerment, freedom, choice and equality. She concludes that the new post-feminist 'sexual contract' on offer to young women can thus be read as a feminist tragedy, what she describes as 'the fall of public woman'.

In 'The Identities of Self-Interest: Performivity, History, Ethics' (Chapter 6), Paul du Gay explores the possibility, seemingly quite foreign to the debates about 'individualization', that different categories and practices of personhood express distinctive ethical comportments, irreducible to common underlying principles. Undertaking a brief historical genealogy of a concept at the heart of the neo-liberal programmes of organizational and personal reform outlined by McRobbie – that of 'self-interest' – du Gay seeks to show how and why self-interested conduct is a multiple not a singular: it does different things in different contexts, not the same thing in each and every context. Indeed, it is put together differently – normatively and technically – in relation to particular 'local' purposes. In contrast to the often a-historic unidimensionalism of contemporary accounts of 'self-interest', including those contained in the 'individualization' thesis, du Gay points to the ways in which early modern conceptions of 'self-interested' conduct were viewed in context as far from selfish and egotistical. Rather than presaging society's ruin, as many contemporary critics would have it, early modern conceptions of 'self-interest', for instance, were aimed precisely as society's salvation, by seeking to offer a mechanism that might help to bring about an end to the ruinous religious civil wars besetting Europe at the time. Rather than interpreting 'self-interest' as intrinsically involving a mean spirited repudiation of the public interest or common good – as the bad other to the good, reflective, deliberative, full human being – du Gay suggests that it is better to look to the particularity of the circumstances, and to the business of descriptions. We might then be able to trace how different forms of self-interested conduct are put together, and thus what they enable the agents they bring into being to 'do' in particular circumstances.

In 'The Constitution of Identity' (Chapter 7), Elliott reviews recent trends in European psychoanalysis – specifically, the theoretical departures of Julia Kristeva, Jean Laplanche and Cornelius Castoriadis – to reframe the question of the imaginative status of identity. Throughout the discussion, he examines the tension between concepts of fantasy and representation on the one hand, and the ideas of creativity, creation and imagination on the other. Among the issues raised are questions about the constitution of representation; the debate in post-Kleinian and post-Lacanian circles over the hypothesis of a proto-fantasy, or instituting representation; and the structuration of representation with reference to primary repression and identification. The current preoccupation with the pre-Oedipal register, and especially the notion of primary repression, is critically appraised, and it is here that Elliott introduces the theorem of *rolling identification* and *representational wrappings of self and other*. This terminological innovation refers in a general way to the study of the imaginary constitution of the subject, linking the psychic origins of the human subject to the foundational force of intersubjectivity and culture.

A related issue in contemporary psychoanalytic approaches to identity stems from the coexistence of imagination and creativity with the complex array of mournful, melancholic and mimetic aspects of subjectivity. In theoretical terms, this was an issue first noted by Freud in his studies of narcissism. In his essay of 1915, 'Mourning and melancholia', Freud reconstructed the connections between love and loss on the one hand, and the limits of identification and identity on the other. The loss of a loved person, he argued, brings with it ambivalence and aggression. Distinguishing between 'normal mourning' and the 'complex of melancholia', Freud considered mourning a normal response to the loss of a loved person. In 'normal mourning', the self incorporates aspects of the other person and then gradually detaches itself from the lost love. By acknowledging the pain of absence, the mourner emotionally draws from the lost love; he or she borrows, as it were, personality traits and feelings associated with the loved person, and in so doing is able to work through these feelings of loss. In the 'complex of melancholia', the individual fails to break from the lost love, keeping hold of the object through identification. Unable to mourn, the melancholic cannot express love and hate directly towards the lost love, and instead denigrates its own ego. Whereas the mourner gradually accepts that the lost love no longer exists, the melancholic engages in denial in order to protect the self from loss.

It now seems increasingly clear that difficulties stemming from mourning and melancholia are not limited to the internal world alone, as if the passions were somehow fully self-contained. Indeed, there are a range of issues – to do with narcissism, mourning, melancholia, denial and displacement – which extend to the core of identity (both individual and collective) and beyond to matters concerning groups, organizations, cultures and nations. In 'Melancholic Identities: Post-traumatic Loss, Memory and Identity Formation' (Chapter 8), Jeffrey Prager traces recent psychoanalytic conceptualizations of mourning and melancholia in terms of the traumatic histories of nations and considers how the survivors of trauma both forget and remember the various horrors of war, terror and genocide. Developing a powerful sociology of mourning, Prager argues that identity and loss are inextricably intertwined. From the AIDS epidemic to the emergence of

International Tribunals of Human Rights, Prager contends that the psychic processes carried within identification, internalization and melancholic identity must be critically confronted in order to avoid endless cycles of traumatic repetition. As he writes, 'Identity, rather than viewed as a kind of eternal reminder of past trauma carried forth into the present, is understood rather as part of a more fluid or mobile self-understanding'.

In Chapter 9, 'Goodbye to Identity?', Stephen Frosh and Lisa Baraister consider the state of subjectivity in the aftermath of post-structuralism and postmodernism as conceived from the standpoint of psychoanalytic theory. Underscoring the psychoanalytic insight that subjectivity is split between consciousness of self and repressed desire, Frosh and Baraitser are nevertheless out to show that the decentring of the subject in contemporary European social theory should be made coterminous with the erasure of identity in social analysis. This important conceptual and political point is explored with reference to a range of contemporary theorists of identity, including Judith Butler, Rosi Braidotti and Jessica Benjamin. Emphasizing the notion of 'Vulnerablity', they focus on the affective and relational unconscious processes that underlie the constructing and reconstructing of identities in the face of enveloping social and political forces in the contemporary age.

In a world of intensive globalization, short-term contracts, ceaseless downsizings and do-it-yourself risk management, the contemporary citizen is constructed as one, astonishingly, able to contain anxiety effortlessly while joining in the difficult work of building and strengthening communities. In Chapter 10 'Cathected Identities', Evans maps the psychodynamics of community activism (in this case, public discourses on sexual offenders) by linking the concept of identity to the psychoanalytic notion of 'cathexis' – the investment of highly charged emotions in something outside and other. Drawing upon the psychoanalytic research of Bion and others on containment, Evans argues that where social conditions are facilitating enough, individuals can maintain basic distinctions between external and internal reality as well as manage pain and fear through emotional toleration. In discussing her case study on reactions and responses to sexual offenders in the UK, Evans argues there was an unhappy fusion between public discourses on sexual offenders and the collective state of mind of a group of protesters who made extreme investments of emotional energy in the idea of the persecutory 'paedophile'. Throughout the discussion Evans demonstrates the ongoing relevance and utility of psychoanalytic theory to grasping political transformations of subjectivity and identity.

Some of the most interesting new cultural ideas surrounding identity have sprung up from psychoanalytic investigations of art. This is not an unusual development within the discourse of psychoanalysis itself since, as Janet Sayers makes evident in her contribution to this volume, a fascination with the aesthetic stretches back to the earliest studies of both Freud and Lacan. The psychoanalytic study of art, or what Sayers terms 'psy-art', underscores the various tensions which are played out at the level of identity in terms of reconciling energy and order, individual and society, creativity and repetition, self and other. In Chapter 11 'Psy-Art: Reimagining Identity', Sayers contrasts the Lacanian account of the formation of the ego with alternative accounts of identity and subjectivity from Freud to the present day. In doing so, she seeks to demonstrate how the art-work might be seen as an allegory for the regeneration of identities in the image of creativity, imagination and the poetic. This is by no means straightforward because, as Sayers suggests, the idea of creativity is itself shot through with ambiguity: psychoanalysis she says 'tells us much more about making our own histories, albeit in circumstances not of our own choosing'.

Identity in Question aims to convey the complexity, contentiousness and significance of current debates over identity in the social sciences and public political life. The book brings together some of the world's leading theorists of identity and its transformations, and the essays collected here represent some of their best work. Mapping the shapes, trajectories and political consequences of identity transformations in a world of intensive globalization is not, however, simply an academic affair. As the contributions to this book make clear, it is also a public and political concern. For as identity moves increasingly to the centre of political life in contemporary societies, so too does discussion and debate over the possibilities for re-imagining in more creative ways how we choose to live, both individually and collectively.

References

Bauman, Z. (1990) *Modernity and Ambivalence*. Cambridge: Polity.
Bauman, Z. (1997) *Postmodernity and its Discontents*. Cambridge: Polity.
Elliott, A. (2004) *Subject to Ourselves* (2nd edn). Boulder, CO: Paradigm.
Frosh, S. (1991) *Identity Crisis*. London: Macmillan.
Hall, S. (1996) 'Who Need Identity?' in S. Hall and P. du Gay (eds), *Questions of Cultural Identity*, London: Sage, pp. 1–17.
Rorty, R. (1989) *Contingency, Irony and Solidarity*. Cambridge: Cambridge University Press.
Smart, B. (1992) *Modern Conditions, Postmodern Controversies*. London: Routledge.

Editor's Introduction

1

Identity in the Globalizing World*

Zygmunt Bauman

'There has been a veritable discursive explosion in recent years around the concept of "identity",' observed Stuart Hall in the introduction to a volume of studies published in 1996. A few years have passed since that observation was made, during which the explosion has triggered an avalanche. No other aspect of contemporary life, it seems, attracts the same amount of attention these days from philosophers, social scientists and psychologists. It is not just that 'identity studies' are fast becoming a thriving industry in their own right; more than that is happening – one may say that 'identity' has now become a prism through which other topical aspects of contemporary life are spotted, grasped and examined. Established issues of social analysis are being rehashed and refurbished to fit the discourse now rotating around the 'identity' axis. For instance, the discussion of justice and equality tends to be conducted in terms of 'recognition', culture is debated in terms of individual, group or categorial difference, creolization and hybridity, while the political process is ever more often theorized around the issues of human rights (that is, the right to a separate identity) and of 'life polities' (that is, identity construction, negotiation and assertion).

I suggest that the spectacular rise of the 'identity discourse' can tell us more about the present-day state of human society than its conceptual and analytical results have told us thus far. And so, rather than composing another 'career report' of contentions and controversies which combine into that discourse, I intend to focus on the tracing of the experiential grounds, and through them the structural roots, of that remarkable shift in intellectual concerns of which the new centrality of the 'identity discourse' is a most salient symptom.

We know from Hegel that the owl of Minerva, the goddess of wisdom, spreads its wings, prudently, at dusk; knowledge, or whatever passes under that name, arrives by the end of the day when the sun has set and things are no longer brightly lit and easily found and handled (long before Hegel coined the tarrying-owl metaphor, Sophocles made clarity of sight into the

*First published in Bauman, *The Individualized Society* (2000). Published here by kind permission of Polity Press.

monopoly of blind Teiresias). Martin Heidegger gave a new twist to Hegel's aphorism in his discussion of the priority of *Zuhandenheit* over *Vorhandenheit* and of the 'catastrophic' origin of the second: good lighting is the true blindness – one does not see what is all-too-visible, one does not note what is 'always there', things are noticed when they disappear or go bust, they must first fall out from the routinely 'given' for the search after their essences to start and the questions about their origin, whereabouts, use or value to be asked. In Arland Ussher's succinct summary, 'The world as world is only revealed to me when things go wrong'. (1955: 80) Or, in Vincent Vycinas's rendition (1969: 36–7), whatever my world consists of is brought to my attention only when it goes missing, or when it suddenly stops behaving as, monotonously, it did before, loses its usefulness or shows itself to be 'unready' for my attempts to use it. It is the awkward and unwieldy, unreliable, resistant and otherwise *frustrating* things that force themselves into our vision, attention and thought.

Let us note that the discovery that things do not keep their shape once and for all and may be different from what they are is an ambiguous experience. Unpredictability breeds anxiety and fear: the world is full of accidents and surprises, one must never let vigilance lapse and should never lay down arms. But the unsteadiness, softness and pliability of things may also trigger ambition and resolve: one can make things better than they are, and need not settle for what there is since no verdict of nature is final, no resistance of reality is unbreakable. One can now dream of a different life – more decent, bearable or enjoyable. And if in addition one has confidence in one's power of thought and in the strength of one's muscles, one can also act on those dreams and perhaps even force them to come true … Alain Peyrefitte (1998: 514–16) has suggested that the remarkable, unprecedented and unique dynamism of our modern capitalist society, all the spectacular advances made by 'Western civilization' over the last two or three centuries, would be unthinkable without such confidence: the triple trust – in oneself, in others, and in the jointly built, durable institutions in which one can confidently inscribe one's long-term plans and actions.

Anxiety and audacity, fear and courage, despair and hope are born together. But the proportion in which they are mixed depends on the resources in one's possession. Owners of foolproof vessels and skilled navigators view the sea as the site of exciting adventure; those condemned to unsound and hazardous dinghies would rather hide behind breakwaters and think of sailing with trepidation. Fears and joys emanating from the instability of things are distributed highly unequally.

Modernity, we may say, specialized in making *zuhanden* things into *vorhanden*. By 'setting the world in motion', it exposed the fragility and unsteadiness of things and threw open the possibility (and the need) of reshaping them. Marx and Engels praised the capitalists, the bourgeois revolutionaries, for 'melting the solids and profaning the sacreds' which had for long centuries cramped human creative powers. Alexis de Tocqueville thought rather that the solids picked for melting in the heat of modernization were already in a state of advanced decomposition and so beyond salvation well before the modern overhaul of nature and society started. Whichever was the case, human nature, once seen as a lasting and not to be revoked legacy of one-off Divine creation, was thrown, together with the rest of Divine creation, into a melting pot. No more was it seen, no more could it be seen, as 'given'. Instead, it turned into a *task*, and a task which every man and woman had no choice but to face up to and perform to the best of their ability. 'Predestination' was replaced with 'life project', fate with vocation – and a 'human nature' into which one was born was replaced with 'identity' which one needs to saw up and make fit.

Philosophers of the Renaissance celebrated the new breathtaking vistas that the 'unfinishedness' of human nature opened up before the resourceful and the bold. 'Men can do all things if they will,' declared Leon Battista Alberti with pride. 'We can become what we will', announced Pico della Mirandola with joy and relish. Ovid's Proteus – who could turn at will from a young man into a lion, a wild boar or a snake, a stone or a tree – and the chameleon, that grandmaster of instant reincarnation, became the paragons of the newly discovered human virtue of self-constitution and self-assertion (see Davies, 1978: 62). A few decades later Jean-Jacques Rousseau would name *perfectibility* as the sole no-choice attribute with which nature had endowed the human race; he would insist that the capacity of self-transformation is the only 'human essence' and the only trait common to us all (see Rousseau, 1986 [1749/1754]: 148). Humans are free to self-create. What they are does not depend on a no-appeal-allowed verdict of Providence, is not a matter of predestination.

Which did not mean necessarily that humans are doomed to float and drift: Proteus may be a symbol of the potency of self-creation, but protean existence is not necessarily the first choice of free human beings. Solids may be melted, but they are melted in order to mould new solids better shaped and better fitted for human happiness than the old ones – but also more solid and so more 'certain' than the old solids managed to be. Melting the solids was to be but the preliminary, site-clearing stage of the modern undertaking to make the world more suitable for human habitation. Designing a new – tough, durable, reliable and trustworthy – setting for human life was to be the second stage, a stage that truly counted since it was to give meaning to the whole enterprise. One order needed to be dismantled so that it could be replaced with another, purpose-built and up to the standards of reason and logic.

As Immanuel Kant insisted, we are all – each one of us – endowed with the faculty of reason, that powerful tool which allows us to compare the options on offer and make our individual choices; but if we use that tool properly, we will all arrive at similar conclusions and will all accept one code of cohabitation which reason tells us is the best. Not all thinkers would be as sanguine as Kant was: not all were sure that each one of us would follow the guidance of reason of our own accord. Perhaps people need to be forced to be free, as Rousseau suspected? Perhaps the newly acquired freedom needs to be used *for* the people rather than *by* people? Perhaps we still need the despots, though ones who are 'enlightened' and so less erratic, more resolute and effective than the despots of yore, to design and fix reason-dictated patterns which would guarantee that people make right and proper uses of their freedom? Both suppositions sounded plausible and both had their enthusiasts, prophets and preachers. The idea of human self-construction and self-assertion carried, as it were, the seeds of democracy mixed with the spores of totalitarianism. The new era of flexible realities and freedom of choice was to be pregnant with unlikely twins: with human rights – but also with what Hannah Arendt called 'total-itarian temptation'.

These comments are on the face of it unrelated to our theme; if I made them here, I did it with the intention of showing that the ostensible unre-latedness is but an illusion, if not a grave mistake. Incompleteness of iden-tity, and particularly the individual responsibility for its completion, are in fact intimately related to all other aspects of the modern condition. However it has been posited in our times and however it presents itself in our reflections, 'identity' is not a 'private matter' and a 'private worry'. That our individuality is socially produced is by now a trivial truth; but the obverse of that truth still needs to be repeated more often: the shape of our sociality, and so of the society we share, depends in its turn on the way in which the task of 'individualization' is framed and responded to.

What the idea of 'individualization' carries is the emancipation of the individual from the ascribed, inherited and inborn determination of his or her social character: a departure rightly seen as a most conspicuous and seminal feature of the modern condition. To put it in a nutshell, 'individu-alization' consists in transforming human 'identity' from a 'given' into a 'task' – and charging the actors with the responsibility for performing that task and for the consequences (also the side-effects) of their performance; in other words, it consists of establishing a '*de jure*' autonomy (though not necessarily a *de facto* one). One's place in society, one's 'social definition', has ceased to be *zuhanden* and has become *vorhanden* instead. One's place in society no longer comes as a (wanted or unwanted) gift. As Jean-Paul Sartre famously put it: it is not enough to be born a bourgeois – one must live one's life as a bourgeois. The same did not need to be said, and could not be said, about the princes, knights, serfs or townsmen of the premodern era.) Needing to *become* what one *is* is the feature of modern living (not of 'modern individualization' – that expression being evidently pleonastic; to speak of individualization and of modernity is to speak of the same social condition). Modernity replaces the *determination* of social standing with a compulsive and obligatory *self*-determination. This, let me repeat, holds for the whole of the modern era: for all periods and for all sectors of society. If this is so – then why has 'the veritable explosion' of concerns with identity occurred in recent years only? What, if anything, happened that was new to affect a problem as old as modernity itself?

Yes, there is something new in the old problem – and this explains the current alarm about the tasks which past generations seemed to handle routinely in a 'matter-of-fact' way. Within the shared predicament of identity-builders there are significant variations setting successive periods of modern history apart from each other. The 'self-identification' task put before men and women once the stiff frames of estates had been broken in the early modern era boiled down to the challenge of living 'true to kind' ('keeping up with the Joneses'): of actively conforming to the established social types and models of conduct, of imitating, following the pattern, 'acculturating', not falling out of step, not deviating from the norm. The falling apart of 'estates' did not set individuals drifting. 'Estates' came to be replaced by 'classes'.

While the estates were a matter of ascription, class membership entailed a large measure of achievement; classes, unlike the estates, had to be 'joined', and the membership had to be continuously renewed, reconfirmed and documented in day-by-day conduct. In other words, the 'disembedded' individuals were prompted and prodded to deploy their new powers and new right to self-determination in the frantic search for 're-embeddedness'. And there was no shortage of 'beds' waiting and ready to accommodate them. Class allocation, though formed and negotiable rather than inherited or simply 'born into' in the way the *estates, Stände* or *états* used to be, tended to become as solid, unalterable and resistant to individual manipulation as the premodern assignment to the estate. Class and gender hung heavily over the individual range of choices; to escape their constraint was not much easier than challenging one's place in the 'divine chain of beings'. If not in theory, then at least for practical intents and purposes, class and gender looked uncannily like 'facts of nature' and the task left to most self-assertive individuals was to 'fit in' into the allocated niche through behaving as its established residents did.

This is, precisely, what distinguished the 'individualization' of yore from the form it has taken now, in our own times of 'liquid' modernity, when not just the individual *placements* in society, but the *places* to which the individuals may gain access and in which they may wish to settle are melting fast and can hardly serve as targets for 'life projects'. This new

5

restlessness and fragility of goals affects us all, unskilled and skilled, uneducated and educated, work-shy and hard-working alike. There is little or nothing we can do to 'bind the future' through following diligently the current standards.

As Daniel Cohen has pointed out, '*Qui débute sa carrière chez Microsoft n'a aucune idée de là où il la terminera. La commencer chez Ford ou Renault s'était au contraire la quasi-certitude de la finir au même endroit*' (1997: 84). It is not just the individuals who are on the move but also the finishing lines of the tracks they run and the running tracks themselves. 'Disembeddedness' is now an experience which is likely to be repeated an unknown number of times in the course of an individual life, since few if any 'beds' for 're-embedding' look solid enough to augur the stability of long occupation. The 'beds' in view look rather like 'musical chairs' of various sizes and styles as well as of changing numbers and mobile positions, forcing men and women to be constantly on the run, promising no rest and none of the satisfaction of 'arriving', none of the comfort of reaching the destination where one can lay down one's arms, relax and stop worrying. There is no prospect of a 'final re-embeddedness' at the end of the road; being on the road has become the permanent way of life of the (now chronically) disembedded individuals.

Writing at the beginning of the twentieth century, Max Weber suggested that 'instrumental rationality' is the main factor regulating human behaviour in the era of modernity – perhaps the only one likely to emerge unscathed from the battle of motivational forces. The matter of ends seemed then to have been settled, and the remaining task of modern men and women was to select the best means to the ends. One could say that uncertainty as to the relative efficiency of means and their availability would be, as long as Weber's proposition held true, the main source of insecurity and anxiety characteristic of modern life. I suggest, though, that whether or not Weber's view was correct at the start of the twentieth century, its truth gradually yet relentlessly evaporated as the century drew to its close. Nowadays, it is not the means that are the prime source of insecurity and anxiety.

The twentieth century excelled in the overproduction of means; means have been produced at a constantly accelerating speed, overtaking the known, let alone acutely felt, needs. Abundant means came to seek the ends which they could serve; it was the turn of the solutions to search desperately for not-yet-articulated problems which they could resolve. On the other hand, though, the ends have become ever more diffuse, scattered and uncertain: the most profuse source of anxiety, the great unknown of men's and women's lives. If you look for a short, sharp yet apt and poignant expression of that new predicament in which people tend to find themselves these days, you could do worse than remember a small ad published recently in the 'jobs sought' column of an English daily: 'Have car, can travel; awaiting propositions'.

And so the 'problem of identity', haunting men and women since the advent of modern times, has changed its shape and content. It used to be the kind of problem which pilgrims confront and struggle to resolve: a problem of 'how to get there?' It is now more like a problem with which the vagabonds, people without fixed addresses and *sans papiers*, struggle daily: 'Where could I, or should I, go? And where will this road I've taken bring me?' The task is no longer to muster enough strength and determination to proceed, through trials and errors, triumphs and defeats, along the beaten track stretching ahead. The task is to pick the least risky turn at the nearest crossroads, to change direction before the road ahead gets impassable or before the road scheme has been redesigned, or before the coveted destination is moved elsewhere or has lost its past glitter. In other words, the quandary tormenting men and women at the turn of the century is not so much how to obtain the identities of their choice and how to have them recognized by people around, but *which* identity to choose and how to keep alert and vigilant so that *another* choice can be made in case the previously chosen identity is withdrawn from the market or stripped of its seductive powers. The main, the most nerve-wracking worry is not how to find a place inside a solid frame of social class or category, and – having found it – how to guard it and avoid eviction; what makes one worry is the suspicion that the hard-won frame will soon be torn apart or melted.

In his by now classic statement of about forty years ago, Erik H. Erikson diagnosed the confusion suffered by the adolescents of that time as 'identity crisis' (a term first coined during the war to describe the condition of some mental patients who 'lost a sense of personal sameness and historical continuity'). 'Identity crisis' in adults, as Erikson put it, is a pathological condition which requires medical intervention; it is also a common yet passing stage in 'normal' personal development, which in all probability will come to its natural end as an adolescent matures. To the question of what the healthy state of a person should be, Erikson answered 'what identity feels like when you become aware of the fact that you do undoubtedly have one': it makes itself felt 'as a subjective sense of an invigorating sameness and continuity' (1974: 17–19).

Either Erikson's opinion has aged, as opinions usually do, or the 'identity crisis' has become today more than a rare condition of mental patients or a passing condition of adolescence: that 'sameness' and 'continuity' are feelings seldom experienced nowadays either by the young or by adults. Furthermore, they are no longer coveted – and if desired, the dream is as a rule contaminated with sinister premonitions and fears. As the two prominent cultural analysts Zbyszko Melosik and Tomasz Szkudlarek have pointed out, it is a curse of all identity construction that 'I lose my freedom, when I reach the goal; I am not myself, when I become somebody' (1998: 89). And in a kaleidoscopic world of reshuffled values, of moving tracks and melting frames, freedom of manoeuvre rises to the rank of the topmost value – indeed, the *meta* value, condition of access to all other values: past, present and above all those yet to come. Rational conduct in such a world demands that the options, as many as possible, are kept open, and gaining an identity which fits too tightly, an identity that once and for all offers 'sameness' and 'continuity', results in the closing of options or forfeiting them in advance. As Christopher Lasch famously observed, the 'identities' sought these days are such as 'can be adopted and discarded like a change of costume'; if they are 'freely chosen', the choice 'no longer implies commitments and consequences' – and so 'the freedom to choose amounts in practice to an abstention from choice' (1979: 29–30), at least, let me add, from a binding choice.

In Grenoble, in December 1997, Pierre Bourdieu spoke of '*précarité*', which '*est aujourd'hui partout*' and '*hante les consciences et les inconscients*'. The fragility of all conceivable points of reference and endemic uncertainty about the future profoundly affect those who have already been hit and all the rest of us who cannot be certain that future blows will pass us by. '*En rendant tout l'avenir incertain*', says Bourdieu, '*la précarité interdit toute anticipation rationnelle et, en particulier, ce minimum de croyance et d'espérance en l'avenir qu'il faut avoir pour se révolter, surtout collectivement, centre le présent, même le plus intolérable. Pour concevoir un projet révolutionnaire, c'est-à-dire une ambition raisonnée de transformer le présent par référence a un avenir projeté, il faut avoir un minimum de prise sur le présent*' (1998: 96–7) – and the grip on the present, the confidence of being in control of one's destiny, is what men and women in our type of society most conspicuously lack. Less and less we hope that by joining forces and standing arm in arm we may force a change in the rules of the game; perhaps the risks which make us afraid and the catastrophes which make us suffer have collective, social origins – but they seem to fall upon each one of us at random, as individual problems, of the kind that could be confronted only individually, and repaired, if at all, only by individual efforts.

There seems to be little point in designing alternative modes of togetherness, in stretching the imagination to visualize a society better serving the cause of freedom and security, in drawing blueprints of socially administered justice, if a collective agency capable of making the words flesh is nowhere in sight. Our dependencies are now truly global, our actions however are, as before, local. The powers which shape the conditions under which we confront our problems are beyond the reach of all the agencies invented by modern democracy in the two centuries of its history; as Manuel Castells put it – real power, the exterritorial global power, flows, but politics, confined now as in the past to the framework of nation-states, stays as before attached to the ground.

A vicious circle, indeed. The fast globalization of the power network seems to conspire and collaborate with a privatized life politics; they stimulate, sustain and reinforce each other. If globalization saps the capacity of established political institutions to act effectively, the massive retreat from the 'body politic' to the narrow concerns of life politics prevents the crystallization of alternative modes of collective action on a par with the globality of the network of dependencies. Everything seems to be in place to make *both* the globalization of life conditions *and* the 'morcellement', the atomization and privatization of life struggles, self-propelling and self-perpetuating. It is against this background that the logic and the endemic illogicality of contemporary 'identity concerns' and the actions they trigger need to be scrutinized and understood.

As Ulrich Beck has pointed out, there are no biographical solutions to systemic contradiction – though it is such solutions that we are pressed or cajoled to discover or invent. There can be no rational response to the rising *précarité* of human conditions so long as such a response is to be confined to the individual's action; the irrationality of possible responses is inescapable, given that the scope of life politics and of the network of forces which determine its conditions are, purely and simply, incomparable and widely disproportionate.

If you cannot, or don't believe you can, do what truly matters, you turn to things which matter less or perhaps not at all, but which you can do or believe you can; and by turning your attention and energy to such things, you may even make them matter – for a time at least ... 'Having no hope', says Christopher Lasch,

> of improving their lives in any of the ways that matter, people have convinced themselves that what matters is psychic self-improvement; getting in touch with their feelings, eating health food, taking lessons in ballet or belly-dancing, immersing themselves in the wisdom of the East, jogging, learning how to 'relate', overcoming the 'fear of pleasure'. Harmless in themselves, these pursuits, elevated to a programme and wrapped in the rhetoric of authenticity and awareness, signify a retreat from politics ... (Lasch, 1979: 23–30).

There is a wide and widening spectrum of 'substitute pastimes', symptomatic of the shift from things that matter but about which nothing can be done to things that matter less or do not matter, but which can be dealt with and handled. Compulsive shopping figures prominently among them. Mikhail Bakhtin's 'carnivals' used to be celebrated inside the home territory where 'routine life' was at other times conducted, and so allowed to lay bare the normally hidden alternatives which daily life contained. Unlike them, the trips to the shopping malls are expeditions to *another world* starkly different from the rest of daily life, to that 'elsewhere' where one can experience briefly that self-confidence and 'authenticity' which one is seeking in vain in routine daily pursuits. Shopping expeditions fill the void left by the travels no longer undertaken by the imagination to an alternative, more secure, humane and just society.

The time-and-effort-consuming activity of putting together, dismantling and rearranging self-identity is another of the 'substitute pastimes'. That activity is, as we have already seen, conducted under conditions of acute insecurity: the targets of action are as precarious as its effects are uncertain. Efforts lead to frustration often enough for the fear of ultimate failure to poison the joy of temporary triumphs. No wonder that to dissolve personal fears in the 'might of numbers', to try to make them inaudible in the hub-bub of a boisterous crowd, is a constant temptation which many a lonely 'identity-builder' finds it difficult to resist. Even stronger is the temptation to pretend that it is the similarity of individual fears that 'makes a commu-nity' and so one can make company out of solitude.

As Eric Hobsbawm recently observed, 'never was the word "community" used more indiscriminately and emptily than in the decades when commu-nities in the sociological sense became hard to find in real life (1994: 428)', 'Men and women look for groups to which they can belong, certainly and forever, in a world in which all else is moving and shifting, in which noth-ing else is certain (1996: 40)'. Jock Young supplies a succinct and poignant gloss: 'Just as community collapses, identity is invented (1999: 164)'. 'Identity' owes the attention it attracts and the passions it begets to being a *surrogate of community*: of that allegedly 'natural home' which is no longer available in the rapidly privatized and individualized, fast globalizing world, and which for that reason can be safely imagined as a cosy shelter of secu-rity and confidence, and as such hotly desired. The paradox, though, is that in order to offer even a modicum of security and so to perform its healing role, identity must belie its origin, must deny being just a surrogate, and best of all needs to conjure up a phantom of the self-same community which it has come to replace. Identity sprouts on the graveyard of communities, but flourishes thanks to its promise to resurrect the dead.

The 'era of identity' is full of sound and fury. The search for identity divides and separates; yet the precariousness of the solitary identity-building prompts the identity-builders to seek pegs on which they can hang together their individually experienced fears and anxieties and perform the exorcism rites in the company of others, similarly afraid and anxious indi-viduals. Whether such 'peg communities' provide what they are hoped to offer – a collective insurance against individually confronted risks – is a moot question; but mounting a barricade in the company of others does supply a momentary respite from loneliness. Effective or not, something has been done, and one can at least console oneself that the blows are not being taken with hands down. As Jonathan Friedman put it, in our globalizing world 'one thing that is not happening is that boundaries are disappearing. Rather, they seem to be erected on every new street corner of every declining neighbourhood of our world (1999: 241)'.

Boundaries are not drawn to fence off and protect already existing identities. As the great Norwegian anthropologist Frederick Earth explained – it is exactly the other way round: the ostensibly shared, 'communal' identities are by-products of feverish boundary-drawing. It is only after the border-posts have been dug in that the myths of their antiquity are spun and the fresh cultural/political origins of identity are carefully covered up by the genesis stories. This stratagem attempts to belie the fact that (to quote Stuart Hall again) what the idea of identity does not signal is a 'stable core of the self, unfolding from the beginning to end through all the vicissitudes of history without change (1996: 3).

Perhaps instead of talking about identities, inherited or acquired, it would be more in keeping with the realities of the globalizing world to speak of *identification*, a never-ending, always incomplete, unfinished and open-ended activity in which we all, by necessity or by choice, are engaged. There is little chance that the tensions, confrontations and conflicts which that activity generates will subside. The frantic search for identity is not a residue of preglobalization times which are not yet fully extirpated but bound to become extinct as the globalization progresses; it is, on the contrary, the side-effect and by-product of the combination of globalizing and individualizing pressures and the tensions they spawn. The identification wars are neither contrary to nor stand in the way of the globalizing tendency: they are a legitimate offspring and natural companion of globalization and, far from arresting it, lubricate its wheels.

References

Bourdieu, P. (1998) 'La précarité est aujourd' hui partout', in *Contrefeux*. Paris: Liber-Raisons d' Agire. (Translated as *Acts of Resistane* (1998), Cambridge, Polity.)

Cohen, D. (1997) *Richesse du monde, pauvretés des nations*. Paris: Flammarion.

Davies, S. (1978) *Renaissance View of Man*. Manchester: Manchester Universtiy Press.

Erikson, E. (1974) *Identity: Youth and Crisis*. London: Faber and Faber.

Friedman, J. (1999) 'The hybridization of roots and the abhorrence of the bush', in M. Featherstone and S. Lash (eds), *Spaces of Culture*. London: Sage.

Hall, S. (1996) 'Who needs "identity"?', in S. Hall and P. du Gay (eds), *Questions of Cultural Identity*. London:Sage.

Hobsbawm, E. (1994) *The Age of Extremes*. London: Michael Joseph.

Hobsbawm, E. (1996) 'The cult of identity politics', *New Left Review*, 217: pp. 38–47.

Lasch, C. (1979) *Culture of Narcissism*. New York: Warner.

Melosik, Z. and Szudlarek, T. (1998) *Kultura, Tozsamosc I Edukacja*. Krakow: Impuls.

Peyrefitte, A. (1998) *La société de confiance. Essai sur les origins du dévelopment*. Paris: Odile Jacob.

Rousseau, J-J (1986 [1749/1754]) *The First and Second Discourses*. New York: Harper and Row.

Ussher, A. (1955) *Journey Through Dread*. New York: Devin-Adair.

Vycinas, V. (1969) *Earth and Gods*. The Hague: Martinus Nojhoff.

Young, J. (1999) *The Exclusive Society*. London: Sage.

2

Losing the Traditional: Individualization and 'Precarious Freedoms'*

Ulrich Beck and Elisabeth Beck-Gernsheim

What does 'individualization of lifestyles' mean?

'Only the day before yesterday, only four years ago, a grand experiment for humanity that had lasted forty years came to an end here.' These words were spoken in Luther's town of Wittenberg by Friedrich Schorlemmer at the end of 1993.

> Seventeen million Germans lived in the walled province in enforced collectivization. A one-party state was seen as the highest form of freedom, individual-ization was damned as subjectivism. A risk-taking approach to the future was rejected in the name of 'scientific' optimism. The 'victors of history' were to set the norms and strive towards a unitary society (the socialist community). Human beings, understood as ceaselessly active communal creatures, were fed on the safe goal of communism, which was guaranteed by scientific laws. People were not allowed to decide anything because there was nothing left to decide, because history had already decided everything 'up there'. But they did not need to decide, either.
>
> Now, in freedom, they may and must decide for themselves; all the existing institutions have collapsed, all the old certainties are gone. The joy of freedom is at the same time a falling into a void. Now let everyone look after himself. What are the rules? Who's in charge? Those who have, and who know how to increase what they have. Seventeen million people have reached this point, but the West's caravan moves on, calling out: 'Come with us. We know the way. We know the goal. We don't know any way. We don't know any goal. What is certain? That everything's uncertain, precarious. Enjoy our lack of ties as freedom.' (Schorlemmer, 1993: 1)

The development in China is different, yet in many ways similar. There, too, the collective system that provided a guaranteed income, the 'iron rice-bowl', is breaking down. Earlier, people had hardly any scope for choice in

---

*First published in Heelas, Lash, and Morris (eds) (1996) *Detraditionalization*. Published here with the kind permission of Blackwell Publishers.

their private or professional life, but the minimal safety net of Communism offered them state-subsidized accommodation, training and health care. It is this state care from the cradle to the grave, tied to the work collective in the factory or on the land, that is now disintegrating. Its place is being taken by contracts linking income and job security to ability and performance. People are now expected to take their lives into their own hands and to pay a market price for services they receive. 'The constant refrain among urban Chinese is that they can no longer keep up with the quickened pace of life. They are confused by shifting values and outlooks on such fundamentals as careers, marriage and family relations' (Sun, 1993: 5).

Whatever we consider – God, nature, truth, science, technology, morality, love, marriage – modern life is turning them all into 'precarious freedoms'. All metaphysics and transcendence, all necessity and certainty are being replaced by artistry. In the most public and the most private ways we are helplessly becoming high-wire dancers in the circus tent. And many of us fall. Not only in the West, but in the countries that have abruptly opened their doors to Western ways of life. People in the former GDR, in Poland, Russia or China, are caught up in a dramatic 'plunge into modernity'.

Such examples, seemingly remote to citizens of the old Federal German Republic, point nevertheless to a dynamic that is familiar to us also. Schorlemmer's address contains the catch-word 'individualization'. This concept implies a group of social developments and experiences characterized, above all, by two meanings. In intellectual debate as in reality these meanings constantly intersect and overlap (which, hardly surprisingly, has given rise to a whole series of misunderstandings and controversies). On the one hand, individualization means the disintegration of previously existing social forms – for example, the increasing fragility of such categories as class and social status, gender roles, family, neighbourhood, and so on. Or, as in the case of the GDR and other states of the Eastern bloc, it means the collapse of state-sanctioned normal biographies, frames of reference, role models. Wherever such tendencies towards disintegration show themselves the question also arises: which new modes of life are coming into being where the old ones, ordained by religion, tradition or the state, are breaking down?

The answer points to the second aspect of individualization. It is, simply, that in modern societies new demands, controls and constraints are being imposed on individuals. Through the job market, the welfare state and institutions, people are tied into a network of regulations, conditions, provisos. From pension rights to insurance protection, from educational grants to tax rates, all these are institutional reference points marking out the horizon within which modern thinking, planning and action must take place.

Individualization in this sense, therefore, certainly does not mean an 'unfettered logic of action, juggling in a virtually empty space'; neither does it mean mere 'subjectivity', an attitude which refuses to see that 'beneath the surface of life is a highly efficient, densely woven institutional society'.[1] On the contrary, the space in which modern subjects deploy their options is anything but a non-social sphere. The density of regulations informing modern society is well known, even notorious (from the MOT test and the tax return to the laws governing the sorting of refuse). In its overall effect it is a work of art of labyrinthine complexity, which accompanies us literally from the cradle to the grave.

The decisive feature of these modern regulations or guidelines is that, far more than earlier, individuals must, in part, supply them for themselves, import them into their biographies through their own actions. This has much to do with the fact that traditional guidelines often contained severe restrictions or even prohibitions on action (such as the ban on marriage, in pre-industrial societies, which prevented members of non-property-owning groups from marrying; or the travel restrictions and the recent obstructions to marriage in the Eastern bloc states, which forbade contact with the 'class enemy'). By contrast, the institutional pressures in modern Western society tend rather to be offers of services or incentives to action – take, for example, the welfare state, with its unemployment benefit, student grants or mortgage relief. To simplify: one was born into traditional society and its preconditions (such as social estate and religion). For modern social advantages one has to do something, to make an active effort. One has to win, know how to assert oneself in the competition for limited resources – and not only once, but day after day.

The normal biography thus becomes the 'elective biography', the 'reflexive biography', the 'do-it-yourself biography'.[2] This does not necessarily happen by choice, neither does it necessarily succeed. The do-it-yourself biography is always a 'risk biography', indeed a 'tightrope biography', a state of permanent (partly overt, partly concealed) endangerment. The façade of prosperity, consumption and glitter can often mask the nearby precipice. The wrong choice of career or just the wrong field, compounded by the downward spiral of private misfortune, divorce, illness, the repossessed home – all this can merely be called bad luck. Such cases bring into the open what was always secretly on the cards: the do-it-yourself biography can swiftly become the breakdown biography. The preordained, unquestioned, often enforced ties of earlier times are replaced by the principle: 'until further notice'. As Bauman (1993) puts it:

> Nowadays everything seems to conspire against ... lifelong projects, permanent bonds, eternal alliances, immutable identities. I cannot build for the long term on my job, my profession or even my abilities. I can bet on my job being cut, my profession changing out of all recognition, my skills being no longer in demand. Nor can a partnership or family provide a basis in the future. In the age of what Anthony Giddens has called 'confluent love', togetherness lasts no longer than the gratification of one of the partners, ties are from the outset only 'until further notice', today's intense attachment makes tomorrow's frustration only the more violent.

15

A kind of 'vagrant's morality' thus becomes a characteristic of the present. The vagrant:

> does not know how long he will remain where he is, and it is not usually he who decides the length of his stay. He chooses his goals as he goes along, as they turn up and as he reads them off the signposts. But even then he does not know for sure whether he is going to take a rest at the next stopping-point, or for how long. He only knows that his stay is unlikely to be a long one. What drives him on is disappointment with the last place he stopped at, and the never-dying hope that the next, as yet unvisited place, or perhaps the one after that, will be free of the defects which have spoiled the ones up to now. (Bauman, 1993: 17)

Are such portrayals, as some suspect, signs of egoism and hedonism, of an ego fever rampant in the West? Looking more closely, we find that another feature of the guidelines of modernity is that they act against, rather than for, family cohesion. Most of the rights and entitlements to support by the welfare state are designed for individuals rather than for families. In many cases they presuppose employment (or, in the case of the unemployed, a willingness to work). Employment in turn implies education and both of these presuppose mobility or a willingness to move. By all these requirements individuals are not so much compelled as peremptorily invited to constitute themselves as individuals: to plan, understand, design themselves and act as individuals – or, should they 'fail', to lie as individuals on the bed they have made for themselves. The welfare state is, in this sense, an experimental apparatus for conditioning ego-related lifestyles. The common good may well be injected into people's hearts as a compulsory inoculation, but the litany of the lost sense of community that is just now being publicly intoned once more continues to be spoken of with a forked tongue, with a double moral standard, as long as the mechanism of individualization remains intact and no one either wishes or is able to call it seriously into question.

Here, again, we find the same picture: decisions, possibly undecidable ones, within guidelines that lead into dilemmas – but decisions which place the individual, as an individual, at the centre and correspondingly penalize traditional lifestyles and behaviour.

Seen in this way, individualization is a social condition which is not arrived at by the free decision of individuals. To adapt Jean-Paul Sartre's phrase: people are condemned to individualization. Individualization is a compulsion, albeit a paradoxical one, to create, to stage manage, not only one's own biography but the bonds and networks surrounding it, and to do this amid changing preferences and at successive stages of life, while constantly adapting to the conditions of the labour market, the education system, the welfare state and so on.

One of the decisive features of individualization processes, then, is that they not only permit but also demand an active contribution by individuals.

As the range of options widens and the necessity of deciding between them grows, so too does the need for individually performed actions, for adjustment, coordination, integration. If they are not to fail, individuals must be able to plan for the long term and adapt to change; they must organize and improvise, set goals, recognize obstacles, accept defeats and attempt new starts. They need initiative, tenacity, flexibility and a tolerance of frustration.

Opportunities, dangers and biographical uncertainties that were earlier predefined within the family association, the village community, or by recourse to the rules of social estates or classes, must now be perceived, interpreted, decided on and processed by individuals themselves. The consequences – both opportunities and burdens alike – are shifted onto individuals who, naturally, in the face of such complexity of social interconnections, are often unable to take the necessary decisions in a properly founded way, by considering interests, morality and consequences.

It is perhaps only by comparing generations that we can perceive how steeply the demands imposed on individuals have been rising. In a novel by Michael Cunningham (1991), a daughter asks her mother why she married her father:

> 'You knew that, of all the people in the world, he was the one you wanted to marry?' I asked. 'You never worried that you might be making some sort of extended mistake, like losing track of your real life and going off on, I don't know, a tangent you could never return from?'

But her mother 'waved the question away as if it were a sluggish but persistent fly. "We didn't ask such big questions then," she said. "Isn't it hard on you, to think and wonder and plan so much?"' (1991: 189f).

In another novel by Scott Turow (1991), a meeting between a father and daughter is described in similar terms:

> Listening to Sonny, who was twisted about by impulse and emotion – beseeching, beleaguered, ironic, angry – it struck Stern that Clara [his wife] and he had had the benefit of a certain good fortune. In his time, the definitions were clearer. Men and women of middle-class upbringing anywhere in the Western world desired to marry, to bear and rear children. Et cetera. Everyone travelled along the same ruts in the road. But for Sonny, marrying late in life, in the New Era, everything was a matter of choice. She got up in the morning and started from scratch, wondering about relationships, marriage, men, the erratic fellow she'd chosen – who, from her description, still seemed to be half a boy. He was reminded of Marta, who often said she would find a male companion just as soon as she figured out what she needed one for. (Turow, 1991: 349)

To some, such examples will sound familiar. To others they will seem alien – tales from a distant world. It is clear that there is no such thing as 'the' individualized society. Unquestionably, the situation in cities like Munich or

Berlin is different from that in Pomerania or East Friesland. Between urban and rural regions there are clear differences, which are empirically demonstrable with regard, for example, to lifestyle and family structure.[3] What has long been taken for granted in one as part of normal life can seem odd, irritating, or threatening in the other. Of course, lifestyles and attitudes from the town are spreading to the country – but refractedly, and with a different gloss. Individualization means, implies, urbanization. But urbanization carries the role models of the world out there into the village living room, through the expansion of education, through tourism, and not least through advertising, the mass media and consumerism. Even where seemingly unaltered lifestyles and traditional certainties are chosen and put on show, they quite often represent decisions against new longings and aroused desires.

It is necessary, therefore, to check each group, milieu and region to determine how far individualization processes – overt or covert – have advanced within it. We do not maintain that this development has achieved blanket coverage of the whole population without differentiation. Rather, the catchword 'individualization' should be seen as designating a trend. What is decisive is the systematic nature of the development linked to the advance of modernity. Martin Baethge (1991: 271) writes: 'Something which points towards tomorrow can hardly be representative of today'. Individualization has elements of both – it is an exemplary diagnosis of the present and the wave of the future.

What is heralded, ultimately, by this development is the end of fixed, predefined images of man. The human being becomes (in a radicalization of Sartre's meaning) a choice among possibilities, *homo optionis*. Life, death, gender, corporeality, identity, religion, marriage, parenthood, social ties – all are becoming decidable down to the small print; once fragmented into options, everything must be decided.[4] At best, this constellation reminds us of Baron Münchhausen, who reputedly solved what has now become a universal problem: how to pull oneself out of the swamp of (im)possibilities by one's own pigtail. This artistic state of civilization has been summed up perhaps most clearly (with a pessimistic twist) by the poet Gottfried Benn:

> In my view the history of man, of his endangerment, his tragedy, is only just beginning. Up to now the altars of saints and the wings of archangels have stood behind him; his weaknesses and wounds have been bathed from chalices and fonts. Now is beginning the series of his great, insoluble, self-inflicted dooms. (Benn, 1979: 150)

On the impossibility of living modern life: the de-routinization of the mundane

It is easily said: certainties have fragmented into questions which are now spinning around in people's heads. But it is more than that. Social action needs routines in which to be enacted. One can even say that our thoughts and actions are shaped, at their deepest level, by something of which we are hardly or not at all aware. There is an extensive literature which stresses the relief afforded in this way by internalized, pre-conscious or semi-conscious routines – or more precisely, the indispensable role they play in enabling people to lead their lives and discover their identities within their social coordinates. As Hartmann Tyrell shows, everyday life is concerned primarily with:

> the temporal order of doing ... But it is not only the temporal order as such which matters, but the associated stratum of experiences repeated over and over again, the normal, the regular, the unsurprising. At the same time, daily life is a sphere of reduced attention, of routinized activity, of safe, easy availability, and thus of actions that can be repeated 'again and again'. It is about 'what is done here', sometimes in a decidedly particularist sense, in the family circle, the village, the region, etc. It is about the commonplace and familiar ... what 'everyone does here'. (Tyrell, 1986: 255)

It is precisely this level of pre-conscious 'collective habitualizations', of matters taken for granted, that is breaking down into a cloud of possibilities to be thought about and negotiated. The deep layer of foreclosed decisions is being forced up into the level of decision making.

Hence the irritation, the endless chafing of the open wound – and the defensive-aggressive reaction. The questions and decisions rising up from the floor of existence can be neither escaped nor changed back into a silent ground on which life can be lived. At most, such pacification is achieved temporarily, provisionally; it is permeated with questions that can burst out again at any time. Think, calculate, plan, adjust, negotiate, define, revoke (with everything constantly starting again from the beginning): these are the imperatives of the 'precarious freedoms' that are taking hold of life as modernity advances. Even not deciding, the mercy of having to submit, is vanishing. Sometimes its place is taken by a hybrid, simulating what has been lost: the decision in favour of chance, of not deciding, an attempt to banish doubt which yet is pursued by doubt even in its interior dialogues:

> I thought I'd be pregnant soon. I'd stopped taking precautions. But I couldn't seem to tell anyone, not Bobby or Jonathan. I suppose I was ashamed of my own motives. I didn't like the idea of myself as calculating or underhanded. All I wanted, really, was to get pregnant by accident. The unexpected disadvantage of modern life is our victory over our own fates. We're called on to decide so much, almost everything ... In another era I'd have had babies in my twenties, when I was married to Denny. I'd have become a mother without quite deciding to. Without weighing the consequences. (Cunningham, 1991: 203)

Life loses its self-evident quality; the social 'instinct substitute' which supports and guides it is caught up in the grinding mills of what needs to be thought out and decided. If it is correct that routines and institutions have an unburdening function which renders individuality and decision making possible, it becomes clear what kind of encumbrance, exertion and stress is imposed by the destruction of routine. Ansgar Weymann (1989) points to the efforts the individual makes to escape this 'tyranny of possibilities' – such as their flight into magic, myth, metaphysics. The overtaxed individual 'seeks, finds and produces countless authorities intervening in social and psychic life, which, as his professional representatives, relieve him of the question: "Who am I and what do I want?" and thus reduce his fear of freedom' (1989: 3). This creates the market for the answer factories, the psycho-boom, the advice literature – that mixture of the esoteric cult, the primal scream, mysticism, yoga and Freud which is supposed to drown out the tyranny of possibilities but in fact reinforces it with its changing fashions.

It is sometimes claimed that individualization means autonomy, emancipation, the freedom and self-liberation of humanity.[5] This calls to mind the proud subject postulated by the philosophy of the Enlightenment, who will acknowledge nothing but reason and its laws. But sometimes anomie rather than autonomy seems to prevail – a state unregulated to the point of lawlessness. (Emile Durkheim, in his classic study of anomie, sees it as the 'evil of missing boundaries', a time of overflowing wishes and desires, no longer disciplined by social barriers (1993: 289, 311.) Any generalization that seeks to understand individualized society only in terms of one extreme or the other (autonomy or anomie) abbreviates and distorts the questions that confront us here. This society is characterized by hybrid forms, contradictions, ambivalences (dependent on political, economic and family conditions). It is also characterized, as we have said, by the 'do-it-yourself biography' which – depending on the economic situation, educational qualifications, stage of life, family situation, colleagues – can easily turn into a 'breakdown biography' (Hitzler, 1988; Beck and Beck-Gernsheim, 1994). Failure and inalienable freedom live in close proximity and perhaps intermingle (as in the 'chosen' lifestyle of 'singles').

At any rate, the topics that individuals wear themselves out on project into the most diverse spheres of life. They may be 'small' questions (such as the allocation of housework), but may also include 'large' questions regarding life and death (from prenatal diagnosis to intensive medical care). The abolition of routine thus releases questions of a very different social and moral weight. But they all bear on the core of existence. One can even say that decisions about lifestyles are 'deified'. Questions that went out of use with God are re-emerging at the centre of life. Everyday life is being post-religiously 'theologized'.

A secular line can be drawn: God, nature, social system. Each of these categories and horizons of meaning to an extent replaces the previous one; each stands for a particular group of self-evident assumptions and provides a source of legitimation for social action, which can be seen as a sequence of secularized necessities. As the dams become permeable and are breached, what was once reserved for God or was given in advance by nature is now transformed into questions and decisions which have their locus in the conduct of private life. (With the successes of reproductive medicine and human genetics the anthropology of the human species is even being drawn quite literally into the area of decision making.) To this extent, from the viewpoint of cultural history, it can be said that modernity, which dawned with the subject's claim to self-empowerment, is redeeming its promise. As modernity gains ground, God, nature and the social system are being progressively replaced, through greater and lesser steps, by the individual – confused, astray, helpless and at a loss. With the abolition of the old coordinates a question arises that has been decried and acclaimed, derided, pronounced sacred, guilty and dead: the question of the individual.

What is new in individualization processes? The example of the social history of marriage

In his book *The Civilization of the Renaissance in Italy*, published in 1860, Jakob Burckhardt wrote that in the Middle Ages human consciousness lay

> dreaming or half awake, beneath a collective veil. The veil was woven of faith, illusion and childish prepossession, through which the world and history were seen clad in strange hues. Man was conscious of himself only as a member of a race, people, party, family, corporation – only through some general category. In Italy, this veil first melted into air, an objective treatment and consideration of the state and of all the things of this world became possible. The subjective side at the same time asserted itself with corresponding emphasis; man became a spiritual individual, and recognized himself as such. (Burckhardt, 1987: 161)

Paradoxically, Burckhardt's description of the Renaissance has features of postmodernism. Everything is taken over by fashions: the politically indifferent private person comes into being; biographies and autobiographies are written and invented; women are educated according to masculine ideals. The highest praise which could then be given to great Italian women was that they had the mind and the courage of men. From the standpoint of the nineteenth century, Burckhardt notes, something emerged which 'our age would call immodesty' (1987: 428).

Anyone reading this and similar accounts will ask: what is new and specific in the individualization processes of the second half of the twentieth century?[6] To give a concise and direct answer, what is historically new is that something that was earlier expected of a few – to lead a life of their own – is now being demanded of more and more people and, in the limiting case, of all people. The new element is, first, the democratization of individual-ization processes and, second (and closely connected), the fact that basic conditions in society favour or enforce individualization (the job market, the need for mobility and training, labour and social legislation, pension pro-visions, and so on).

This history of the spread to pre-eminence of individualizations can be illustrated by various social phenomena and formations. Such will now be done by means of an exemplary sketch of the social history of marriage. To state our thesis at the outset: whereas marriage was earlier first and fore-most an institution *sui generis* raised above the individual, today it is becom-ing more and more a product and construct of the individuals forming it. Let us now trace this historical curve in more detail. As late as the seven-teenth and eighteenth centuries, marriage was to be understood not from below to above but from above to below, as a direct component of the social order. It was a socially binding mode of living and working which was largely inaccessible to individual intervention. It prescribed to men and women what they had to do and not to do even in the details of daily life, work, eco-nomic behaviour and sexuality. (Of course, not everyone complied. But the social mesh of the family and village community was tight, and the possi-bilities of control were omnipresent. Anyone who infringed the prevailing norms therefore had to reckon with rigorous sanctions.) To overstate slightly: marriage was a kind of internalized 'natural law' which – hallowed by God and the authority of the church, secured by the material interests of those bound together within it – was, so to speak, 'executed' in marriage. This emerges clearly through what seems to be an example of the contrary – a hard-won divorce reported by Gisela Bock and Barbara Duden:

> In the early 18th century, in the Seine/Maine region of France, two people appeared before the responsible church court: Jean Plicque, a vintner in Villenoy and Catherine Giradin, his wife. Seven months earlier she had with difficulty achieved a separation of bed and board on grounds of absolute incompatibility. Now they came back and declared that it would be not only better but 'much more advantageous and useful for them to live together than to remain apart'. This couple's realization is typical of all rural and urban households: husband and wife were dependent on each other because and as long as there was no possibility of earning a livelihood outside joint family work. (Bock and Duden, 1977: 126)

This couple's realization points up a situation that (despite all the diversity) seems to have been typical of pre-industrial society. Apart from church and monastery, there was no basis for material existence outside marriage. Marriage was not held together by the love, self-discovery or self-therapy of two wage-earners seeking each other and themselves, but was founded on religious obligation and materially anchored in the marital forms of work and life. Anyone who wishes to understand the meaning of this institution of marriage must leave aside the individuals and place at the centre the overarching whole of an order finally founded on God and the afterlife. Here marriage did not serve individual happiness, but was a means for achieving succession, hereditary family rule in the case of the nobility, and so on. The stability of the social order and hierarchy depended on it in a very tangible way.

With the beginning of the modern age the higher meanings superimposed on forms of social existence were loosened. The trend towards individuality – first in the middle-class 'market individual' founded on private capital – called into question the gravity of collective identities and action units, at least latently. With the separation of the family from the economic sphere, the working, economic unit of husband and wife was ruptured. Characteristically, the response to this dissolution of the material basis of the marriage community was a heightening of the moral and legal underpinnings of marriage. Here, again, marriage is justified 'deductively', that is from above to below, but now with a moral exclamation mark, as a cornerstone of the bourgeois-Christian world order. A draft of the German Civil Code, published in 1888, states: 'A German Civil Code, following the general Christian view among the people, will have to start from the assumption that in marital law it is not the principle of the individual freedom of the spouses that prevails, but that marriage should be seen as a moral and legal order independent of the will of the spouses' (cited by Blasius, 1992: 130).

'Not the principle of ... individual freedom', but an 'order independent of the will of the spouses': the threatening possibility resonates implicitly in the negation. However, the community is a one-sided one. The wife is expressly forbidden to use her own name. Her surname thus becomes that of her husband. In exemplary fashion, the general element is equated with power – here, that of the husband. As late as 1956 we read in a judgement: 'Rather, Article 6 GG allows equal rights to come into play in family law only to the extent that our traditional concept of the family, as determined by Christianity, remains intact. All exaggerated individualistic tendencies are thereby denied an effect on marital law ... This must also apply to marital law as it relates to names' (cited by Struck, 1991: 390). Here we already find the exorcising formulation about the 'exaggerated individualistic tendencies' that has lost nothing of its topicality. By it the Beelzebub of individualism was supposed to be sprinkled and driven out with the holy water of tradition.

Family registers from an unopened treasure trove of idealized family images proclaimed, as it were, *ex cathedra*. Two of them will be juxtaposed here: one from the time of National Socialism and one from the 1970s in the German Federal Republic. The contrast could hardly be more radical. The prefatory remarks make clear the individualistic conversion that has taken place in Germany – even officially – within three decades.

23

In the register from the early 1940s we read: 'Prefatory note: Marriage cannot be an end in itself, but must serve a greater goal, the increase and survival of the species and the race. Adolf Hitler'.[7] This sounds like a command and was no doubt intended as one. The racial doctrine of National Socialism is an extreme example of the 'counter-modernization' which stages a masquerade of the past in order to push back the 'decadent' tendencies of modernity (Beck, 1993: Chapter 4). It aims – using every means – to establish the unquestioned world of a re-integrated blood community. Marriage thus becomes a branch office of the state, a miniature state, the 'germ-cell of the state'. It is the place where the 'German race' is reproduced.

The commentary in the family register from the 1970s seems expressly to countermand the one just quoted. Here we read that 'the task of marriage under private law is not to see itself primarily as serving other aims beyond it, but to find its main purpose in marriage itself'.[8] Today's marriage manual no longer talks about the 'Christian world order and its values' or of 'state goals', and still less of the 'survival of the race'. Instead, it makes explicit the switch that has taken place from a view directed at the whole to one focused on people. The state even seems to slap its own wrist in warning the spouses entrusted to it not to do what up until then had been state law and policy regarding marriage, namely to follow 'traditional models':

> Caution is advised in face of the dangerous temptation to accept traditional models of marriage and of the family without question as 'natural', causing them to become fossilized in law. The rapid development of our modern industrial society, the increasing number of working women, the expected further reduction of working hours, the changing character of professions, etc. compel the legal system to adopt an open-minded, unprejudiced attitude towards new embodiments of marriage and the family.[9]

The voice of sociology is audible here. This may even be a case of the (legendary) 'trickling down', the 'disappearance' of sociology – here, in the family register – which indicates its successful effect.

However, the newly weds would also find the following 'blessing' quoted in their marriage manual in a chapter on 'The Dissolution of Marriage': 'Once their disputes have reached a certain stage, they (the spouses) seem to each other like two surgeons operating on each other without anaesthetic, who "get better and better at knowing what hurts"'.[10] This is witty and apt and could hardly contrast more dramatically with the 'racial marriage' or the 'Christian marriage' still legally binding in the 1950s. Furthermore, it could not show more clearly the radical change from the interpretation of marriage as something beyond the individual to the exclusively individual interpretation. Here, not only does an official text mention the dissolution of marriage in the same breath as the contract, marriage is also institutionalized as an individualized programme. The why, what and how long of marriage are placed entirely in the hands and hearts of those joined in it. From now on there is just one maxim defining what marriage means: the script is the individualization of marriage. The individual code of marriage is, so to speak, legally ordained.

This makes two things clear. First, even the old forms of marriage, now that they have been bureaucratically disowned, must be chosen and lived at one's personal risk. Even the marriage guidance manual contains, in effect, the warning that marriage – like excessive speed on a winding road – is a risky personal undertaking for which no insurances are valid. And second, no one can now say what goes on behind the oh-so-unchanging label of 'marriage' – what is possible, permitted, required, taboo or indispensable. The world order of marriage is from now on an individual order which must be questioned and reconstructed by individuals as they go along.

To forestall any misunderstanding: even the new, individual order of marriage is not a mere product of individualization and its wishes. Rather, it is bound to institutional edicts – for example those of the legal system, which are central. It depends on the requirements of the educational system, the labour market, old-age pensions (with the last presupposing that today both partners – and not just the husband, as earlier – have their own independent biographies as earners and their own financial security). Even with regard to the twosome, therefore – that seemingly completely private, intimate sphere – individualization does not by any means imply that the increased freedom of choice is the same thing as a breakdown of order.[11] Rather, what we see here, as elsewhere, is what Talcott Parsons has called 'institutionalized individualism' (1978: 321). Freely translated, this means that in modern life the individual is confronted on many levels with the following challenge – you may and you must lead your own independent life, outside the old bonds of family, tribe, religion, origin and class, and you must do this within the new guidelines and rules which the state, the job market, the bureaucracy, and so on lay down. In this sense marriage, too, in its modern version, is not merely an individual order but an 'individual situation dependent on institutions' (Beck, 1986: 210).

Perspectives and controversies of an individual-oriented sociology

All sociology splits into two opposed views of the same thing. The social dimension can be regarded either from the standpoint of individuals or from that of the whole (society, state, the common good, class, group, organization, and so on) (cf. Bolte, 1983). Both standpoints are founded on the structure of social action, which can be analysed either in terms of the agents or in terms of the social structure. However, that both standpoints are equally possible, equally necessary, or equally original does not mean that they are equally valuable or have equal rights; still less does it mean that they are identical. Rather, each of these viewpoints relativizes, criticizes the other (subtly, but with abundant consequences): anyone who analyses society from the standpoint of the individual does not accept its form at a particular time as a preordained, unalterable datum, but calls it into question. Here, sociological thought is not far from the 'art of mistrust', to use a formulation of Berger (1977: 40), adapted from Nietzsche. Indeed, it tends to 'destabilize' existing power relationships, as Bauman (1991: 17), for example, puts it. By contrast, where the so-called 'operational requirements' of society (or subdivisions of it) provide the framework of reference, they are often presented to the outside world simply as the inner happiness of the ego. To apply this happiness there are funnels (known as 'duties') and institutions for pouring it through these funnels, for purposes of intimidation: schools, courts, marriages, organizations, and so on.

The prevailing sociology has usually made things easy for itself by cutting off the questions that arise here with the strict injunction, backed up by thick volumes, that individuals can only be or become individuals within society. In this way they continually repress the idea: what would happen if these individuals wanted a different society, or even a different type of society?

The old sociology, still well endowed with university chairs, is armed against this idea: the general interest, congealed as structure, is condensed and glorified as Parsonian 'functional prerequisites'. From such prerequisites – as from a cornucopia of secularized ethical duties – pour forth 'role patterns', 'functions', 'demands', 'subsystems', equally remote from God and the earth, divorced from action and yet its precondition, which are to be applied as a standard to the confusion and refractoriness of individuals, to yield judgements such as 'normal', 'deviant', 'erroneous' and 'absurd'.

Accordingly, the 'individualistic' perspective on society has up to now been usually dismissed as presumptuous and self-contradictory. There is talk – using an up-to-date idiom – of 'demand inflation' and the 'ego society'. The decay of values is deplored, while it is forgotten that such decay is as old as Socrates. The GDR had exemplary experience of the inverse question and foundered on it: what happens to institutions without individuals? What does it mean when individuals withdraw their assent from the institutional elite? The same question was urgently posed in Italy in 1993 (and in France, Sweden, Finland, Germany, the USA, and so on) and the answer was the same: the political systems tremble. Where the functionalist viewpoint, based on system theory, is dominant, a 'subject-oriented' sociology often appears not only deviant but subversive. For it can sometimes reveal that the party and institutional elites are riders without horses.

Neither is it true, of course, that both conceptions of the social order are incomplete in themselves and need to supplement each other. But before such a need for harmony smoothes over a conflict which has not yet been fought openly, it should be pointed out here that for some centuries the view of the totality has suppressed that of individuals. In light of this it is time to turn the tables and ask the question – what kind of society comes into being after the demise of the great political camps and the party political consensus?

In other words, the two points of view remain until further notice incompatible: they are even becoming, through a modernization which is setting individuals and their demands and dilemmas free, more and more irreconcilable, and are giving rise to antithetical explanations, methods, theories and intellectual traditions.

It will be objected that this is not a meaningful antithesis. Entities which presuppose each other analytically, individuals and society, cannot be described as a social conflict. Moreover, both viewpoints lay claim to both viewpoints. He who embraces the 'whole' (of society) – the functionality of social formations – in his field of vision, self-evidently claims to include the standpoint of individuals as well. If necessary, this is presented as the morally correct standpoint, that which must be asserted against the false self-consciousness of individuals in their own well-understood interests. Whereas, conversely, every variant of subject- or individual-oriented sociology naturally also offers statements and explanations about the intrinsic reality of social formations and systems, their structure, stage management, and so on.

What was shown in the preceding section through the example of marriage applies generally: the antithesis between the individual- and system-based viewpoints should be understood as a historical development. If, in traditional, pre-industrial societies, we can still, perhaps, assume a fairly balanced relationship between the two frames of reference, this pre-established harmony breaks down with the unfolding of modernity. This is the central theme of sociology in Emile Durkheim and Georg Simmel. But both still assume that it is possible to integrate individualized society, as it were transcendentally, through values. Such a possibility, however, became more unrealistic the more individuals were released from the classical forms of integration in groups, including family and class. What is emerging today can be called, with Hans Magnus Enzensberger, 'the average exoticism of everyday life':

> It is most obvious in the provinces. Market towns in Lower Bavaria, villages in the Eifel Hills, small towns in Holstein are populated by figures no one could have dreamed of only thirty years ago. For example, golf-playing butchers, wives imported from Thailand, counter-intelligence agents with allotments, Turkish Mullahs, women chemists in Nicaragua committees, vagrants driving Mercedes, autonomists with organic gardens, weapons-collecting tax officials, peacock-breeding smallholders, militant lesbians, Tamil ice-cream sellers, classics scholars in commodity futures trading, mercenaries on home

leave, extremist animal-rights activists, cocaine dealers with solariums, dominas with clients in top management, computer freaks commuting between Californian data banks and nature reserves in Hesse, carpenters who supply golden doors to Saudi Arabia, art forgers, Karl May researchers, bodyguards, jazz experts, euthanasists and porno producers. Into the shoes of the village idiots and the oddballs, of the eccentrics and the queer fish, has stepped the average deviationist, who no longer stands out at all from millions like him. (Enzensberger, 1992: 179)

Under such conditions, institutions are founded on antiquated images of individuals and their social situations. To avoid endangering their own power, the administrators of these institutions maintain the status quo at all costs (supported by a sociology operating with the old conceptual stereotypes). An amusing consequence of this is that the political class regards the individuals 'out there' as no less stupid and brazen than the society of individuals considers the political class. The question as to which of them is right can, in principle, be easily decided. The idea that only the party elite and the bureaucratic apparatus knows what is what and that everyone else is imbecilic is one that characterized the Soviet Union – until it collapsed.

'This society', Enzensberger writes of the German Federal Republic:

is no longer capable of being disappointed. It registered very early, very quickly what's going on in Bonn. The way the parties present themselves also contributes to this cynical view. The politicians try to compensate for the loss of their authority, the erosion of power and trust, by a huge expenditure on advertising. But these wasteful battles are counter-productive. The message is tautolo-gous and empty. They always say only one thing, which is, 'I am I' or 'We are we'. The zero statement is the preferred form of self-presentation. That naturally confirms people's belief that no ideas can be expected from this caste ... When the posters say: 'It's Germany's future', then everyone knows that these are empty words, at most it's about the future of the milk subsidy to farmers, of the health insurance contributions or benefits. The Federal Republic is relatively stable and relatively successful not because of, but despite being ruled by the people who grin down from the election posters. (Enzensberger, 1992: 233, 228)

The theory of individualization takes sides in political debate in two ways: first, it elaborates a frame of reference which allows the subject area – the conflicts between individuals and society – to be analysed from the standpoint of individuals. Second, the theory shows how, as modern society develops further, it is becoming questionable to assume that collective units of meaning and action exist. System theories, which assume an existence and the reproduction of the social independence of the actions and thoughts of individuals, are thereby losing reality content. To exaggerate slightly: system theory is turning into a system *metaphysics* which obstructs the view of the virulent social and political process whereby, in all spheres of activity, the content, goals, foundations and structures of the 'social' are having to be renegotiated, reinvented and reconstructed.[12]

A sociology which confronts the viewpoint serving the survival of institutions with the viewpoint of individuals is a largely undeveloped area of the discipline. Almost all sociology, through a 'congenital bias', is based on a negation of individuality and the individual. The social has almost always been conceived in terms of tribes, religions, classes, associations, and above all, recently, of social systems. The individuals were the interchangeable element, the product of circumstances, the character masks, the subjective factor, the environment of the systems – in short, the indefinable. Sociology's credo, to which it owes its professional identity, states over and over again that the individual is the illusion of individuals who are denied insight into the social conditions and conditionality of their lives.

The works of world literature, the great narratives and dramas that have held the epochs in thrall, are variations of this doctrine of the higher reality and dignity of the general, social dimension, the indivisible unit of which – as the term *individere* itself implies – is the individual. But is a science of *individere* actually possible? Is not a 'sociology of the individual' (unless it contents itself with the social history of that concept, in the context of discourse theory) a self-contradiction, a pig with wings, a disguised appeal for sociology to abolish itself?

One does not need to go to the opposite extreme to see that many of the main concepts of sociology are on a war footing with the basic idea of individualization theory: that traditional contexts are being broken up, reconnected, recast, and are becoming in all cases decidable, decision dependent, in need of justification. Where this historical development is asserting itself, the viewpoints from 'above' and 'below', from the social whole and from the individual, are diverging. At the same time, the questions stirred up by system theory's perspective are still in force and even take on increased importance as they become more unmanageable. Take, for example, the declining birth rate, which can only be deciphered if seen against the background of the changed wishes, hopes and life plans of men and women. On the level of society as a whole, it brings with it a whole string of secondary consequences and questions (education policy, labour market management, pensions, local planning, immigration policy, and so on). Individuals, their preferences and aversions, are becoming the interference factor, that which is simply incalculable, a constant source of irritation, because they upset all calculations – education quotas, study plans, pension calculations, and the like. Among politicians and administrators, and the academic experts who prepare their texts, this heightens the suspicion of irrationality, since it keeps turning the current legal, administrative and computing formulae into wastepaper. Where hitherto-accepted assumptions are found wanting, the clamour about 'mood democracy' and the 'elbow society' begins. Norms and moral standards are set. But the tidal wave of new life designs, of do-it-yourself and tightrope biographies, cannot be either held back or understood in this way. The scurrying of the individualized lifestyles, elaborated in the personal trial-and-error process (between training, retraining, unemployment and career, between hopes of love, divorce, new dreams of happiness), is unamenable to the need for a standardization of bureaucratized political science and sociology.

No one denies that important matters are thought about and initiated by these disciplines as well. But what was previously regarded as background noise to be neglected is now being seen, more and more undeniably, as the basic situation. The frame of reference of institutionalized state politics and administration, on the one hand, and that of individuals trying to hold together their biography fragments, on the other, is breaking apart into antagonistic conceptions of 'public welfare', 'quality of life', 'future viability', 'justice' and 'progress'. A rift is opening between the images of society prevalent in politics and institutions and those arising from the situations of individuals struggling for viable ways of living.

In this tension-laden field, sociology must rethink its concepts and its research routines. In the face of Enzensberger's 'average exoticism of everyday life', together with what is now formulated with scholarly caution as the 'pluralization of lifestyles', old classifications and schemata are becoming as ideologically suspect as they are necessary to the institutional actors. Take, for example, the studies which 'prove' that the increasingly numerous non-marital partnerships are really pre-conjugal communities and that post-conjugal communities are actually only a preliminary form of the next marriage, so that marriage can be proclaimed the transcendental victor throughout all this turbulence. Such consolations have their market and their grateful customers: the turmoils of individualization, their message runs, are a storm in surviving marriage's teacup.

This confirms the old adage that the echo coming back out of the wood is the same as the shout that went into it. Anyone who 'maritalizes' alternative ways of living should not be surprised if he sees marriages wherever he looks. But this is a prime example of blind empiricism. Even methodical brilliance, that is able to avoid calling its categorical framework into question, becomes a second-hand bookshop stocked with standard social groups, which only exist as an ideal: though as such they are very much alive.[13]

Prospect: how can highly individualized societies be integrated?

Individualization has a double face: 'precarious freedoms'. Expressed in the old, wrong terms, emancipation and anomie form together, through their political chemistry, an explosive mixture. The consequences and questions erupting in all parts of society are correspondingly deep reaching and nerve deadening; they increasingly alarm the public and preoccupy social scientists. To mention only a few: how do children grow up when there are fewer and fewer clear guidelines and responsibilities in families? Can connections be made with the growing tendency towards violence among young people? Is the age of mass products and mass consumption coming to an end with the pluralization of lifestyles and must the economy and industry adapt themselves to products and product fashions that can be combined individually, with corresponding methods of production?

Is it at all possible for a society in the drifting sand of individualization to be registered statistically and analysed sociologically? Is there any remaining basic unit of the social, whether this is the household, family or commune? How could such units be defined and made operational? How should the various political spheres – for example, local politics, traffic policy, environmental policy, family or welfare policy – react to the diversification and transitoriness of needs and situations? How must social work (and its educational content) change when poverty is divided up and, as it were, distributed laterally among biographies? What architecture, what spatial planning, what educational planning does a society need under the pressure of individualization? Has the end come for the big parties and the big associations, or are they just starting a new stage of their history?

Behind all these irritating questions, a basic question is making itself more and more clearly heard: is it still at all possible to integrate highly individualized societies? As is shown by the rebirth of nationalism, of ethnic differences and conflicts in Europe, there is a strong temptation to react to these challenges with the classical instruments of encapsulation against 'aliens', which means turning back the wheels of social modernization. No doubt the acceptance of violence against foreigners in the streets (for example) may indeed be explained in this way. In Germany as in other Western European states an uprising against the 1970s and 1980s is in progress, a *Kulturkampf* of the two modernities. Old certainties, just now grown fragile, are again proclaimed – from everyday life to politics, from the family to the economy and the concept of progress. The highly individualized, find-out-for-yourself society is to be replaced by an inwardly heterogeneous society outwardly consolidated into a fortress, and the demarcation against 'foreigners' fits in with this calculation.

To put the matter ironically: since men can no longer, 'unfortunately', deny the right of women to vote, since women's desire for education can only with difficulty be held in check, since everything that might be useful in this regard proves awkward, a perhaps quite serviceable alternative route is being taken – not quite consciously but not quite unconsciously either. It involves achieving the same goals through the dramaturgy of violence and nationalism. Here the breaching of the taboo on violence by right-wing extremists has a basis of which little account has been taken: namely, the counter-revolt, pent up in the West too, against the individualization, feminization and ecologization of everyday life. Quite incidentally, violence reinstates the priorities of orthodox industrial society – economic growth, a faith in technology, the nuclear family, gender hierarchy – banishing the tiresome spirits of permanent questioning. Or seeming to do so.

But nailing down the status quo or even doing a backward *salto mortale* could not, at the end of the twentieth century, provide a basis of legitimacy. The same is true of the three ways of integrating highly industrialized societies that are mentioned again and again in the debate. They, too, are becoming uncertain, fragile, unable to function in the longer term.

The first is the possibility of what might be called a transcendental consensus, an integration through values, which was the driving force of classical sociology from Durkheim to Parsons. Opposing this today is the realization that the diversification of cultural perceptions and the connections people have to make for themselves eat away the very foundations on which value communities can feed and constantly renew themselves.

Others, second, contrast to this integration through values an integration founded on joint material interests. If an avowal of common values (which, of course, always has a narrowing, repressive side) is no longer possible, it is replaced in a highly developed society by the share in prosperity that is felt by broad sections of the population, binding them into that society. According to this theory, the cohesion of the old federal republic rested primarily on the growing 'economic cake', whereas the new, enlarged republic – where recession, shortage and poverty are starting to take control – faces severe tests. But even disregarding this topical development, the basic assumption is itself questionable. To hope that only material interests and institutional dependence (consumption, job market, welfare state, pensions) create cohesion is to confuse the problem with the solution, making a virtue (desired by theory) out of the necessity of disintegrating groups and group allegiances.

Third, national consciousness itself is no longer able to provide a basis for stable integration. This is not only shown by the polarizations generated by the 'national project'. It is also, as Rene König wrote as early as 1979, 'much too abstract in relation to real and very tangible fissures' (1979: 364); it is simply no longer able to reach and bind these splits. In other words, with the mobilization of ethnic identities, it is precisely national integration which breaks down:

> This can be called a 'relapse into the middle ages', and the disintegration of the existing large societies into separate, opposed local powers can be seen as the decay of the old 'nations' – a process which has been a reality in some parts of the old and new worlds for some time now. Here, the old path from alliances to empires is reversed; the great

empires sometimes split up into federative formations, or the individual parts split off
along lines determined by political, ethnic or other factors. (ibid.: 364f)

So what is left? In conclusion, we would like to indicate at least the possibility of a different kind of integration and to put it forward for discussion.
To summarize our basic idea: if highly individualized societies can be bound
together at all, it is only, first, through a clear understanding of precisely this
situation and second, if people can be successfully mobilized and motivated
for the challenges present at the centre of their lives (unemployment, the
destruction of nature, and so on). Where the old sociality is 'evaporating',
society must be reinvented. Integration therefore becomes possible if no
attempt is made to arrest and push back the breakout of individuals. This
can happen if we make conscious use of the situation and try to forge new,
politically open, creative forms of bond and alliance. The question of
whether we still have the strength, the imagination – and the time – for this
'invention of the political' (Beck, 1993, 2005) is, to be sure, a matter of life
and death.

In one of his last major essays, König sketched a positively Utopian role
for sociology in this connection. He believed it could contribute to integration through enabling the highly complex society to reflect and observe
itself creatively and methodically. He criticized the 'ruling class of today' in
the strongest terms because it had 'lived entirely on a legitimacy borrowed
from old elites and had added nothing of its own'. In this situation, König
goes on, 'sociology could make this highly complex thematic context transparent ... Admittedly, integration could not then be achieved on the institutional level' – either ethnically, socially, economically or through state
nationalism. 'To an extent, it can only be implemented "in thought".'
Therefore, it could be achieved 'only within the framework of a new philosophy, which no longer revolved around "being" and "becoming", but
around the chances for human beings under the conditions that have been
described' (1979: 367; cf. Peters, 1993).

What König proposes is in fact very topical – an integration to be attained
'in thought', in the struggle for new existential foundations for industrial civilization. Post-traditional societies threatening the cohesion of this
civilization can only become integrable, if at all, through the experiment
of their self-interpretation, self-observation, self-opening, self-discovery,
indeed, their self-invention. Their future, their ability to have and shape a
future, is the measure of their integration. Whether they can succeed in this
is, of course, questionable. Perhaps it will turn out that individualization and
integration are in fact mutually exclusive. And what of sociology? Is it really
able to make an intellectual contribution to pluralist societies? Or will it
remain stuck in its routines, obliterating the big outlines of change and
challenge with its minute calculations of developmental trends?

In his novel *The Man without Qualities* (1961), Musil distinguishes between a sense for reality and a sense for possibility. He defines the latter as 'the capacity to think how everything could "just as easily" be, and to attach no more importance to what is than to what is not'. Someone who sees possible truths, Musil goes on, has, 'at least in the opinion of their devotees ... something positively divine, a fiery, soaring quality, a constructive will ... that does not shrink from reality but treats it, on the contrary, as a mission and an invention ... Since his ideas ... are nothing else than as yet unborn realities, he too of course has a sense of reality; but it is a sense of possible reality' (1961: 12).

Undoubtedly, sociology, too, ought to develop such a sense of possible reality – but that is another matter.

Notes

1 Respectively, this is how Ostner and Roy (1991: 18) and Karl Ulrich Mayer (1991: 88) understand individualization; for a summary of the debate on individualization, see Beck (1994).

2 Ronald Hitzler (1988) writes about 'do-it-yourself biography' (*Bastelbiographie*), Anthony Giddens (1991) about 'reflexive biography', and Katrin Ley (1984) about 'elective biography' (*Wahlbiographie*).

3 Hans Bertram and Clemens Dannenbeck (1990); Hans Bertram, Hiltrud Bayer and Renate Bauereiss (1993); Gunter Burkart and Martin Kohli (1992).

4 Peter Gross refers to the multi-options society (1994), *Multioptionsgesellschaft*. (Frankfurt: Suhrkamp).

5 E.g. Gunter Burkart (1993).

6 Cf., for example, Dumont (1991); Macfarlane (1979); Morris (1972); Foucault (1984).

7 *Familienstammbuch mil Ahnenpass*, Paul Albrechts Verlage, Stulp and Berlin, no date (c. 1940), cf. p. 3; for the interrelations between individualization, family, sex roles and love, see Beck and Beck-Gernsheim (1994).

8 *Stammbuch*, published by Bundesverband der Deutsches Standesbeamten, e.V., Verlag fur Standesamtwesen, Berlin and Frankfurt, no date (c. 1970), no page references.

9 Ibid.

10 Ibid.

11 Zapf (1992) expressly opposes this widespread misunderstanding (cf. 1992: 190).

12 Cf. the theory of reflexive modernization in Beck (1993), especially Chapter 3; and Beck, et al. (1994).

13 The pragmatic a priori method of mass data sociology is worth noting: quantitative methods presuppose pre-formed categories and concepts (even if they are nominally deactivated). However, a society which is individualizing itself eludes these standardizations imposed by research method (which is already giving rise to unmanageable complications in the introduction of flexible working time and work contracts, for example). It is therefore difficult for a sociology proud of its technical virtuosity to jump over its own shadow and address questions of a self-individualizing society. But at the same time it becomes clear

here once again how woefully sociology has so far neglected the question of what kind of sociological empiricism, of scholarly and social self-observation, is appropriate to a society caught in the drought and sand drift of individualization. Cf. Beck and Allmendinger (1993).

References

Baethge, M. (1991) 'Arbeit, Vergesellschaftung, Identität – zur zunehmenden normativen Subjectivierung der Arbeit', in W. Zapf (ed.), *Die Modernisierung Moderner Gesellschaften*. Frankfurt/M.: Campus.

Bauman, Z. (1991) *Thinking Sociologically*. Oxford: Blackwell.

Bauman, Z. (1993) 'Wir sind wie Landstreicher – die Moral im Zeitalter der Beliebigkeit', *Süddeutsche Zeitung*, 16–17 November.

Beck, U. (1986) *Risikogesellschaft. Aufdem Weg in eine andere Moderne*. Frankfurt/M.: Suhrkamp. (Translation (1992). *Risk Society*. London: Sage).

Beck, U. (1993) *Die Erfindung des Politischen*. Frankfurt: Suhrkamp. (Translation (1997) *The Reinvention of Politics*. Cambridge: Polity.)

Beck, U. (1994) 'The debate on the "individualization theory"', in B. Schäfers (ed.), *Sociology in Germany – Development, Institutionalization, Theoretical Disputes*. Opladen: Leske Verlag, pp. 191–200.

Beck, U. (2005) *Power in the Global Age*. Cambridge. Polity.

Beck, U. and Allmendinger, J. (1993) *Individualisienmg und die Erhebung Sozialer Ungleichheit*. Munich: DFG research project.

Beck, U. *schrift für Soziologie*, 3(June): 178–87.

Beck, U. and Beck-Gernsheim, E. (1994) *The Normal Chaos of Love*. Cambridge: Polity.

Beck, U., Giddens, A. and Lash, S. (1994) *Reflexive Modernization – Politics, Tradition and Aesthetics in the Modern Social Order*. Cambridge: Polity.

Benn, G. (1979) *Essays und Reden um der Farsungder Eastdrucke*. Frankfurt/M.: Fischer.

Berger, P. L. (1977) *Einladungzur Soziologie*. Munich: Deutsche Taschenbuch Verlag.

Bertram, H. and Dannenbeck, C. (1990) 'Pluralisierung von Lebenslagen und Individualisierung von Lebensführungen. Zur Theorie und Empiric regionaler Disparitäten in der Bundesrepublik Deutschland', in P. A. Berger and S. Bradil (eds), *Lebenslagen, Lebensläufe, Lebensstile*. Göttingen: Schwartz, pp. 207–29.

Bertram, H., Bayer, H. and Bauereiss, R. (1993) *Familien-Atlas, Lebenslagen und Regionen in Deutschland*. Opladen: Leske und Budrich.

Blasius, D. (1992) *Ehescheidung in Deutschland im 19. und 20. Jahrhundert*. Frankfurt: Fischer Taschenbuch Verlag.

Bock, G. and Duden, B. (1977) 'Arbeit aus Liebe – Liebe als Arbeit in Frauen und Wissenschaft', *Beiträge zur Berliner Sommeruniversität für Frauen*, July 1986. Berlin: Courage Verlag, pp. 118–99.

Bolte, K.M. (1983) 'Subjektorientierte Soziologie – Plädoyer für eine Forschungsperspektive', in K. M. Bolte and E. Treutner (eds), *Subjektorientierte Arbeits – und Berufssoziologie*. Frankfurt/M.: Campus, pp. 12–36.

Burckhardt, J. (1987) *Die Kultur der Renaissance in Italien*. Stuttgart: Reclam.

Burkart, G. (1993) 'Individualisierung und Elternschaft – das Beispiel USA', *Zeitschrift für Soziologie*, 3(June): 159–77.

Burkart, G. and Kohli, M. (1992) *Liebe, Ehe, Elternschaft*. Munich: Piper.

Cunningham, M. (1991) *A Home at the End of the World*. Harmondsworth: Penguin.

Dumont, L. (1991) *Individualismus – Zur Ideologie der Moderne*. Frankfurt/M.: Campus.

Durkheim, E. (1993) *DerSelbstmord*. Frankfurt: Suhrkamp (*Suicide: A Study in Sociology*, trans. J. A. Spaulding and G. Simpson. New York: Free Press).

Enzensberger, H. M. (1992) *Mediocrity and Delusion: Collected Diversions* (trans. Martin Chalmers). London: Verso.

Foucault, M. (1984) *Le Souci de Soi*. Paris: Gallimard.

Giddens, A. (1991) *Self-Identity and Modernity*. London: Polity.

Gross, P. (1994) *Die Multioptionsgesellschaft*. Frankfurt: Suhrkamp.

Hitzler, R. (1988) *Kleine Lebenswelten – EinBeitrag zum Verstehen von Kultur*. Opladen: Westdeutscher Verlag.

König, R. (1979) 'Gesellschaftliches Bewusstsein und Soziologie', in G. Lüschen (ed.), *Deutsche Soziologie seit* 1945. Special edition 21. Opladen: Westdeutscher Verlag, pp. 358–70.

Ley, K. (1984) 'Von der Normal – zur Wahlbiographie', in M. Kohli and G. Robert (eds), *Biographie und Soziale Wirklichkeit*. Stuttgart: Metzler, pp. 239–60.

Macfarlane, A. (1979) *The Origins of English Individualism: The Family, Property and Social Transition*. New York: Cambridge University Press.

Mayer, K. U. (1991) 'Soziale Ungleichheit und Lebensläufe', in B. Giesen and C. Leggewie (eds), *Experiment Vereinigung*. Berlin: Rotbuch, pp. 87–99.

Morris, C. (1972) *The Discovery of the Individual, 1050–1200*. Toronto: University of Toronto Press.

Musil, R. (1961) *The Man without Qualities*. London: Seeker & Warburg.

Ostner, I. and Roy, P. (1991) *Späte Heirat – Ergebnis biographisch unterschiedlicher Erfahrungen mil 'Cash' und 'Care'*. Project proposal to Deutsche Forschungsgemeinschaft (DFG), Bremen.

Parsons, T. (1978) *Religion in Postindustrial Society: In Action, Theory and the Human Condition*. New York: Free.

Peters, B. (1993) *Die Integration Moderner Gesellschaften*. Frankfurt/M.: Suhrkamp.

Schorlemmer, F. (1993) 'Der Befund ist nicht alles'. Contribution to debate on *Bindungsverlust und Zukunftsangst in der Risikogesellschaft*, 30 October, in Halle (manuscript).

Struck, G. (1991) 'Die mühselige Gleichberechtigung von Mann und Frau in Ehenamensrecht', *Neue Justiz*, 9: 390–2.

Sun, L. H. (1993) 'Freedom has a price, Chinese discover', *International Herald Tribune*, 14 June.

Turow, S. (1991) *The Burden of Proof*. Harmondsworth: Penguin.

Tyrell, H. (1986) 'Soziologische Anmerkungen zur historischen Familienforschung', *Geschichte und Gesellschaft*, 12: 254–73.

Weymann, A. (1989) 'Handlungsspielräume im Lebenslauf', in A. Weymann (ed.), *Handlungsspielräume. Untersuchungen zur Individualisientng und Institutionalisierung von Lebensläufen in der Moderns*. Stuttgart: Enke.

Zapf, W. (1992) 'Entwicklung und Sozialstruktur moderner Gesellschaften', in H. Korte and B. Schafers (eds), *Einführung in Hauptbegriffe der Soziologie*. Opladen: Leske and Budrich.

3

The Global New Individualist Debate: Three Theories of Individualism and Beyond

Anthony Elliott and Charles Lemert

Individualism has become so prevalent in talk among modern people that many will be surprised to learn that the word is of relatively recent vintage – not much earlier than the 1830s when a great French social thinker and observer of American life gave the word a still-cogent meaning:

> Individualism is a novel expression, to which a novel idea has given birth ... Individualism is a mature and calm feeling, which disposes each member of the community to sever himself from the mass of his fellow-creatures, and to draw apart with his family and friends. (Tocqueville, 1976 [1835]: 98)

What was novel about the idea and the word in the 1830s was that Tocqueville, himself quite a serious individual thinker, was commenting on the social consequences of a moral and political principle that gave rise to the modern world. The idea was that the proper and primary condition of the human individual in society is a state of composure within and without comfort among those few to whom one is most closely bound. To achieve this idyllic state the individual must 'sever himself from the mass of his fellow-creatures and draw apart' (Tocqueville, 1976 [1835]: 98).

Tocqueville's definition begins to suggest the degree to which, prior to the modern world, individualism was far from a normal first-consideration when people thought about the purpose of their lives. Individualism, as a commonplace moral ideal, was not just unique to the modern world, but in many ways its prevalence has been one of modernity's identifying social facts. This is why, years later, we recall Tocqueville's nineteenth century observations with interest, and why the fate of the moral individual and his freedoms (or lack thereof) has long been a worry of social critics in the twentieth, and now into the twenty-first.

In this chapter, we will sketch a social-theoretical account of some key notions of individualism that have influenced public political debate. Given that the concept of individualism is one of the most widely used in the social sciences and humanities, any summary treatment of scholarly research would be only superficial. Accordingly, we situate our discussion of individualism throughout this chapter in the context of changing relations between identity and globalization. The snapshots of individualism presented here are crucial for grasping social changes currently sweeping the globe, as well as the basis upon which we develop hypotheses regarding the emergence of a new individualism in the final sections of the chapter. There are three contemporary, compelling, and widely discussed theories of individualism with respect to issues regarding the globalization of life, meaning, self-actualisation and identity. We describe these as *manipulated individualism*, *isolated privatism*, and, *reflexive individualization*. We conclude by contrasting these theories with our own account of *the new individualism*.

Manipulated Individualism

How should individualism be characterized? Individualism in the present age has been cast by some within a broader field of historical and economic determinations and, with some degree of oversimplification, two variant perspectives may be recognized here. A first group consists of those who argue that public life is contaminated with the manipulation of human capacities by transnational corporations and global elites. A second group argues that social control or political domination within our individualist culture is more complex and paradoxical than some Orwellian dystopic of the unconstrained powers of Big Brother; instead, political domination arises from an acute contradiction within the very global, technological frameworks that shape individualism's ideological needs. Such critics thus seek to juxtapose the intensification of globalization processes and the impersonality of large-scale institutions with the corrosion of intimacies of personal life. Needless to say, each of these conceptual orientations have influenced the other, although the political differences between them remain reasonably clear.

We can find an interesting starting point for such orientations in the classical sociology of George Simmel. In his *Fundamental Problems of Sociology* (1950), Simmel spoke of a 'new individualism' stemming from the modern metropolis and the money economy. Liberated from the grip of tradition (or what Simmel called 'the rusty chains of guild, birth right and church'), the meanings that motivate modern people are no longer fixed through external categories, but rather arise through an intensification of processes of strong self-definition. 'The individual', writes Simmel, 'seeks his *self* as if he did not yet have it, and yet, at the same time, is certain that his only fixed point is this self' (1950: 79). Simmel's self-actualising individual is all about the work of self-assembly, self-construction, liveliness and playfulness; in short, life lived as artfulness. And yet, while enlightening and exciting, this modernist approach to individualism also implies its opposite, a negation of meaning and the total loss of personality. There is a sense in which modern culture is at once enabling and constraining, which Simmel seeks to plot through the extremities of our individualist age. In a metropolitan, urban world – under the pressures of the city crowd and the alienating structures of economic exchange – individual identities are necessarily egoistic, calculating and blasé. In such a way, people seek reassurance of their independence and power in an overwhelmingly indifferent and impersonal world. The overemphasis placed on individualism is thus, on Simmel's reckoning at least, a 'retracted acuity' (1968 [1896]: 68), the expression of unfreedom rather than liberation.

In contrast to the liberal concept of moral individualism, with its ideal of a flowering, all-round development of individual human powers, what arises from this critical orientation is a relentless focus on exploitative social relations. The study of the material and emotional devastation that capitalism has unleashed is especially interesting in this context, and arguably the single most important body of ideas that addresses social division and alienation comes from the German tradition of critical theory – sometimes referred to as the 'Frankfurt School'. Broadly Marxist in orientation, it was the Frankfurt School's strong interest in identity (and especially new forms of individualism) that necessitated a shift away from class struggle and materialism narrowly conceived. The key perspectives advanced in German critical theory – particularly evident in the writings of Max Horkheimer, Theodor Adorno and Herbert Marcuse – were shaped largely by the twentieth-century experience of fascism, particularly the Nazi reign of terror in Western Europe. For the Frankfurt School's social analysts, or for those whose approach has been influenced in some significant way by this school of thought, the individual is viewed as an instrument of domination and alienation. A variety of terms were introduced to capture this crippling constitution of individualism under conditions of advanced capitalism, from Adorno's (1950) critique of 'the authoritarian personality' to Marcuse's portrait of 'one-dimensional man'.

In the Frankfurt School's sociology, if there is one area that stands out in terms of dramatizing the transformed social conditions in which individualism operates in our own time it is that of mass culture. The critical theorists were especially interested in how individuals are shaped as consumers through the mass media, which in their analyses demands both the manipulation and domination of mass consciousness. Tracing the dynamics of irrational authoritarianism in communications media, the critical theorists suggested that popular culture is manufactured under conditions that reflect the interest of media conglomerates. 'The culture industry' wrote Adorno, 'intentionally integrates its consumers from above' (2001: 98).

Technology itself, even the use of household technologies such as radios and televisions, determines the responses and reactions of individuals. This rigid control of mass media, for the early critical theorists, is itself the result of a broadcast language of command – in which the reflectiveness of the individual is instantly nullified. As Adorno puts this, 'The repetitiveness, the selfsameness, and the ubiquity of modern mass culture tend to make for automatized reactions and to weaken the forces of individual resistance' (2001: 160). In some ways, Adorno's comments offer a suggestive critique of the broadcast activities of such diverse media companies as MTV, CNN and TimeWarner. Yet there are many obvious respects in which the relation between markets and consumers is not as neatly unified as some formulations of the critical theorists suggest. Still, there is little doubt that Frankfurt School theory has provided an inspired approach to various aspects of the relationship between individualist identities and media entertainment – particularly as regards film, TV and even jazz, as well as other forms of popular music.

The ideas of the Frankfurt School have been taken up in a number of ways to make sense of our age of rampant individualism. For the most part, many writers influenced by the assumptions of critical theory have tended to view individualism and a preoccupation with identity as an outcrop of monopoly capitalism and the processes of commercialisation. It fell to what has been called the second generation of critical theorists to develop a more sociologically sophisticated critique of the cultural consequences of the spread of globalizing social forces into the private sphere as a whole. Today the most prominent critical theorist is Jürgen Habermas, who has put forward a sweeping and challenging social theory of how the accelerating pace of modernization reshapes the boundaries between public and private life. Though Habermas's analysis of the changing boundaries between public and private life is sociologically dense and historically complex, the broad thrust of the argument, succinctly put, is this. In the societies of early or market capitalism, individuals performed a vital role in mediating between the differentiated spheres of the state and civil society through interpersonal interaction, business dealings and civic association. The model of the so-called 'public sphere' that Habermas defends is, essentially, one that can be traced to the life of the *polis* in classical Greece. In ancient Greece, the public sphere was constituted as a profoundly dialogical arena, a place where individuals came to meet to engage in a public discourse of critical reason and to debate issues of common interest.

Habermas's account of democratic and public participatory processes takes its cue from reasoned debate, logical thinking and consensus; indeed, his critique of the rise of the bourgeois public sphere draws parallels between the *polis* of classical Greek city-states and the literary salons and coffee houses of early eighteenth-century Europe, where different groups met to exchange opinions on a dizzying array of ideas and ideologies. As the state came to penetrate more and more into the economy and civil society, however, the public sphere – so valued by Habermas – entered into a period of unprecedented decline. The global expansion of capitalism, and the associated intensification of commodification, spelt the disintegration of the public sphere. This became shrunken, according to Habermas, as the corrosive and bureaucratizing logic of capitalist society came to eat away at the practical and civic agencies of everyday life as well as eroding the influence of broader cultural traditions.

For Habermas, this is how it is in our own time – but perhaps even more so. The impact of new communication technologies, like television, cable and satellite, is viewed as weakening both the private sphere and civic association; the public sphere itself becomes desiccated. Though he does not address these concerns in any great detail in his more recent writings, Habermas does explicitly recognize the potential gains to democracy that were generated by the advent of electronic media; he acknowledges that the dramatic proliferation of communication technologies and media services might contribute to the democratizing potentials of cosmopolitanism; and he also recognizes that some commentators view the Internet and digital interactive technology as heralding a second spectacular age for a revitalized and democratic public sphere. Yet Habermas, for the most part, remains unconvinced. The use of the Internet and related interactive technology may create new forms of publicness, but this is a degradation of genuine civic engagement and public political debate. It is degradation as individuals today mostly engage with mass communications and mass culture in privatized terms, as isolated selves obsessed with mediated spectacles. 'In comparison with printed communications', writes Habermas:

> 'the programmes sent by the new media curtail the reactions of their recipients in a peculiar way. They draw the eyes and ears of the public under their spell but at the same time, by taking away its distance, place it under "tutelage", which is to say they deprive it of the opportunity to say something and to disagree ... The sounding board of an educated stratum tutored in the public use of reason has been shattered: the public is split apart into minorities of specialists who put their reason to use non-publicly and a great mass of consumers whose receptiveness is public but uncritical.' (Habermas, 1989 [1962]: 170–5)

Our age of mediated conversation (TV chat shows, radio talkback) is one of politics trivialized. As Habermas writes, 'today the conversation itself is administered'; the privatized appropriation of such mediated conversation is such that it may be pointless to speak of a robust public sphere at all. Indeed, in his mature writings, Habermas writes of a 'colonization' of the private sphere by the rationalizing, bureaucratizing forces of large-scale institutions (Habermas, 1989 [1962]: 164).

There are quite a number of criticisms of the thesis of manipulated individualism, both of Frankfurt School thinking and of authors working within a broadly critical theory tradition. Some critics argue that, while advocates of such a line of thinking are mostly accurate in their description of the socio-economic shifts of the present day, what they nevertheless fail to do is put those shifts into context at the level of the individual. Few would deny, for instance, that the rise of mass culture and consumerism hasn't, in some sense or another, contributed to a pervasive instrumentalism within private affairs and social relations. And yet it's surely too simplistic to suggest, as some authors indebted to contemporary critical theory have, that what people make out of popular culture and communication media is entirely controlled by corporate power or manipulated through ideology. Equally contentious is the assumption that individuals are increasingly powerless in the face of global forces, with all this implies for a downgrading of human agency, resistance and social knowledgeability. As Cambridge sociologist John B. Thompson queries:

> Why do members of the life-world *not* perceive that what they are threatened by is the uncontrolled growth of system complexities, rooted ultimately in the dynamics of capital accumulation and valorization? Why do they not resist this growth directly and demand, in an open and widespread way, the transformation of the economic system which underlies it? (Thompson, 1995: 167)

Thompson's remarks are directed at Habermas, but equally apply to variants of the thesis of manipulated individualism.

Isolated Privatism

Individualism as isolated privatism is, as we define it here at any rate, more culturalist than sociological. Its major protagonists describe modern culture as heralding the death of personal autonomy, involving the replacement of authentic, reflective subjectivity with a narcissistic, hedonistic attitude towards other people and the wider world. Whereas theories of manipulated individualism tend to concentrate on the overshadowing of selfhood by large-scale institutional forces, adherents of the thesis of isolated privatism derive their notions from transformations in ideology, culture, art and literature as well as in economic life. While the former group of social critics recasts the material foundations of life in terms of the restructuring of capitalism and globalism, the latter would theorize today's world more in terms of cross-cultural fertilisations and psychological upheavals.

Many of the leading figures of the thesis of isolated privatism (though they would no doubt reject such a label) are to be found not in Europe, but in the USA. In a widely influential treatment of how contemporary cultural life has become progressively uncoupled from politics and the economy,

Daniel Bell (1993) shows how a modernist ideological context of secular Puritanism transmuted into consumerist imperatives of purchasing and pleasure-seeking. In stimulating consumer desires, multinationals and business conglomerates today encourage people to think only of their own private satisfactions, which in turn weakens the spirit of active citizenship. Yet despite the cultural supremicism of consumer freedom, Bell contends that today's hyper-individualist idiom enters into an embarrassing contradiction with the moral fabric of society. A similar capacious moralizing characterizes the work of Allan Bloom, who lambastes what he calls – in defensive, mildly anxious tones – our 'culture of moral relativism'. Like Bell, Bloom says the contemporary epoch inaugurates an isolated privatism at the level of the individual; but Bloom in particular harbours a neoconservative suspicion of social changes such as the rise of feminism and sexual permissiveness, which he sees as culturally regressive. People today, writes Bloom, are 'spiritually unclad, unconnected, isolated, with no inherited or unconditional connection with anything or anyone' (1988: 87).

If individuals today are unable to muster the commitment necessary to sustain interpersonal relationships and civic participation, this is because an unchecked narcissism empties out both the emotional depths of the self and the affective texture of interpersonal communication. Thus Richard Sennett, in *The Fall of Public Man* (1978), explains the demise of public life as a consequence of pathological narcissism and character disorders. The deadening of public political space, says Sennett, arises not simply from impinging forces of commodification or bureaucratisation, but from the dominance of notions of self-fulfilment, sensual gratification and self-absorption at the expense of social bonds. An equally influential version of the thesis of societal narcissism has been put forward by the late American historian Christopher Lasch, who speaks of a 'minimal self' in an age of survivalism. Lasch's self is one that is focused on the experience of living 'one day at a time', of everyday life as a 'succession of minor emergencies' (Lasch, 1985).

Robert Bellah and a group of Californian academics, standing somewhere in the middle of the left-liberal wing of individualism theory, believe that much of the language of contemporary individualism profoundly constrains the ways in which people think about their identities, relationships with others and also involvements with the wider world. In *Habits of the Heart* (1996), a book that explores the relationship between culture and character in contemporary America, Bellah and his associates argue that the balance between public commitments and private attachments has tipped overwhelmingly in favour of the latter at the expense of the former. Through in-depth interviews with Americans from various walks of life, Bellah and his associates hold that the fierce individualism pervading American culture today is in danger of producing selves either obsessed with material gain and private success on the one hand or pseudo forms of commitment to, and concern for, our fellow citizens on the other. Here we have what we might call a popular conception of individualism, or at least a popular-academic take on the political costs of an individualist culture. It is therefore all the more perplexing that hardly any of this critique captures the changing, conflicting trends of globalization and identity.

Interestingly Bellah and his associates, who contextualize practices of individualism in terms of cultural tradition, political ideology and social history, see the problems facing our society less in terms of invasive economic forces eating away at the fabric of social practices and cultural traditions, and rather as a lifting of individualist ideologies to the second power. They speak of many of their interviewees as being trapped in a language of isolating individualism, a language that ultimately distorts human capacities for genuine personal growth, ongoing commitments to others and an involvement in public affairs. 'We are concerned' they write 'that individualism may have grown cancerous ... that it may be threatening the survival of freedom itself' (1996: *xlii*).

Yet Bellah and his associates are constrained by their liberal definition of individualism to dismiss as distorting or pathological any kind of social practices that do not fit with their rather traditionalist understanding of the civic-regarding character of the public sphere. Hence, their laments about consumption orientated lifestyles, TV culture and the packaged good life. But this, notwithstanding its liberal sneering and lofty academic remoteness, falsely assumes that the language of 'public' and 'private', or 'the cultural' and 'the personal', is adequate for comprehending the global webs in which forms of identity and individualism are today constituted. Part of the problem, in our view, stems from the overvaluation Bellah and his associates place on religious and republican traditions as unquestionable sources for spontaneous and enriching forms of self-definition. Conversely, they can find precious little of this in what they term 'utilitarian individualism' and 'expressive individualism'. They are thus left celebrating an image of individualism from a bygone age, one that idealizes individual rationality and logical reasoning and likewise denigrates spontaneous subjectivity and emotional literacy. This ultimately manoeuvres them into the absurd position of saying that the writings of, say, Tocqueville, or the actions of cultural heroes like cowboys, speak to authentic individuation; whereas they would argue that our culture of therapy and our appetite for consumerism are only pseudo-individualistic in form.

In Robert D. Putnam's *Bowling Alone – The Collapse and Revival of American Community* (2001), the same sweeping generalisations take on a decidedly popul.arist flavour. According to Putnam, the crisis of the American Community is that of broken bonds and deteriorating democracy. He uses the metaphor of 'bowling' to capture recent social changes through which individuals are more and more disconnected from family life, friends, colleagues, neighbours and the social system itself. Here's Putnam's argument in a nutshell: where people once bowled in league teams, during their leisure time after work, now they bowl alone, as solitary entertainment. Putnam makes similar claims to Lasch and Bellah about the need to avoid cultural nostalgia, but it is interesting that his analysis proceeds from juxtaposing the communal character of yesteryear with the impersonality of today's world. Civic engagement as opposed to disconnected individualism, co-operative community as opposed to commercialised competition, genuine relationships as opposed to episodic encounters: these are the oppositions through which Putnam summarizes the decline of social life.

American feminist and sociologist Arlie Hochschild's book *The Commercialization of Intimate Life* (2003) similarly warns of the emotional dangers of global consumer capitalism for our experiences of identity, gender, sexuality and family life. Much like Lasch and Sennett before her, she believes that globalization is eating away at the fabric of private life, degrading individualism into self-obsession and unchecked narcissism. For Hochschild, the new global galaxy of digital communications, market institutions and transnational corporations give rise to what she calls 'a spirit of instrumental detachment'. Isolated, adrift, anxious and empty: these are the defining emotional contours of the individual self in a globalizing world. Especially evident today is what Hochschild calls a 'cultural cooling' affecting people's attitudes towards sex, relationships and love. She contrasts the patriarchal world of yesteryear, where rigid, predefined gender relationships ruled, with the new postmodern world of more open communication and fluid boundaries between the sexes. Paradoxically, the vanished world of till-death-do-us-part seems to have provided for greater emotional warmth than the cooler emotional strategies demanded by today's. Examining in detail women's best-selling advice books for clues as to this cultural cooling of intimate life, Hochschild speaks of an 'abduction of feminism'. With the spirit of feminism now displaced onto private life, Hochschild's 'perfectly packaged woman' is one who is taking her cue from the postmodern sexual revolution – as represented in *Sex and the City*. Diet, dress sexy, dye your hair and get a face-lift: such is the relentless media advice, says Hochschild, on how women should negotiate today's high-risk relationships market.

Whichever variant you choose in the debate over isolated privatism one thing is clear: contemporary culture remakes the individual ego-centric, and so also in the shadow of a narcissistic-like society. Self-enclosed, self-obsessed, market-style identities are cultivated by late modern or postmodern culture: a surface concern with self, others and the wider world, much like surfing the Net, is the only game in town. Yet while we don't deny that privatism – the privatisation of human experience – isn't an undoubted characteristic of contemporary cultural conditions, we fundamentally disagree with the elitist and anachronistic assumptions that individualism today is rendered merely surface-orientated, media-driven and focused on personal or unpolitical issues. For one thing, ours is a time of collapsing distinctions between public and private life, of the erasure of traditional distinctions between private issues and political matters, but that also brings with it new experiences of where culture and politics actually reside. The cultural characterization of pathological narcissism, from Lasch to Hochschild, is ill-suited to analysing current patterns of individualism, primarily since global transformations render self-identity itself a profoundly political arena. Many such transformations date from the late 1960s and early 1970s, where a number of genuinely transnational social movements – feminism, gay and lesbian rights, indigenous movements and environmentalism – ushered in a widespread acceptance of the politicization of issues previously portrayed as private. Today popular culture, however distasteful or degraded it is to some cultural critics, is where millions of people negotiate some of the central political issues of the day, to do with contested notions of gender, sexuality, race, ethnicity and on and on.

Criticizing individuals for their ongoing interest and engagement with communications media and popular culture on the grounds that this represents a retreat from the public sphere and genuine citizenship is also too simplistic. In conditions of globalization, in which media networks and new communications technologies powerfully influence many aspects of our lives, popular culture and the mass media are where many encounter political issues and negotiate identities. It's certainly true, as Lasch and others contend, that the mass media is entertainment-orientated, celebrity-driven and sometimes focused on reducing complex political issues to private concerns. Yet the popular media also moves in many directions simultaneously, and there is considerable research to indicate that the interaction between audiences and media messages has become increasingly complex, contradictory and discontinuous in the digital age. It's estimated, for example, that a newspaper today contains as many bits of information as people living in pre-modern societies might have encountered during the course of their lives. There's little doubt that the information revolution has reshaped individualism as we know it, yet the failure to consider with full seriousness the consequences of this communications transformation renders accounts of isolated privatism backward-looking and blinkered.

Reflexive Individualization

We live in a world that places a premium on instant gratification. Thanks to technology-induced globalization, the desire for immediate results – for gratification now – has never been as pervasive or acute. We are accustomed to sending email across the planet in seconds. To shopping in stores stocked with goods from all over the world. And to drifting through relations with other people (both intimate and at work) without long-term commitment. The vanished world of self-restraint has truly been replaced with a culture of immediacy.

If globalization raises our lust for instant gratification to the second power, it also powerfully reshapes – as theories of manipulated individualism and isolated privatism make clear – the way we conceive of our individualism and ourselves. Awareness of a new individualism unleashed by the forces of globalization is also a key concern that unites a variety of intellectuals trying to grasp the novel ways societies 'institutionalize' these transformed relations of private and public, self and society, individual and history. This brings us to the theory of individualization. The ideas of authors and activists associated with notions of individualization are perhaps best described as centre-left politically and strongly sociological, since social forces play such a large role in them. For proponents of the theory of individualization, the social vision of intrusive large-scale governmental forces and capitalistic conglomerates into the tissue of daily life and the personal sphere is not sufficient for grasping the core opportunities and risks of contemporary culture. Rather than 'big institutions' ruling the lives of 'small individuals' – a social vision especially to the fore in variants of the thesis of manipulated individualism – the theory of individualization holds that people today are only partly integrated into the social network. The leading thinker associated with this approach, German sociologist Ulrich Beck, argues that people today must constantly undertake the work of inventive and resourceful self-building and self-design in order to avoid their identities breaking into pieces. Explicitly rejecting the notion of individualism, Beck's ideas emphasize the global transformations of everyday life and of the relationship of the individual self to society.

In his groundbreaking study *The Reinvention of Politics* (1997), a riposte to the theories of both manipulated individualism and isolated privatism, Beck contends that the making of identities today is an innovative institutionalized process, not an outcrop of inner desires or the forces of socialization. Beck sketches something he calls 'institutional individualization', in which people's ability to create a biographical narrative – and continuously revise their self-definition – becomes fundamental to our age of pervasive globalization. In a world of interconnected information technologies and diversified communication networks, he argues, people are always revising, reworking and reinventing their personal habits and identities in the light of knowledge about the state and direction of the world.

At the centre of Beck's work is the claim that the shift from tradition to modernity has unleashed a profoundly novel process of self-formation, one that notwithstanding regional differences and cultural variations is everywhere similar. According to Beck, traditional societies gave people little room for individual autonomy as categories of meaning were pre-given. Religion is perhaps the obvious example here. In modern, secular society, by contrast, the construction of identity and individualism becomes detached from history, particularly in the West. It becomes increasingly difficult to rely on traditional frameworks of understanding in the orientation of one's life and activities, principally due to the vast explosion in social possibilities and cultural horizons generated by modernity. Individualization, or the reflexive organization of the self, demands that people explain themselves and become open to discourse or reflective deliberation – both internally and externally. Against this backcloth, Beck tracks the spiralling of insecurities experienced by people the world over in their attempts at self-definition and particularly their ways of coping with globalization. Reflecting on the complex negotiations people make in juggling the conflicting demands of career, family, friends, work and love, Beck opens up new ways of understanding self-experience and individualism. Perceptively, he speaks of an emergent 'self-driven culture'. Of self-designed biographies. And of DIY identities. The French philosopher Jean-Paul Sartre once quipped that it is not enough to be born a bourgeois, rather one must live one's life as a bourgeois. Beck takes this idea and pushes it further. Pressure to become what one is – and especially to demonstrate to family, friends and colleagues that one has truly 'made it' – is perhaps a central defining feature of contemporary Western living. The evidence is all around. In the seemingly unstoppable desire to shop and consume luxury goods. In new conditions of work, where networking, short-term teamwork and instant self-reinvention are all the rage. And also in the craving for instant celebrity, and the packaged good life that goes with it.

It's a provocative thesis, and one that chimes nicely with the vast expansion of media culture, interconnected virtuality and the information technology revolution – all of which have served to provide many with a glimpse of alternative horizons and symbolic possibilities on a scale that did not exist previously. Beck sketches what these big social changes mean for people in the following way:

> 'Individualisation' means, *first*, the disembedding of industrial-society ways of life and, *second*, the re-embedding of new ones, in which the individuals must produce, stage and cobble together their biographies … put in plain terms, 'individualisation' means the disintegration of the certainties of industrial society as well as the compulsion to find and invent new certainties for oneself and others without them. (Beck, 1997: 95)

This search for 'new certainties' in a world of heightened ambivalence is shaped by the interwoven trends of individualization and globalization. But Beck argues that globalization is not a single process; rather, globalization is a complex mix of forces – usually messy, often contradictory – that produce novelties, complexeties and disjunctures in patterns of individualism and forms of identity.

The self today thus becomes a kind of DIY survival specialist, imbuing with expansive and polyarchic meanings a world stripped of pre-given significances and traditionalist structures, rules and processes. The individual self in an age of individualization can find only a privatised, contingent kind of foundation to the activities one sustains in the world, which in turn both defies presumptions about traditional ways of doing things and spurs further the self-design and self-construction of all phases of life. This kind of individualism is for Beck the sole source of meaning and value, though that is not to say that the subject's ceaseless biographical productivity springs from an inner depth, emotional resilience or personality. What constitutes the individuality of the individual self in Beck's sociological doctrine is the ongoing negotiation and strenuous modification of complex identity processes – interlocking networks, civic initiatives, social movements, ethnic and racial clusters, business pyramids, and on and on.

This kind of individualization is not confined only to the private sphere (though this is surely often a common fantasy); individualization is *socially produced*. All processes of individualisation thus become political, even though it is the case that the political consequences of today's DIY-biographies are often better grasped with hindsight. As Beck characterizes the endless push and pull, conflicts and compromises, of individualization: 'Decisions, possibly undecidable decisions, certainly not free, but forced by others and wrested out of oneself, under conditions that lead into dilemmas' (1997: 97).

Towards a new individualism: contextualizing social theory

In what follows, the argument will be developed that the three theories of individualism reviewed above – *manipulated individualism, isolated privatism* and *reflexive individualization* – when blended together in a reflective configuration provide some purchase on a new individualism sweeping the globe today. After detailing some of the historical context underpinning these social theories of individualism, we turn in the next section of this chapter to briefly consider the contours of this new individualism.

Deadly worlds and the manipulated new individualism: after the 1920s

The first of the three attempts to understand what has come to be called the new individualism was, of course, the theories of the German school of critical theory which had their roots in the terrors wrought by Hitler's rise to power in the 1930s and the war and genocide that followed thereafter. There can be no doubt that the evil of Nazi fascism and the slaughter of innocents to which it led was the foremost spectacle that led German social thinkers to realize that social theory had to reevaluate its classical assumptions, in particular those of pure science as the basis for social progress and of the moral individual as the engine of social history. The Nazis themselves used the language and practice of scientific knowledge to execute their final plan of racial purification, which among other of its terrors had the effect of demonstrating just how vulnerable the moral individual is to the influence of a wicked authority. Yet, as terrible as the Holocaust was, there was another realization, widely shared in Europe especially. The unresolved political and economic crises that followed the Great War soon led to the recognition that the old days of a nineteenth-century faith in the ideals of individualism were passé if not gone forever. The moral individual, however fine an ideal, had, in effect, failed to serve as a sufficient moral glue to hold the social whole together; on the contrary, exaggerated individualism was widely thought to have been not only futile before the gathering social storms but even partly responsible for the catastrophe, at least in the sense that individualism did little to hold off the wars, market collapse, and political terrors.

In this regard, the horrors of the First World War, which Europeans still refer to as the Great War, proved decisive. All across Europe, where the Great War had been fought so visibly, social thinkers of all kinds began, early after in the 1920s, to reassess the social and political theories of moral individualism that Tocqueville observed a century before had come under scrutiny, if not suspicion. But in Germany the situation was different in important ways that affected the ability of its leading intellectuals to reassess the traditional as freshly as, even in France and the UK, it was possible. Germany had experienced its defeat in the war with abiding bitterness towards the price the allied nations had imposed, which had led to political and economic instability as it faced the impossible task of social recovery under the financial and political penalties excised by the Treaty of Versailles in 1919. Instability is always the seed bed of political trouble, especially in democracies as ill-formed as Germany's. Hence, Hitler's rise to power and the nightmare that followed. These events are not so easily summarized into a neat causal nexus, but they begin to explain why social theory turned sharply critical of the nineteenth-century values of the knowing and powerful individual of bourgeois culture.

The early founders of the German tradition of thought from which Jurgen Habermas today has descended were forced to flee Germany. Many settled for a time in America where, like Tocqueville before them, they no doubt saw first-hand an old individualism that, in their land, was no longer possible.

What Habermas today calls the colonization of everyday life by the larger social forces is itself a critical theory directly related to Theodor Adorno's deep mistrust of what in the 1940s were the new mass communication cultures created by radio and the first wave of Hollywood cinema. He had seen first-hand how Hitler and the Nazi's used these media essentially to manufacture a goose-stepping mass culture of obedience to authority.

These then were the social realities that led to the widespread idea that the old individualism had given way to a new one in which the social individual, once the ideal of independent calm cut-off from 'the mass of his fellow-creatures', was now, under different conditions, the tragically helpless individual produced by a culture of *manipulated individualism*. The single most striking image of the manipulated individual was one that emerged well after the Second World War, in the 1960s when Herbert Marcuse wrote a celebrated book soundly critical of the mass (now mostly televisual) culture. The book was *One Dimensional Man* (1964), a study of the systematic deadening of the free individual's cultural and political independence. The remaining, shriveled dimension, according to Marcuse, was the mindlessness created by the pervasive intrusions of mass culture. Marx's *rural idiocy* had become Marcuse's *urban imbecility*. The once proud (if arrogant) mature individual of the nineteenth century was now a shell of his former self, with all individualizing qualities eroded by the steady drip of low-brow culture. *I Love Lucy* and *The Brady Bunch* did the work once done by Hitler's tirades – the hollow men T.S. Eliot had forecast in 1925 when the trouble of the first war was already coming to the fore. From these social experiences – that are by no means absent today – came the first important step towards rethinking the old individualism as a new and far from comforting manipulated state of moral life.

The emotional costs of isolated privatism: after the 1950s

The second theory of the new individualism emerged in the years when critical theorists like Marcuse and Habermas were refining theirs, and it came, predictably, from American social theorists (or at least social theorists who, in contrast to Marcuse, both lived in America and thought *as* Americans). The timing of the first foray into this second theory of new individualism, as *isolated privatism*, was early in the 1950s. Ironically, this was a time when, so soon after the second war in Europe, the United States stood tall in a unique global position – a posture, if anything, more strikingly unique than even today when it stands as the only remaining superpower. Yet by 1950 it was already evident that the USA and the Soviet Union were at odds, odds that were dealt in the unsettled peace at Yalta in 1945 in which vague agreements entered into by Franklin Roosevelt, acquiesced to by Winston Churchill, and eagerly sought by Joseph Stalin ceded the Soviets a considerable chunk of Europe's real estate. It would not, however, be fair to say that the Soviets had no claim on Eastern Europe. They had in fact made the crucial difference in their defeat of Hitler on the Eastern Front (a fact that American and British generals resisted mightily). Still, among much else, this gave the Soviets a considerable buffer against the West, including half of Germany. This fact when combined with their military, scientific, and technological capacity made the Soviet Union a rival to American dominance in real political terms, if not economic ones. The Cold War, thus, was both an iron curtain dividing the world *and* a wall that cast a long shadow over Europe and the United States.

In the USA the situation was, in some ways, absurd. America, easily and without question, was the mightiest nation on earth and especially so economically. This was because, in addition to having mobilized its industrial capacity in the war effort, America had once again avoided war on its own land. As a result Asia and Europe, and even the Soviet Union, had suffered the ravages of land and air warfare, leaving their economic infrastructures either limited or, in the cases of continental Western Europe and Japan, all but destroyed. However, because of the perceived threat of Soviet communism, American economic superiority came up against its geo-political limits. No economic rivals in the one aspect; a dangerous and powerful rival in the other. As a result, the Cold War remained cold due to this global imbalance of power that left the door open through which a Siberian shudder crept, chilling the moral bones of the Americans. The theory of military containment had the further unanticipated effect of containing the domestic vitality of American society. The rivalry, as instituted through the Cold War, was founded on little and led nowhere as we now know – nowhere that is but to the Soviet gulags and to America's anti-communism terrors.

It may be that the suffering visited on innocents – including in Korea and later in Vietnam where millions died in the name of this cold war – was the consequence of this contradiction in the global situation. People, including whole nations, feel disaffected or alienated when their worlds make no sense. This was Emile Durkheim's far more elegantly put idea of anomie as a cause of personal violence. America in the 1950s, when the televisual culture that so infuriated Marcuse was coming into its own, was a very strange mix of silliness and outright evil – the silly humour of Milton Berle and *I Love Lucy* and the evil of two gulags (including the American one in which thousands were banished from public life by unfounded accusations that they were communist fellow travelers). Underlying both this silliness and evil in America was its exceptional level of affluence.

The 1950s in America was the period when the middle class replaced the bourgeoisie as the social standard of the Good Society. And this middle class – populated by returning veterans of the war and their new wives and children, underwritten by a booming economy with jobs aplenty (at least for whites), and enhanced by a cornucopia of cheap homes and cars cleaned and serviced by a then astonishing array of new gadgets – this middle class represented the avant garde of a new social world.

This was the Golden Age when, in the USA at least, experts thought that finally the old values of human progress would become manifest. The idea was simple. If the formerly marginal economic classes of men and women (those once consigned to the uncertainties of the working class) could own homes in Levittown, drive one or more cars, take vacations on their boats, spend hours of leisure bowling with others, leave the housework to machines of all kinds, invite Elvis and Uncle Miltie into their homes by TV – then what more could they want? The problem was that the women and their children left in empty suburban towns of no particular cultural life did not enjoy the routine drone of their lives in houses that all looked the same with neighbours who aspired to do what they did. Far from it. Films like Marlon Brando's *The Wild One* in 1953 portrayed the rebelliousness of the new and young middle class. Middle-class affluence put money in the pockets of children, who became economic factors in themselves, which in turn led to the creation of what was soon called youth culture – young people with enough money to own a motorcycle (or, later, to shop at the malls), cut loose from their stultifying (one-dimensional, actually) suburbs to rage against the world. Their moms were, at the time, quieter about their anger which did not emerge until the women's liberation movement a decade later. Meanwhile the husbands and fathers of the middle class were off to their shops and offices, or on the empty road we know from Arthur Miller's *Death of a Salesman*. Say what you like about male privilege (and there can be no doubt that compared to their wives these men did enjoy freedoms), these men worked hard. In their minds they had fought the war that gave these freedoms, and now they worked hard to enjoy their cars and boats, to keep the kids and wives happy. But they too had their doubts.

In fact, in 1950s' America there was plenty of doubt to go around. At home in the suburbs, or in the crushing conformity required in the work-place, there was doubt as to why this newly-founded affluence did not lead to personal happiness. And looking out on the world, there was doubt as to why a good America which had defended freedom twice in the same century, and was now rebuilding both Europe and Japan, was not respected as the supreme world power – a status many thought America had earned and proven, but which the Soviet and Chinese communists seemingly defied at every turn. Thus while the urban imbecility spawned by televisual culture created a veneer of fancy-free living, those who looked closely at Elvis could see Marlon Brando's wild one – a connection that had not escaped the young. Rebellion when it occurs in cultural (as opposed to political) forms is a sign of something wrong; usually a contradiction, often a repugnant cultural expectation, sometimes no more than a vague interior uneasiness that something is broken in the world. One of the more memorable early books on the problem was Keats' *The Crack in the Picture Window* in 1957. All the modest splendour of the new lives and homes with picture windows meant to invite others to see the affluence within was somehow a broken image.

But where does *isolated privatism* come into this strange mix of the American 1950s and after? Today, Robert Putnam writes of bowling alone and means to argue that this once most social of leisure time activities has now declined into the pastime of a stratum of the new individuals. While critics would argue with Putnam's evidence, what remains is that for a long time, since at least the 1950s, American social critics have worried about the *loss* of the *old* individualism of Tocqueville's day. One of the first and most sensational of such critics was David Riesman, who with colleagues published *The Lonely Crowd* in 1950. The title says all that needs to be said. On the surface of the 1950s everyone was crowding together – wearing the same grey flannel suit to the office, living in the same or similar picture window tract homes (even the well off!), seeking out the routine gossip in neighbourhood coffee klatches, looking down the high school hallways for the latest fashion fad or new lingo – all ages among the new and rising middle classes in America were, indeed, caught up in this crowd behaviour. The new word was 'conformism' but what was meant was conforming too much to Tocqueville's 'mass of fellow creatures'. The concern on the part of social critics like Riesman was that behind all the crowd behaviour lay a loneliness that represented the surface emotional state of a fundamental change in the character of individuals. In his language, an empty *other-directedness* had taken over the personal lives of men and women who had once been *inner-directed*.

Naturally, Riesman, like other academic social scientists in his day, was not writing a popular essay (though remarkably this very academic book quickly became an all-time best-seller among books of its kind). What he and many others saw was a fundamental transformation in the social character of modern man (as they would put it in those days) and this transformation threatened to erode the economic and social achievements that had produced all that was good in the modern world. Who were these two 'characters'? The inner-directed man was none other than, yes, the man of nineteenth-century individualism, but a type of individual who, late in the nineteenth century (and well before the new middle classes arose after World War Two) was no longer free to indulge the lofty bourgeois comforts of Tocqueville's individual. The individual had already been transformed – into the self-starting entrepreneur, a man with little time to reflect on the comforts of private life because he was so engaged in the business of hard work, producing for profit in the bourgeoning capitalist system. This man was none other than that ideal type that German sociologist Max Weber illustrated in his description of Benjamin Franklin – the modern man himself. Frugal, self-motivated, goal oriented, hard-working, disciplined, and set firm upon a life of capital gain which he saw as a way of contributing to the building up of the modern world. Weber published his famous essay on this modern man whom Riesman would come to call inner-directed. *The Protestant Ethic and the Spirit of Capitalism* appeared (in installments) in Germany in 1904 and 1905. Ever after, social scientists took it as a gospel of social-psychology – that the modern person was modern by virtue of his individualism, an individualism that throve on an inner-directed self by work in and on the exterior world.

By 1950, Riesman and others, having been taught to take Weber's description of modern man as gospel (and not unreasonably so), saw a very different sort of character – the conforming individual who gave his life over to hard work, yes, but a half-century after Weber, the hard work that post-war social critics observed had become, they thought, the work of someone performing as a team-worker, an individual who supported the company goals, one who could be counted upon to live according to the conforming values of the culture, one whose wife and children were 'normal' in number and kind, and so on. Believing this as they did, social critics of the American 1950s had every reason to be concerned. To all appearances the affluence of the time had yielded a comfortable physical life, with enough leisure time to play, thus to work less, and enough surplus cash to spend, thus to buy and consume. Where Weber saw a producer, Riesman saw a consumer – and he was not wrong. Americans did have money to spend and they spent it with a vengeance. On cars, clothes, trinkets, just plain stuff that could magically adorn their homes and bodies. There was truth in the observation. Something was changing as we now know, as the great American commercial invention from that time – the shopping mall – has spread throughout the world. Postmodern man is, first and foremost, a shopper! He, or she, may hate the attribution, as much as she or he hates the credit card debt that grows beyond repeal, but it is very hard to deny.

This then is where the concern over *isolated privatism* first arose. The American social critics were, in a sense, not all that different from the German critical theorists. In the 1960s Herbert Marcuse was living in California. He saw and experienced what Riesman and others had been commenting upon. The difference however lay in the causes to which these effects were attributed. Marcuse, with his German sensibilities, saw a one-dimensionality imposed from the outside by the evils of mass culture. Riesman et al., and notably the sociologist Erving Goffman, put the blame or the responsibility on the individual, for what Goffman called being a self who presents himself in social settings by means of a native skill at impression management. In this respect (though not in others) the American theory of *isolated privatism* and the European one of *manipulated individualism* were (and are) two sides of the same social coin, deflated by a decline in the market value of the old individualism. For the European critical theorists the threat to the individual was evident and out in the open – the fissures in European social and political structures aggravated by wars and depression, and brought home metonymically by Hitler. For the Americans the threat was more subtle, but just as devastating – abroad their national power was, if not weak, at least vulnerable to challenge; at home, all the affluence in their domestic worlds, could not keep the kids, then the women, then the men from rebelling, rebellions ironically wrought not by deprivation but by an excess that remained (as their older values taught) unsatisfying. Come home from a day at the mall and what do you have? Tired feet, unbearable debt, and (more often than not) worthless stuff bought on sale that in the dulling light of home is fit only for consignment to the back of the closet. This is hardly a holocaust, but it is in its way a kind of interior terror that can have the effect of eroding the individual's self-confidence.

Worn down shoppers, like today's couch potatoes, cannot even begin to think of themselves as the source of moral and political power in the world. This was Marcuse's main point. Thus, leaving aside the fact that when push comes to shove Americans tend to see the individual as the source of social action (as Europeans tend to see the social as the source of individual power or its loss), what remains is that today's theories of a new individualism in the USA descend from a uniquely American social experience that was undeniably (if temporarily) different from Europe's. In the 1950s Americans were building miles and miles of highway whereby lonely individuals could flee from block upon block of tract homes. Meanwhile Europeans were, literally, rebuilding society as a whole. No wonder then that on the European side of the Atlantic the new individualism was thought to have been manufactured by an evil that had to be eliminated from the social structures in which it grew, while on the Western side of the same ocean it was viewed as a failure of American moral will.

The globalized individual – risks and costs: after the 1990s

The third of the three theories of the new individualism doubtless has its roots in many of the same histories that led to the first two. By the late 1990s proponents of the first two theories of the new individualism were either dead or retired and aging. The third group of social critics, mostly European and mostly British (either by birth or immigration), are of a younger generation (even as they themselves are no longer young in years). They are of that generation which Americans called the baby boomers. A kind of shorthand for those brought up in the false affluence of the 1950s – too young to ride with Marlon Brando's wild bunch, but old enough in the 1960s to see their mothers turn into feminists or hear their fathers talk of Woodstock or Selma. The experiences of this generation were different in Europe, where a definite seriousness of social purpose was necessarily more the order of the day. Yet by the end of the twentieth century, what they saw and heard in youth had simultaneously prepared them for dramatic changes in the world about them while failing even to begin to describe the transformations that appeared in the 1990s and into the twenty-first century. The speed at which globalization (both the concept and the reality) transformed daily life made the events of their youth appear as buggy rides in contrast.

Early in the 2000s we do not yet know how far and how fast globalization will take us, nor even, when and if it comes to a rest, the inertia will hurl us down on the murderous rocks of social collapse or settle us on a soft cushion of economic comfort. People argue both sides of the story. They agree only in the word they use to name it – globalization – which may turn out to be unwise if only because the worlds they describe so differently seem so utterly incommensurable. Yet, in one additional respect, these two views (and the countless variants between) do seem to agree on two things: that the world today is risky (who could deny it after 9/11?) and that the risks, being beyond the control of our familiar national cultures, require us, as individuals, to adjust. A small accord, but interesting just the same. Whether some are right to call this adjustment *self-reflexivity* is itself another matter. What we at least, if not all the disputants, can agree on for now, is that globalization requires a new way of being and behaving in the world.

Richard Sennett (actually more of an isolated privatism theorist in spite of his recent ties with the British proponents of risk society) has said in *The Corrosion of Character* (1998) that the fathers of his generation normally took and kept the same job with the same firm or institution all through their adult lives until retirement, while their children grew into an entirely different world. Today in the West that ideal is gone, and is deteriorating even in Japan where corporate loyalty is a matter of honour. From about the 1970s onwards, when economic crises arising from the manipulated costs of petroleum hit hard the then-still industrial world, men and women (and note here also that in the USA it had become necessary even for middle-class women to join the workforce) had to have several careers. For many women, it became a matter of living as a homemaker during their twenties, then going back to school to train for a new career that, once entered, led from place to place: from teaching to real estate, from law school to corporate management, from medicine to academic research. This of course was a pattern that was already flourishing among men – one that has in the adult years of the baby boomer generation became standard, and for many tragically common as globalization sent capital and jobs abroad, leaving many workers in their fifties without employment.

When social conditions require individuals to think differently about their lives, they must begin with thoughts about who they are and who they wish they were. For an individual to adjust to changed social conditions (even those that seem routine, such as a decline in the industrial sector in which one has worked for years), she must *reflect* – look back, that is, on the self she has been inhabiting. This, in a word, is the self-reflexive attitude of the new individualism as it has come to be early in the 2000s; and, it hardly needs to be said, *self-reflexivity* will be all the more intense and essential when the changing world all about is filled with risks – risks that prevent any life, even among the well-heeled, from reclining into self-satisfaction. In a sense, social life has always been, and will always be, a matter of risk. Individuals, whatever comforts they have or desire, cannot and do not control the larger social realities. Many of the old bourgeois individualists of the 1830s saw their sons or grandsons off to death in the Civil War of the 1860s. Yet, as terrible as civil and world wars may be, the long run of history has shown that in time they relent and peace, if not always prosperity, returns.

Globalization and the new individualism

Ours is the era of a new individualism: our current fascination for the instant making, reinvention and transformation of selves is, in some sense or another, integral to contemporary living. Living in the global age of a new individualism requires individuals capable of designing and directing their own biographies, of defining identities in terms of self-actualisation and of deploying social goods and cultural symbols to represent individual expression and personality. In the current social circumstances – in which our lives are reshaped by technology-induced globalization and the transformation of capitalism – it is not the particular individuality of an individual that's most important. What's increasingly significant is how individuals create identities, the cultural forms through which people symbolise individual expression and desire, and perhaps above all the speed with which identities can be reinvented and instantly transformed. It is this stress on instant transformation – and in particular the fears and anxieties it is designed to displace or lessen – that distinguishes our account of the new individualism from the foregoing theories of individualism.

Consider, for, example, contemporary representations of individualism in popular culture and the media, particularly the selling of 'lifestyles' and of DIY-identities to mass audiences. Apple Computer's 1998 'Think Different' campaign illustrates this well:

> Here's to the crazy ones. The misfits. The rebels. The troublemakers. The round pegs in the square holes. The ones who see things differently. They're not fond of rules. And they have no respect of the status quo. You can praise them, quote them, disbelieve

them, glorify them or vilify them. But the only thing you can't do is ignore them. Because they change things. They invent. They imagine. They heal. They explore. They create. They inspire. They push the human race forward. Maybe they have to be crazy ... we make tools for these kinds of people. Because while some see them as the crazy ones, we see genius. (Apple Computers, 1998)

Whatever else individualism may offer – and in the 'Think Different' campaign the promises are undeniably large and varied, from imagination to rebellion to craziness – identity embodies a palpable cultural contradiction. Apple drew a direct connection between its hi-tech aesthetics and individual expression. Between the technological revolution and personal genius. And yet this campaign, paradoxically, was selling individuality to a mass audience.

How did such a cultural contradiction come about? How can it be that individualism – which, one might think, is by definition opposed to cultural regulation or social consensus – has ended up, in some social contexts, opposed to autonomy? There are a number of key sociological factors involved in the rise of a new individualism (for further discussion see Elliott and Lemert, 2005), but in what follows we briefly note two: 'want-now' consumerism and globalization.

The twenty-first century craze to reinvent ourselves constantly is fast becoming a dangerous addiction that can ruin lives. Today this is nowhere more evident than in the pressure consumerism puts on us to 'transform' and 'improve' every aspect of ourselves: not just our homes and gardens but our careers, our food, our clothes, our sex lives, our faces, minds and bodies. In our quick-fix society, people want change and, increasingly, they want it instantly. There are various market-directed solutions that now offer the promise of instant transformation. More and more, such market-directed solutions – from self-help to therapy culture, from instant identity makeovers to plastic surgery – are reduced to a purchase mentality. There's an emerging generation of people whom might be called the 'Instant Generation' and who treat individualism as on a par with shopping: consumed fast and with immediate results. Today's 'want-now' consumerism promotes a fantasy of the self's infinite plasticity. The message from the makeover industry is that there's nothing to stop you reinventing yourself however you choose. But your redesigned sense of individualism is unlikely to make you happy for long. For identity enhancements are only fashioned with the short term in mind. They are just until 'next time'.

We see this social trend all around us, not only in the rise of plastic surgery and the instant identity make-overs of reality TV but also in compulsive consumerism, speed dating and therapy culture. In a world that places a premium on instant gratification, the desire for immediate results has never been as pervasive or acute. We have become accustomed to emailing others across the planet in seconds, buying flashy consumer goods with the click of a mouse, and drifting in and out of relations with others without long-term commitments. Is it any wonder that we now have different expectations about life's possibilities and the potential for change?

But there's also a deeper set of social forces at work in this branding of cosmetic surgery as a consumer lifestyle choice. The root of the problem is largely cultural, driven by a new corporate ethos that flexible and ceaseless reinvention is the only adequate response to globalization. The fast, short-term, techy culture of globalization is unleashing a new paradigm of self-making. In a world of short-term contracts, endless downsizings, just-in-time deliveries and multiple careers, the capacity to change and reinvent oneself is fundamental. A faith in flexibility, plasticity and incessant reinvention – all this means we are no longer judged on what we have done and achieved; we're now judged on our flexibility, on our readiness for an instant makeover. The culture of short-termism promoted by globalization puts pressure on people to try to 'improve', 'transform' and 'reinvent' themselves. Driven by desire and the fear of such a metamorphosis, individuals desperately attempt to 'refashion' themselves as more efficient, fast, lean, inventive and self-actualizing than they were previously. Day-in day-out, society in the era of this new individualism is fundamentally shaped by this fear of disposability.

Not all that long ago, anyone who wanted such instant change – say, plastic surgery or online speed-dating – would have been recommended therapy in the first instance. Today, by contrast, there is a widespread acceptance that the new individualism is beneficial and even desirable. Yet this social transformation has not been heralded by a shift in psychological understanding. It is, rather, symptomatic of a pervasive addiction to the ethos of instant self-reinvention. And the flipside of today's reinvention craze is the fear of personal disposability.

Perhaps the most distinctive feature of the new individualism is the playing out of these positive and negative features – the cultural trends towards freedom and alienation – against a backcloth of the *demise of social context*. Today, people in the polished cities of the West make sense of experience on the edge of a *disappearance of context*. As science and new technologies offer alternative paradigms and possibilities for social life, we have replaced the old contexts of tradition and custom with a focus on our individual selves. This shift in focus from the old rules and boundaries to the internal world of the individual is now central to the contemporary mood. The main legacy of this cultural trend is that individuals are increasingly expected to produce context for themselves. The designing of life, of a self-project, is deeply rooted as both a social norm and cultural obligation.

In the brave new world of globalization, new information technologies and multinational capitalism, however, individualism has changed in three crucial ways. Firstly, the undermining of traditions and in particular traditional ways of living has, as one might expect, enormously expanded the range of personal choice and opportunity for many people. As modern societies are more and more 'detraditionalized' (to use a term coined by Anthony Giddens), pre-existing ways of doing things become less secure, less taken for granted. It could be said that this is just a matter of the old rules and boundaries governing personal and social life dissolving, but we think not. For the import of traditions today has a reflexive aspect. Take marriage, for example. Not so long ago, marriage was widely seen as a sacred union 'till-death-do-us-part'. By contrast marriage today, against a backdrop of both the sexual revolution and divorce rates soaring throughout the West, has been transformed for many into a kind of temporary arrangement – as something that can be discarded. Leaving to one side the issue of whether this has been progressive or regressive, we think that what's important here is the new sense of uncertainty that such change has bred. For the likelihood of divorce must now be 'factored in' by everyone contemplating getting married, a reckoning that renders marriage different from what it was in the past. At the same time, however, such changes also open our individualist culture to wider challenges, extending the terrain of emotional life beyond the inviolable character of tradition. What most complicates the thread of individualism in this connection is the *experimental feel* that much of what we do in our private and social lives takes on.

The second crucial way in which the ideology of individualism changes in our own time is as a consequence of privatization. The neoliberal crusade to free individual initiative from the controls of the state has in recent years seen the ravages of cutbacks in welfare provisions or services, as well as the spread of a more market-led business orientation to the institutions of government on both sides of the Atlantic. Privatism as a result becomes of central importance to large areas of contemporary urban life, especially so in an age of increased mobility and digital technologies. The shrinking of communal ties and relations as a consequence of privatism is one reason why Don Watson, in *Death Sentence* (2003), suggests economic rationalism has debased our public language. Welfare agencies try to provide better 'outcomes' for 'customers'; hospital managers develop 'best-practice scenarios'; vice-chancellors review variable university fees in order to deliver improved 'educational product'. Watson's point is that a debased managerial language infects social life around the globe.

But the problem is more pervasive than that of any mere infection. For individualism today is intrinsically connected, we argue, with the growth of *privatized worlds*. Such worlds privatized propel individuals into shutting others and the wider world out of their emotional lives. Under the impact of privatism, the self is denied any wider relational connection at a deeply unconscious level, and on the level of day-to-day behaviour such 'new individualisms' set the stage for a unique cultural constellation of anguish, anxiety, fear, disappointment and dread. Yet to connect individualism to the new social conditions of enforced privatization is not to say that we are witnessing the end of collective ideals or, in a wider sense, the public sphere. Rather, the privatizing of identities – what we term the new individualism – becomes fundamental to the way individuals, groups and institutions organize social things. This is the case whether people yearn for either a public, cosmopolitan or a more traditional lifestyle. As market forces penetrate ever more deeply into the tissue of social life, what we can see taking place today is a shift from a politized culture to privatized culture. People, increasingly, are seeking personal solutions to social problems – in the hope of shutting out the risks, terrors and persecutions that dominate their lives in the global age.

The third important change in the way individualism has changed is at once ironic and less definite than the former two. Individualism as it came to be understood since Tocqueville's observations in the 1830s was, for the most part, a value of the middle and upper classes in the European diaspora. But this does not mean that people on the social and economic margins of public life are ignorant of the lifestyles of the dominant classes. Still, the classically free individual as the man who removes himself from the masses is necessarily a way of life possible only to people of means, to those able to attain and maintain a bourgeois life. The poor may aspire to such freedom, but neither the tenant farmer nor the factory worker is in a position to achieve it. Freedom, like individualism, is largely a conceit of the privileged who naively measure the differences they enjoy from the ways of the poor according to their impression that the poor simply do not know how to behave.

One of the striking facts of the current situation is the paradox that as the rich grow more distant from the poor in economic terms the poor encroach more on the privileged cultures of the better off. Globalization is, at least, about economics and culture. At the same time, those who think it is nothing but good tend to collapse the two, as those who think it is nothing but bad distinguish them too harshly; the reality is that the economic and the cultural are each powerful forces that sometimes move in concert, sometimes in tension, but most often in complex and surprising ways. Economically the global nature of international capital has led to a net loss for the world's poorest even as it may have propelled some into the comfortable social and economic classes. While culture in the form of mediated experiences and consumption desires has brought the rich and poor closer together in the paradoxical sense that the poor cannot achieve the standards of the well off, they can and do have a better understanding of how the other half lives.

There is ample evidence that poverty has devastating consequences for children and their families. Depression, post-traumatic stress disorder, obesity, lung and heart diseases, and starvation are rampant among the very poor, and especially when they are simultaneously exposed to violence as they are. None of these disorders of the world's social inequalities has declined, but it may be that to them is now added the affliction suffered more apparently by the middle and upper classes – that of isolation arising from being cut off from the social benefits that the poor can now plainly see in the cities and towns where they beg or from which they flee. Over time, the poorer and more marginal social groups have tended to be the bearers of traditions – religious and ethnic most especially. Thus, the growth of religious activism in the most impoverished regions of Africa, the Caribbean, the Middle East, and Asia is but one of the obvious instances of a cultural reaction to the inequalities of the modern world. One result has clearly been the emotional cost of the epidemic of social isolation that is always more severely visited on the poor. It makes little sense, however, to refer to the isolation of the poor as privatization if the private is taken as the interior spaces to which the individual retreats. But it does make sense if the formerly very different isolation of the poor from the means of success and self-esteem is crushed in the vacuum created by the flight of the new rich from the pains of human despair.

References

Adorno, T. (1950) *The Authoritarian Personality*. New York: Harpers.

Adorno, T. (2001) *The Culture Industry* (2nd edn) New York: Routledge.

Beck, U. (1997) *The Reinvention of Politics*. Cambridge: Polity.

Bell, D. (1993) *Communitarianism and its Critics*. Oxford: Oxford University Press.

Bellah, R., Madsen, R., Sullivan, W., Swindler, A. and Tipton, S. (1996) *Habits of the Heart: Individualism and Commitment in American Life*. Berkeley and Los Angeles: University of California Press.

Bloom, A. (1988) *The Closing of the American Mind*. New York: Simon and Schuster.

Elliott, A. and Lemert, C. (2005) *The New Individualism: The Emotional Costs of Globalization*. London: Routledge.

Habermas, J. (1989 [1962]). *The Structural Transformation of the Public Sphere: An Inquiry into a Category of Bourgeois Society* (trans T. Burger,). Cambridge, MA: MIT.

Hochschild, A. (2003) *The Commercialization of Intimate Life*. Berkeley and Los Angeles: University of California Press.

Keats, J. (1957) *The Crack in the Picture Window*. Boston: Houghton Mifflin.

Lasch, C. (1985) *The Minimal Self: Psychic Survival in Troubled Times*. New York: Norton.

Marcuse, H. (1964) *One Dimensional Man: Studies in the Ideology of Advanced Industrial Society*. Boston, MA: Beacon.

Putnam, R. D. (2001) *Bowling Alone: The Collapse and Revival of American Community*. New York: Simon and Schuster.

Riesman, D., Glazer, N. and Denney, R. (1950) *The Lonely Crowd: A Study of the Changing American Nature*. New Haven, CT: Yale University Press.

Sennett, R. (1978) *The Fall of Public Man*. New York: Norton.

Sennett, R. (1998) *The Corrosion of Character*. New York: Norton.

Simmel, G. (1950) 'Fundamental problems of sociology', in K. H. Wolff (ed.), *The Sociology of Georg Simmel*. New York: Free Press, pp. 1–25.

Simmel, G. (1968 [1896]) 'Sociological aesthetics', in *The Conflict in Modern Culture and Other Essays* (trans. P. Etzkorn). New York: Teachers College Press, pp. 68–80.

Thompson, J. B. (1995) *The Media and Modernity: A Social Theory of the Media*. Cambridge: Polity.

Tocqueville, A. de (1976 [1835]) *Democracy in America*. (P. Bradley (ed.) and H. Reeve (trans)). New York: Knopf.

Watson, D. (2003) *Death Sentence: The Decay of Public Language*. Milsons Point, NSW: Random House Australia.

4

Heeding Piedade's Song: Feminism and Sublime Affinity

Drucilla Cornell

In this chapter, I will pursue the ethical claim that in our struggle to build transnational feminist alliances, we must at times forsake the drive that we have to 'know' each other; if by knowledge we imply an objectifying relationship that allows us to securely place an object under the concept of reason. We are all familiar with the critiques of a certain strand of feminism that aspires to give us a new concept of woman, since such a concept would simply reinstate the rigid gender identities that have so effectively entrapped women and men. Indeed, some feminists have come to question whether the category of woman or even of gender is of any use, not just in feminist politics, but even in social science broadly construed. For the purposes of discussion, I want to emphasize that at times, I think we need to embrace concepts of reason, including analytic reason, in the pursuit of social justice. But we must do so in a way that remains faithful to what Dipesh Chakrabarty has called a 'double consciousness', (2000: 240), so that we may always remind ourselves that the language of social science carries within it the danger of erasing plural ways of being human that are inherent in the 'worlding' of the earth, to use Heidegger's language. A 'worlding' that should allow us to know when we move from participation to observation and analysis in order to maintain a critical reflection on any process through which we represent our world.

Although it is beyond the scope of my chapter, I do want to at least introduce the distinction between a concept and a category. A concept involves us in an appeal to universal validity, or in a weaker form, to the sedimented meanings that allow us to firmly identify a class or grouping through a set of either ideal or essentialized properties or attributes. (We will shortly return to Kant's use of concepts in his *Critique of Pure Reason*.) A category, on the other hand, makes specific generalizations, often based on highly elaborated frameworks, in which an analysis of a given object of study is both positioned and justified. But in this chapter, I will focus on sublime affinity as a way for us to enact our solidarity with one another in a feminist alliance – I would wish to stay true to Chakrabarty's 'double consciousness' that recognizes the need for such doubling in our struggles for social justice. This means, for example, that there are circumstances in which it is important to make use of gender as an analytic category that can help us both to observe and to understand our social reality. More broadly put, I do think there are circumstances in which we should employ determinate judgment in our knowledge of the world that we achieve through understanding, but that ultimately, it not understanding or even a critical reflection of reason upon itself which we should rely on in feminist political struggles (Chakrabarty, 2000).

Let me turn now to some of Kant's ideas that I will use throughout the chapter. First let me distinguish the use of the imagination in cognition and its deployment in reflective from aesthetic judgment. The ground of our knowledge is the transcendental imagination in which we intuit our world as always already in space and time. The transcendental imagination gives us the world of presentation and with it all things that can be known. The cognition of objects, which is for Kant what constitutes determinate judgment as such in the first critique, is carried out through a mediation in which the judgment consists in matching up the categories of the understanding with the raw material supplied by sensibility. Kant famously argued that this determination demands a schematization of the objects to be subsumed under the categories carried out by the imagination. The schema is a mediating representation that, to use Kant's words, is 'homogenous with the category, on the one hand, and with the appearance, on the other, and that thus makes possible the application of the category to the appearance' (Kant, 1998: *A138/B177*). We need to be able to imagine the abstract content of a concept so that we can adequately apply it to its various manifestations that, despite seeming differences, instantiate the concept. Kant provides the following example: 'The concept of dog signifies a rule whereby my imagination can trace the shape of such a four-footed animal in a general way, i.e., without being limited to any single and determinate shape offered to me by experience, or even to all possible images that I can exhibit in concreto' (Kant, 1998: *A131/B180*). Kant refers to this schematic representation of a dog as a template (or as he sometimes calls it, a monogram) for dog-hood, that links the concept to our sensible images of such an animal. In this case, understanding de-limits the role that the imagination can play. In other words, the cognition of objects serves a mediating role central to determinative judgment, in that its schemata make possible the subsumption of particulars under concepts, i.e., dogs under dog-hood. Understanding legislates the form of representation, and the schematizing aims of imagination are limited by the aims of cognition. Although this may seem abstract and far from feminist struggles, we can begin to deepen the profound suspicion that some feminists have of knowledge through concepts, including any concept of woman or even of women, because the imagination, in order to cognize the group, will inherently schematize and idealize the factors that are to be given substantiality in the concept itself. In other words, if we had a concept of woman, we would limit our imagination in terms of how and who we might be through the re-imagining and re-symbolization of the feminine within sexual difference. If feminism is ultimately to concern itself with women as subjects, then there is a deep sense in which we do not want to seek in advance concepts that would limit the imagination in its portrayal of the richness of that subjectivity.

Aesthetic reflection in Kant, in both the beautiful and the sublime, alternatively does not ascribe objective properties to things as determinate judgment does, but rather cultivates a subjective relationship between imagination and its object. Although I will not spend much time on the aesthetic judgment of taste in this chapter, I do want to emphasize that the difference between the judgment of taste and the judgment of the sublime does implicate a different role for the imagination. There is a specific sense in which the formalism of Kant's idea of aesthetic judgment in taste limits the imagination. Apprehending and reflecting on an object's form will necessarily involve exploring the temporal and spatial relations among its various parts, since the transcendental imagination is in the end what gives us our world. If the spatial and temporal form of an object spontaneously accords with the faculty of concepts, which is inevitably dependent on the form of space and time, then that form gives pleasure in the sense that we spontaneously feel the unity of our faculties. Concepts, it's important to note, are not brought to bear directly on aesthetic judgment; instead the imagination freely plays over the object so as to feel the harmony of cognition with sensibility, the harmony between the free imagination and the lawfulness of understanding, which takes us back to the attribution to a beautiful object of a purposiveness. This purposiveness is ultimately produced as a new way to regard the object as a formal unity that invents the harmony we seek out. It does so by creating in us a feeling that we can freely reach an accord between our faculties by allowing an imagination not properly determined by any concept, yet one that must still synchronize with the limits of the understanding if the object is to please us as we sink in the possibility that our understanding does not need to alienate us from our sensibility. On this reading, Kant's famous appeal to a *sensus communis*, so as to confirm the inter-subjective validity of aesthetic judgments, does not take us to any established community or communities. Instead, it appeals to a possibility that is available to all of us, precisely because we are rational creatures that think through the ground of the transcendental imagination, and therefore the feeling of pleasure we get from the harmony of our cognitive powers can be agreeable to all such creatures because it points to a cognitive relation common to all.

A judgment of the sublime, in contrast to beauty, is generated in us when an object defies the imagination's effort, an effort required because of its relationship to reason to present our world as a whole and the objects in it as comprehensible. Here we need to briefly review why affinity has transcendental purchase in Kant. Kant asks how particular instances are made possible by the pre-conceptual work of productive imagination. His answer is as follows: 'the basis for the possibility of the manifold's association, insofar as this basis lies in the object, is called the manifold's affinity' (Kant, 1998: A113). The imagination proceeds through three principles of synthesis. These are apprehension, reproduction, and recognition. The synthesis of reproduction provides the possibility that presentations are associable and comparable as such. In other words, if we did not reproduce an image that differentiates between dog-hood and cat-hood, we would not know the actual difference between dogs and cats. As a result, we could not recognize this specificity and difference between the two creatures. We need reproduction in order to get the recognition we need to organize what we apprehend under categories. Affinity is the pre-conceptual relationship that we imagine as there between diverse objects so that we can not only know objects but also know the relationships between them. But the transcendental purchase of affinity is that it gives us a world in which objects are in relation to one another, and it's precisely the conceptually undetermined relationships that take us back to imagined connections of the relata to which we now give a non-conceptual and new and different sense.

But this 'whole', precisely because its basis is pre-conceptual, can never itself be fully conceptualized. Reason reaches the limits of its aspiration exactly as it attempts to encompass all the faculties, and ultimately to find its way to fully rationalize the schemata. Sublime imagination and reason ultimately confront each other as what is unbounded by comprehensibility. In the mathematical sublime, the failure of the imagination to comprehend what is being presented to it turns on its inability to retain an ever-growing volume of apprehension. Apprehension explodes comprehensibility, and the imagination falters before what it is being asked to take in. Under the breakdown of the imagination, we find ourselves instead confronted with an overwhelming, indeterminate multitude of connotation. The meanings that sublime reflection ascribes both to art works and to aesthetic ideas more generally, must remain indeterminate and open ended, precisely because they can never be schematized or even harmonized as the imagination invents an object that seems to us as one with our understanding and our sensibility. If the judgment of taste links, but does not fully determine, imagination's relationship to the understanding, sublime reflection links the imagination to the ideas of reason, ideas which presume a totality that Kant's whole critical work demands that we apprehend as beyond the reach of the understanding, precisely because the understanding itself is grounded in intuitions that give us a pre-conceptual world which is at the same time the basis for all conception.

Sublime reflection produces uncanny relations among phenomena that seem to have no obvious connection, and by so doing, opens us to a differential affinity of relata, an affinity that denies schematization or determination by any definite concept. In the sublime, everyday concepts fail us and we must struggle to make a different kind of sense of the uncanny. The imagination necessarily fails us in sublime reflection, and as we've seen, reason ultimately has to appeal to the imagination in its aspiration to totality, therefore we can only trace out the meaning of the ideas of reason through aesthetic ideas that can at best represent them, but never capture them. To quote Kant: 'By an aesthetic idea I mean the representation of the imagination which induces much thought, yet without the possibility of any definite thought whatever, i.e., concept, being adequate to it, and which language, consequently, can never get quite on level terms with or render completely intelligible. It is easily seen, that an aesthetic idea is the counterpart (pendant) of a rational idea which, conversely, is a concept, to which no intuition (representation of the imagination) can be adequate' (Kant, 2006: SS 49). In a very particular sense, an aesthetic idea portrays an expressive relation to reason, even though the sublime reflection both inspires, and is inspired by, the unhinging of the bounds of both reason and the imagination in any single concept. The relationship then between reason and sublime reflection lies at the heart of Kant's unique understanding of why and how respect for our rational capacities is not only inspired by the sublime, but is also necessary if a judgment of sublimity is to arise. There is a sense then, at those moments of failure of comprehension, that we are returned to the dignity of reason's aspirations to apprehend the totality that grounds and lays before us the world as such. But we can never reach back so as to ascertain its graspability by our concepts. It is precisely at this moment of failure that we respect the grandness of reason's aspirations as we also confront the limits of what we can ever fully know.

This complex relationship between the sublime and a respect for reason explains Kant's famous quote:

> In the immeasurableness of nature and incompetence of our faculty for adopting a standard proportionate to the aesthetic estimation of the magnitude of its realm, we found our own limitation. But with this we also found in our rational faculty another non-sensuous standard, one which has that infinity itself under it as unit, and in comparison with which everything in nature is small, and so found in our minds a pre-eminence over nature even in its immeasurability ... In this way external nature is not estimated in our aesthetic judgment as sublime so far as exciting fear, but rather because it challenges our power (one not of nature) to regard as small those things of which we are wont to be solicitous (worldly goods, health, and life), and hence to regard its might (to which in these matters we are no doubt subject) as exercising over us and our

personality no such rude dominion that we should bow down before it, once the question becomes one of our highest principles and of our asserting or forsaking them. Therefore nature is here called sublime merely because it raises the imagination to a presentation of those cases in which the mind can make itself sensible of the appropriate sublimity of the sphere of its own being, even above nature. (Kant, 2006: SS 28)

It is no exaggeration to write that in Kant, it is the tension between reason's aspirations, imagination's failure of comprehension, and our respect for both that yield the feeling of sublimity. In determinate judgment, we subsume particulars under universally valid concepts, universally valid for creatures who have to think through the world in terms of time and space, and whose cognitive faculties are inevitably divided in the tasks they serve under the rubric of the understanding. In the case of aesthetic judgment, however, there are no concepts under which to place particulars. I need to stress this, because some commentators have suggested that aesthetic reflection broadens our mind, and indeed broadens our concepts. But a broad concept would still be a concept in Kant, and it's precisely not the task of aesthetic judgment to generate concepts. Not even aesthetic ideas, which open the space for reflection on the ideas of reason, should ever be allowed to interfere with the non-schematic operations of aesthetic reflection more broadly defined.

It is this uncanny sense of ourselves and the affinity of our affective relationships that I believe is crucial to feminism. Ethical feminism, as I have defined it, inverts the relationship between the positive and the ethical in this sense. Ethical feminism promotes the recognition that who we are and how we have been as women who make our own histories will always slip beyond the grasp of our current conceptual knowledge precisely because of the way in which hegemonic patriarchal conceptions of women make the imagination of us as those subjects next to impossible (Cornell, 1991). What I mean by the ethical here, is precisely the demand put on us, and particularly those of us who are white women in the rich countries of the North, to recognize that when we seek to 'understand' women, and this so easily happens when we try to 'comprehend' women of other cultures, we fall all too easily into what Chakrabarty reminds us is the inherent, objectifying tendency in a modernity that always understands others as objects of our knowledge, and judges them by the categories and concepts through which we grasp our world (Chakrabarty, 2000). As I've stated earlier in this chapter, I am with Chakrabarty, and indeed with Kant, that we should not forsake analysis and determinate judgment, but we should always recognize the incompleteness of both, particularly in our confrontation with the sublimity of 'the infinite incommensurabilities through which we struggle – perenially, precariously, but unavoidably – to "world the earth" in order to live within our different sense of ontic belonging' (Chakrabarty, 2000: 254).

Ethical feminism is for me an ethical, aesthetic imperative which demands that we accept our responsibility to constantly question our habits, to spin new extensions of webs of meaning, and to respect the open efflorescence of significance given in the rich field of ontic orientations that we now face in our world. Can we dream that the overwhelming complexity of the divergent ways in which human beings 'world their world' and still aspire to another dream, that of a reconciled humanity that aspires to the idea of Kant's ultimate idea of reason, the idea of humanity itself is possible? Perhaps we can, if we dare to dream of paradise.

In Toni Morrison's novel *Paradise* (1999), a diverse group of women (Mavis, Gigi, Seneca, and Pallas) find their way to a former religious school once under the leadership of one Mary Magna. As the novel begins, Mary Magna is still alive, although fading under the burnout of extreme old age, the flame of her life fanned by her devoted friend Connie. Connie was a 'stray' child found by Mary Magna in Brazil and brought to the United States to serve with her in her religious school. The women who wend their way to the convent are running away from the past, a world in which they were ensnared in patterns of abuse and neglect. They do not share anything in common other than that they are runaways. We know from the first sentence of the novel that one of them is white; later on, we are told that Connie is Brazilian. The convent itself is made up of women who have literally straggled in, and after Mary Magna's death, Connie retreats into her basement, only rarely engaging with the women who have set up their home under her roof. The convent is outside a town called Ruby, formed by a devoted group of black men – devoted to their God and to each other as '8-rocks' – whose almost blue-black colour is read by them as a symbol of their racial purity. An illegitimate affair between Connie and one of the founders of Ruby is not the only contact that the convent has with the town. Women from Ruby find solace and female treatment there. And indeed, Connie first comes to terms with the extent of her spiritual power by raising from the dead one of the young men who had driven out along the road beside the convent.

Ultimately, as we will see, Morrison is contrasting two very different views of identity. The men of Ruby can clearly not conceive of these women as other than a threat to their identity, their God, and their town. For them to maintain their identity, the women must be driven out, if not simply killed. But under the spiritual rituals led by Connie, who renames herself Consolata Sosa, the women find a way to a different identification with each other. This identification is other to strays and runaways, now transformed by what it demanded or more accurately did not demand of them. The women gaze at Consolata as she calls them into the ritual space that will 'reform' them as belonging to a new covenant in the convent. The women are drawn in, even as they question Connie: 'What is she talking about, this ideal parent, friend, companion in whose company they were safe from harm? What is she thinking, this perfect landlord who charged nothing and welcomed anybody; this granny goose who could be confided in or ignored, lied to or suborned; this play mother who could be hugged or walked out on depending on the whim of the child?' (Morrison, 1999: 262).

In her tales, Consolata Sosa remembers the world of African religion, and more specifically of the Candomble houses which she came out of and allows herself to return to by claiming her own spiritual power and the traditions in which it is rooted.

> Then, in words clearer than her introductory speech (which none of them understood), she told them of a place where white sidewalks met the sea and fish the color of plums swam alongside children. She spoke of fruit that tasted the way sapphires look and boys using rubies for dice. Of scented cathedrals made of gold where gods and goddesses sat in the pews with the congregation. Of carnations tall as trees. Dwarfs with diamonds for teeth. Snakes aroused by poetry and bells. Then she told them of a woman named Piedade, who sang but never said a word. (Morrison, 1999: 263–4)

For those unfamiliar with the rituals of Candomble, Consolata takes her 'children' that are in disarray into an embrace that can hold them all by allowing them to return to the site of their trauma and to re-imagine themselves apart from it. Morrison's symbolism here is that Consolata is the daughter of Yemoja who is, in the Yoruba Pantheon, both the goddess of the ocean and the patron orisa of the 'Gelede' Society. The 'Gelede' Society, in the original Yoruba religion that comes from Nigeria, celebrates the powerful women witches of the world, who had both the power to help build society and the power to destroy it. Yemoja is the ultimate manifestation of female spiritual power, and therefore, metaphorically at least, she is the 'greatest witch of all'.

Consolata's first command to the women is that they draw a template of themselves. As we have seen in Kant, a template or a monogram is a schematization of what is shared in common by the objects of the manifold so that it can be intuited as things within the conceptual unity. But here the template is where the women will draw what does not yet exist, and what cannot be conceptualized. In current psychoanalytic language, each woman has suffered a severe wound to the imagined image of herself through profound trauma. In the template they will draw out a new self, one no longer hunted and haunted, but they cannot do this without being returned to the self before the trauma which is, at least when psychoanalytically conceived, the no-self. This imagined no-self, this chance to go again and become a person differently, and perhaps a person at all for the first time, is what Morrison describes in the undergoing by each woman of a shared ritual. The first step in that ritual is the loud dreaming in which their identifications blend with one another.

That is how the loud dreaming began. How the stories rose in that place. Half-tales and the never-dreamed escaped from their lips to soar high above guttering candles, shifting dust from crates and bottles. And it was never important to know who said the dream or whether it had meaning. In spite of or because their bodies ache, they step easily into the dreamer's tale. They enter the heat in the Cadillac, feel the smack of cold air in the Higgledy Piggledy. They know their tennis shoes are unlaced and that a bra strap annoys each time it slips from the shoulder. The Armour package is sticky. They inhale the perfume of sleeping infants and feel parent-cozy although they notice one's head is turned awkwardly. (Morrison, 1999: 264)

But the loud dreaming is ultimately a call to draw out a different self from within the ritualistic connection that now supports them in a new promise of who they can be. They turned their templates into art works in which their re-imagined body is now reinterpreted by the others as giving expression to a history and to an experience that had no capacity to make itself into their world before they drew it and then explained it.

Life, real and intense, shifted to down there in limited pools of light, in air smoky from kerosene lamps and candle wax. The templates drew them like magnets. It was Pallas who insisted they shop for tubes of paint, sticks of colored chalk. Paint thinner and chamois cloth. They understood and began to begin. First with natural features: breasts and pudenda, toes, ears, and head hair. Seneca duplicated in robin's egg blue one of her more elegant scars, one drop of red at its tip. Later on, when she had the hunger to slice her inner thigh, she chose instead to mark the open body lying on the cellar floor. They spoke to each other about what had been dreamed and what had been drawn. Are you sure she was your sister? Maybe she was your mother. Why? Because a mother might, but no sister would do such a thing. Seneca capped her tube. Gigi drew a heart locket around her body's throat, and when Mavis asked her about it, she said it was a gift from her father which she had thrown into the Gulf of Mexico. Were there pictures inside? asked Pallas. Yeah. Two. Whose? Gigi didn't answer. (Morrison, 1999: 265)

In her initial opening to the ritual that forms the new covenant in which each woman's personhood is supported, Consolata appeals to a unity of the good and bad mother, a unity again which was the sublime affinity, not a concept, of what these figures are or even should be in some limited moral sense. 'Here me, listen. Never break me in two' (Morrison, 1999: 263). This imagined affinity of the 'good and bad', Eve as Mary's mother and Mary as the daughter of Eve, symbolizes the bringing together of parts of themselves subsumed in a self-blame that each woman had buried in order to survive her traumatic past. Described at the end of the ritual, the woman are returned to a kind of joy in their relationship to the great waters, rivers, and oceans that Consolata evokes in her ritual. These dancing women have found themselves in a re-imagined covenant in which each is returned through ritual to an originary rebirth out of the water that first contained them.

Heeding Piedade's Song

Consolata started it; the rest were quick to join her. There are great rivers in the world and on their banks and the edges of oceans children thrill to water. In places where rain is light the thrill is almost erotic. But those sensations bow to the rapture of holy women dancing in hot sweet rain. They would have laughed, had enchantment not been so deep. If there were any recollections of a recent warning or intimations of harm, the irresistible rain washed them away. Seneca embraced and finally let go of a dark morning in state housing. Grace witnessed the successful cleansing of a white shirt that never should have been stained. Mavis moved in the shudder of rose of Sharon petals tickling her skin. Pallas, delivered of a delicate son, held him close while the rain rinsed away a scary woman on an escalator and all fear of black water. Consolata, fully housed by the god who sought her out in the garden, was the more furious dancer, Mavis the most elegant. Seneca and Grace danced together, then parted to skip through fresh mud. Pallas, smoothing raindrops from her baby's head, swayed like a frond. (Morrison, 1999: 283)

Morrison evokes the possible viewer who might have stopped by the convent during the ritual and would have seen the women in the magnificence of their freedom. The viewer would have been puzzled by what she saw; so uncanny and so unfamiliar would be the sight of these women who were at peace with each other and with themselves, and with the rain. As Morrison writes, maybe this visitor would have had the flash of an insight that the convent women were no longer 'haunted'. The viewer confronts the sublimity of these women now imagined to be free, and as she does so confronts what is most unfamiliar – a covenant based not on restrictive identities who have to abject what is unlike themselves, but on the promise of a reconciled life with each other and with nature, and what is promised in the sublimity of that imagined reconciliation if not paradise.

This covenant worked out in ritual certainly does not proceed under the concept of woman. Yet the ritual itself explicitly turns on the 'material' of the feminine imaginary. Famously, Jacques Lacan defined the feminine imaginary as what was pushed under by the symbolic order, leaving only the residue of the psychical fantasy of woman in place of the ultimate object of desire, the mother-Other which is always there for the subject. The fantasy split off into 'good' and 'bad' woman, so as to tame that unbearable desire, is exactly what Consolota puts into play at the beginning of her ritual. Her reminder, Eve as Mary's mother, Mary as the daughter of Eve, is to seek to reclaim both good and bad woman in the process of re-imagining the significance of both. Simple identification along the lines of good and bad is as a result broken up, and the women can then own up to, and live differently with, the 'bad' girl they have always abjected in themselves. Lacan, of course, would not have believed that such a ritual could heal, nor that women could ever live beyond being haunted by the inexpressibility of their feminine sexual difference, and hunted by men if they try to break up the symbolic order so as to alter themselves in a new field of desire and significance (Lacan, 1982). Yet of course, Lacan had no experiences with the rituals of the Yoruba-based religion, or more specifically, of the Candomble traditions and practices of Brazil. Morrison invites us to imagine such a ritual in all its sublimity. And yet it's not just the ritual and loud dreaming that are sublime; it is the full acknowledgment of each woman by every other of the intensity of her suffering that is itself sublime. Time itself is lost as the women engage in the re-workings of their feminine imaginary. As Morrison writes, 'January folded. February too. By March, days passed uncut from night as careful etchings of body parts and memorabilia occupied them. Yellow barrettes, red peonies, a green cross on a field of white. A majestic penis pierced with a Cupid's bow. Rose of Sharon petals, Lorna Doones. A bright orange couple making steady love under a childish sun' (Morrison, 1999: 265).

I wrote at the beginning of this chapter that we should not seek a new concept of woman because it limits this imaginative play with the feminine imaginary in the name of a series of known attributes that can be grasped as what a woman *is*, and with that grasping, a limit is placed on who a woman could be. Simply put, we do not seek a new concept of woman, because we do not wish to limit the play of the imagination in sublime reflection. Sublime reflection allows us to explode the sedimented meanings we associate with the name woman, and even with the name women. In a deep sense, what matters is the singularity of each woman's past; and yet that past only comes to mean for each woman as she re-imagines herself through turning her template, her idealized person, into something she now shapes.

Does race and ethnicity play out in this re-identification? We know that all the women are not black. So if there is race and ethnicity in the Convent, it remains as the marks on the flesh which themselves have to be re-imagined, in the re-making of who they are, together. If we wanted to use psychoanalytic terminology here, the women are re-making themselves through their sexual difference and not despite it. I have distinguished elsewhere between identity, position, and identification (Cornell, 2002: 98–100). In ritual, these women explicitly play with the meaning of the identification 'woman' as it comes to them in all the bits-and-pieces of the images of the feminine imaginary. But they also have an identity for the men in the town as women. They are positioned as the ultimate bad women, who dare witchcraft and threaten with the power of their orisas, the identified phallic stability of the town. This convent, with the fear and awe it inspires, had to be a woman's convent. It was only such a convent that could threaten the men of Ruby, precisely because their covenant, their paradise, is incompatible with the safe and stern phallic home the men have identified as their only hope for redemption from a racist world. Their terror of the women explodes in the meeting the men hold to take the decision that these women must be hunted down and removed of all their contaminating influence, so that the town could once again be in its purity.

It was a secret meeting, but the rumors had been whispered for more than a year. Outrages that had been accumulating all along took shape as evidence. A mother was knocked down the stairs by her cold-eyed daughter. Four damaged infants were born in one family. Daughters refused to get out of bed. Brides disappeared on their honeymoons. Two brothers shot each other on New Year's Day. Trips to Demby for VD shots common. And what went on at the Oven these days was not to be believed. So when nine men decided to meet there, they had to run everybody off the place with shotguns before they could sit in the beams of their flashlights to take matters into their own hands. The proof they had been collecting since the terrible discovery in the spring could not be denied: the one thing that connected all these catastrophes was in the Convent. And in the Convent were those women. (Morrison, 1999: 11)

The specificity of these women's lives is neither reducible to some overarching concept of woman, nor is it based in a simple notion of their difference. Difference, in other words, is not a spelled out; marked, feminine difference that can be used as a standpoint of critique for either universalist humanist notions, or even as the basis of some attempt to ascribe universality to the concept woman. As Adam Thurschwell and I wrote in 1987,

> In a related manner, the gynocentric critique of universalist feminism is a critique of the identity category that (mistakenly) accepts this category for what it claims to be. We fully share the motivations that inspired this critique, but have attempted to show that understood properly, the stark choice between universality and absolute difference is a misrepresentation of the interlocking interplay of sameness and difference. Furthermore, it is a false choice: the gynocentric response reinscribes itself in the same repressive logic of identity that it criticizes in universalist feminism. We condemn a reified gender differentiation not in the name of some 'universal human nature', but because it would confine us to certain socially designated personality structures, and because it misrepresents the self-difference of the gendered subject. It restricts the play of difference that marks every attempt to confirm identity. (Cornell and Thurschwell, 1996 [1987]: 160–1)

We have seen that, for Kant, aesthetic ideas seek to express what can never be conceptualized, including the ideas of reason themselves. In Morrison's novel, paradise evokes a number of aesthetic ideas that force us towards new insights and visions which defy total comprehension. These insights push us towards drawing out new networks of affinity, including the affinity the women find in their being-together in their dance in the rain. But Paradise, in the most profound sense, is itself an aesthetic idea. Its promise is clearly beyond any notion of it. But it is just such a promise that Morrison evokes as always a possible new covenant, a new way of relating to nature, and a different, ethically altered humanity. Paradise, as itself an aesthetic idea, can only be brought into shape as ultimately what denies the very process of shaping itself. Imagination falters before what it most seeks to envision. And so as we strive to evoke paradise as an aesthetic idea, we also have to acknowledge that all such expressions are imperfect, that they break down under the very demand of what the aesthetic idea longs for but cannot realize in any form of knowledge. Paradise is even irreducible to the great Kantian ideal of humanity, which regulates us as moral creatures as we aspire to live together in the kingdom of ends. For in this beyond, we not only find the magnificent sternness of the moral law, a sternness that the men of Ruby believe themselves to ever try to live by, we find the happiness of the rain dance, we find what Adam Thurshwell and I defined as reconciliation: the coincidence of love and freedom. This is a promise that Consolata envisioned with Piedade's songs. Piedade's song and Consolata's insight allow her to ascend to the practice of healing, and even of breathing life back in to what appears to be dead. For in a sense, isn't that what the ritual gave to the women? Another site of who they might be together, and with the world around them? As an aesthetic idea, always incomplete in its imagined affinity that leaves human beings at peace with all that is, paradise undermines the very shapes it seeks to actualize.

Was paradise ever there? Did the story happen? Was Consolata really a witch who could raise the dead? I ask you to imagine with me, if you can, that other space of our being-together, through an affirmation of our sexual difference that itself never claims to be anything other than a vision, that as it glimmers necessarily fades if we try to hold on to it too strongly. If we listen hard enough, can we hear Piedade's songs, even if there is no actual sound that goes with them? When Richard Misner, the politically inspired minister of Ruby, returns to the convent with Anna to see what is left, they find nothing there. Consolata had been shot; so had the 'white woman'. The others supposedly ran into the garden. Anna and Richard take some eggs from the hen house and then they see it, or rather sense it. Anna says she heard a door close; Richard saw a window. On the way home, they laugh about who's the pessimist, who's the optimist. But both 'knew' that for a minute they had had insight, and that insight led them to the sublime questions that they, and of course we, rarely want to confront. 'Whether through a door needing to be opened or a beckoning window already raised, what would happen if you entered? What would be on the other side? What on earth would it be? What on earth?' (Morrison, 1999: 305). Perhaps paradise. Do you dare to open that window? Can you bear to hear Piedade's song? Morrison herself has dared to open that window, returning us to an initial imaging of Piedade, Yemoja, and her circle in the Gelede society, Osun and her enchanted waters, which always allow us to see ourselves differently. Did this initial imagining force the story on the writer? Does it make us confront unbearable hope and dread as we open the window or shut the door? Do we dare to try to imagine the sublimity of that story of paradise, told through figures of women of overwhelming power? If we do so dare, then it will be our story, our imagining, and our struggle. And if we do dare then there is hope, because for a moment at least we have insight into the full force of the promise of paradise. I leave Morrison with the last word.

> In ocean hush a woman black as firewood is singing. Next to her is a younger woman whose head rests on the singing woman's lap. Ruined fingers troll the tea brown hair. All the colors of seashells – wheat, roses, pearl – fuse in the younger woman's face. Her emerald eyes adore the black framed in cerulean blue. Around them on the beach, sea trash gleams. Discarded bottle caps sparkle near a broken sandal. A small dead radio plays the quiet surf.

> There is nothing to beat this solace which is what Piedade's song is about, although the words evoke memories neither one has ever had: or reaching age in the company of the other; of speech shared and divided bread smoking from the fire; the unambivalent bliss of going home to be at home – the ease of coming back to love begun.

> When the ocean heaves sending rhythms of water ashore, Piedade looks to see what has come. Another ship, perhaps, but different, heading to port, crew and passengers, lost and saved, atremble, for they have been disconsolate for some time. Now they will rest before shouldering the endless work they were created to do down here in paradise. (Morrison, 1999: 318)

References

Chakrabarty, D. (2000) *Provincializing Europe: Postcolonial Thought and Historical Difference*. Princeton: Princeton University Press.

Cornell, D. (1991) *Beyond Accommodation: Ethical Feminism, Deconstruction, and the Law*. New York: Routledge.

Cornell, D. (2002) *Between Women and Generations: Legacies of Dignity*. New York: Palgrave Macmillan.

Cornell, D. and Thurschwell, A. (1996 [1987]) 'Feminism, negativity, intersubjectivity', in D. Cornell and S. Benhabib (eds), *Feminism as Critique: Essays on the Politics of Gender in Late-Capitalist Societies*. Minneapolis: University of Minnesota Press.

Kant, I. (1998) *Critique of Pure Reason*. (P. Guyer and A. Wood, eds and trans). Cambridge: Cambridge University Press.

Kant, I. (2006 [1790]) *The Critique of Judgement* (J. C. Meredith, trans). Oxford: Oxford University Press.

Lacan, J. (1982) *Feminine Sexuality and the Ecole Freudienne*. New York: Palgrave Macmillan.

Morrison, T. (1999) *Paradise*. New York: Plume.

5

Top Girls? Young Women and the Post-feminist Sexual Contract*[1]

Angela McRobbie

Since early decisions on education and employment influence later possibilities, it is only younger women who are able to make many of the major work and life decisions in a context of legally enforceable equal opportunities. Age is thus crucial in new forms of difference and inequalities between women. (Walby, 1997: 41)

The education of girls is probably the most important catalyst for changes in society. Augusto Lopez-Claros, Chief Economist, at the World Economic Forum, quoted in the *Guardian* 18 May 2005, p. 208.

And now it's quite clear that the danger has changed. (Foucault, 1984: 344)

Resurgent patriarchies and gender retrenchment

This analysis of a 'new sexual contract' now seemingly available to young women, takes, as a starting point, some passing comments by a number of feminist theorists in the last few years. First, there is Butler's mention, in regard to her rich and complex equivocations on gay marriage and her reflections on the politics of kinship, that there has been a decline in radical sexual politics (Butler, 2005). Second, there is Mohanty's important argument in her article 'Under Western Eyes Revisited', that the restructuring of flexible global capitalism now relies heavily on the willing labour of girls and women and that this entails both a decisive re-definition of gender relations and also forms of retrenchment on the part of 'patriarchies and hegemonic masculinities' (Mohanty, 2002). Mohanty argues that young women are allocated a pivotal role in the new global labour market, but this coming forward coincides with the fading away of feminism and the women's movement, such that post-Beijing, the most significant site for pursuing struggles for gender justice has been the anti-globalization movement. But, when she wrote 'Under Western Eyes' there had been, she recalls, 'a very vibrant, transnational, women's movement, while the site I write from today is very different' (2002: 499). Mohanty suggests that the general shift in

*First published in *Cultural Studies*, Vol. 21, Nos. 4–5 July/September 2007, pp. 718–737. Published here with the kind permission of Routledge.

global politics towards the right, and the decline of social welfarist models, coincide with 'processes that recolonise the culture and identity of people' (2002: 515). (The word 'recolonise' is relevant to the argument I will present here.)

Both of these observations by Butler and Mohanty chime also with my own recent focus on gender, media and popular culture. I have argued that emerging from largely First World scenarios, the attribution of apparently post-feminist freedoms to young women most manifest within the cultural realm in the form of new visibilities, becomes, in fact, the occasion for the undoing of feminism (McRobbie, 2004). The various political issues associated with feminism are understood to be now widely recognized and responded to (they have become feminist common sense) with the effect that there is no longer any place for feminism in contemporary political culture. But this disavowal permits the subtle renewal of gender injustices, while vengeful patriarchal norms are also re-instated. These are easily overlooked, or else a blind eye is turned to them, because they are overshadowed by the high-visibility tropes of freedom now attached to the category of young women through processes of female individualization achieved through a range of recommended technologies of self. On these grounds my own account of post-feminism is equated with a 'double movement': gender retrenchment is secured, paradoxically, through the wide dissemination of discourses of female freedom and (putative) equality. Young women are able to come forward on condition that feminism fades away.

Sylvia Walby's (2002) rationale for the shift away from earlier and more autonomous forms of feminist practice to an engagement with mainstream politics on a national and global stage stands in sharp contrast to this analysis of the new constraints of female equality. It is because there have been various feminist successes that it is now appropriate to re-position feminist politics within the mainstream. Feminism has had a major impact in the field of global human rights and has in effect transformed the human rights agenda. It has also been effective at the level of the UK nation state so that gender issues are now thoroughly integrated into the wider political field. These changes, along with the participation of women in work, give rise to a new 'gender regime'. Walby's model is therefore accumulative, in terms of gains which have been made, and linear, in that feminism moves from localized actions and autonomy into the world stage, and because of this presence and participation, and in light of the possibilities which emerge from globalization, feminism itself changes to comprise advocacy networks, alliances, and coalitions which are capable of being organized to meet particular or culture-specific requirements. Walby endorses a kind of multifaceted, gender mainstreaming politics on the basis of institutional recognition. She offers a persuasive (if top down) and positive account of the professionalization and institutionalization of feminism. In addition her own engagement with women's policy issues (eg., the UK government's Women's Budget Group) is important.

But this model of gender regime is quite different from that posed in the pages that follow. This is because Walby implies that institutionalization and capacity building, and indeed participation as well as the growth of feminist expertise and the presence of women professionals on the world stage, have come about in a progressive way. She does not engage with the wider and punitive conditions upon which female success is predicated. Nor is she alert to the new constraints which emerge as the cost of participation, and, more generally, the re-shaping of gender inequities which are an integral part of resurgent, global, neo-liberal, economic policies. Walby acknowledges women's place as producers in the global economy but overlooks their importance as consumers of global culture, even though it is within the commercial domain that processes of gender re-stabilization are most in evidence.

With these recent feminist perspectives acknowledged, this chapter asks the question, how do we account for the range of social, cultural and economic transformations which have brought forth a new category of young womanhood? If such changes find themselves consolidated into a discernible trend in the UK (and elsewhere) in the last ten to fifteen years, what are we to make of the decisive re-positioning of young women this appears to entail? Transformations such as those described below tend to be seen as positive, and they are palpable reminders that women's lives have improved. But the feminist perspective presented here is alert to the dangers which arise when a selection of (mostly liberal) feminist values and ideals appear to be inscribed within a more profound and determined attempt, undertaken by an array of political and cultural forces, to re-shape notions of womanhood to fit with new or emerging (neo-liberalized) social and economic arrangements. And within a context where in Europe and in the USA there has been a decisive shift to the right, this might also be seen as a way of re-stabilizing gender relations against the disruptive threat posed by feminism. It's not so much turning the clock back as turning it forward to secure a post-feminist gender settlement, a new sexual contract.[2] The recent explosion of discourse about the category of girl or young women enacts and brings into being these processes of gender re-stabilization.

The meanings which now converge around the figure of the girl or young women (which, from a UK cultural perspective, have global export value, including films like *Bridget Jones's Diary* and *Bend It Like Beckham*) are now more weighted towards capacity, success, attainment, enjoyment, entitlement, social mobility and participation. The dynamics of regulation and control are less about what young women ought not to do, and more about what they can do. The production of girlhood now comprises a constant stream of incitements and enticements to engage in a range of specified practices which are understood to be both progressive but also consummately and reassuringly feminine. What seems to underpin these practices is a suggestion that young women have now won the battle for equality, they have gained recognition as subjects worthy of governmental attention, and this has replaced any need for the feminist critiques of what Mohanty labels hegemonic masculinities.[3]

The girl emerges across a range of social and cultural spaces as a subject truly worthy of investment. Within the language of Britain's New Labour government, the girl who has benefited from the equal opportunities now available to her can be mobilized as the embodiment of the values of the new meritocracy. This term has become an abbreviation for the more individualistic and competitive values promoted by New Labour, particularly within education. Nowadays, a young woman's success seems to promise economic prosperity on the basis of her enthusiasm for work and having a career. Thus a defining feature of contemporary girlhood is the attribution of capacity, summed up, as Anita Harris describes, in the Body Shop phrase the 'can do' girl (Harris, 2004).[4] This begs the question – what is at stake in this process of endowing the new female subject with capacity? The attribution of both freedom and success to young women, as a series of interpellative processes, takes sharply differentiated forms across the seemingly more fluid boundaries of class, ethnicity and sexuality. This produces a range of entanglements of racialized and classified configurations of youthful femininity.[5] While there is a good deal more work to be done on the specificities of these re-figurations of femininity, within changed but nonetheless re-stabilized landscapes of class and race, and indeed where change is the instrument of re-stabilization, the point to be made here is that the celebratory discourse of opportunity and achievement is the means by which this change is realized. From being assumed to be headed towards marriage, motherhood and limited economic participation, the girl is now a social category understood primarily as being endowed with economic capacity. Within specified social conditions and political constraints, young, increasingly well-educated women, of different ethnic and social backgrounds, now find themselves charged with the requirement that they perform as economically active female citizens. They are invited to recognize themselves as privileged subjects of social change, and perhaps they might even be expected to be grateful for the support they have received. The pleasingly lively, capable and 'becoming' young woman, whether black, white or Asian, is now an attractive harbinger of social change.

The post-feminist masquerade

Young women have been hyper-actively positioned in relation to a wide range of social, political and economic changes of which they themselves appear to be the privileged subjects. We might now imagine the young woman as a highly efficient assemblage for productivity. (This too marks a shift, as women now figure in governmental discourse as much for their productive as reproductive capacities). The young woman has government ministers encouraging her to avoid low paid and traditionally gendered jobs like hairdressing. She is an object of concern when a wide discrepancy is revealed between high levels of academic performance, yet a pervasive, low self-esteem.[6] She also merits the attention of government on the basis of the inequalities of pay and reward in the labour market, which are reminders that there is indeed still a role for government to play in supporting women's rights. She is addressed as though she is already 'gender aware', as a result of equal opportunities policies in the education system. With all of this feminist influence somehow behind her, she is now pushed firmly in the direction of independence and self reliance (Budgeon, 2001; Harris, 2004). This entails self-monitoring, the setting up of personal plans and searching for individual solutions. These female individualization processes require that young women become important to themselves. In times of stress, the young woman is encouraged to seek therapy, counselling or guidance. She is thus an intensively managed subject of the post-feminist, gender-aware, biopolitical practices of a new governmentality (Rose, 1999). But here we might inquire as to what gender values underpin these concerns. Does this strategy affirm new 're-traditionalized' styles of normative femininity to be adhered to, despite these winds of gender change (Adkins, 2002; Probyn, 1997). Rather than exploring these processes through the concept of a re-traditionalization, my preference is to draw on strands of thinking from psycho-analytic feminism and examine gender re-positioning through the idea of a post-feminist masquerade. This I take to be a containment strategy adopted on behalf of the (patriarchal) Symbolic when faced with a possible disruption to the stable binaries of sexual difference.

We might ask is the masquerade (as first defined by Riviere in 1929, and then returned to by Butler in 1990/1999) one of the now self-conscious means by which young women are encouraged to collude with the re-stabilization of gender norms so as to undo the gains of feminism and dissociate themselves from this now discredited political identity (see the attached advertisement for *Grazia* magazine in the *Guardian* 17 January 2006).

Riviere's famous essay of 1929 is one piece of writing which feminists have frequently returned to.[7] As a psychoanlyst, Riviere was interested in how 'women who wish for masculinity may put on a mask of womanliness to avert anxiety and the retribution feared from men' (Riviere, 1986[1929]: 35, quoted in Butler, 1999: 65). Riviere understands womanliness and masquerade to be indistinguishable; there is no naturally feminine woman lurking underneath this mask. I want to propose that the post-feminist masquerade is a strategy or device for the re-securing of patriarchal law and masculine hegemony. The masquerade exists as a mode of feminine

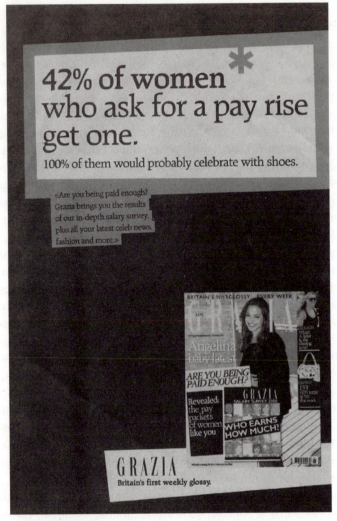

Figure 5.1 Grazia advertisement in the *Guardian* (17 January 2006). Courtesy *Grazia* magazine

inscription, an interpellative device, at work and highly visible across the commercial domain as a familiar (even nostalgic), lighthearted (unserious), refrain of femininity. It has recently been re-instated into the repertoire of femininity ironically.[8] This signals that the hyper-femininity of the masquerade which would seemingly re-locate women back inside the terms of traditional gender hierarchies, by having her wear spindly stilettos, 'pencil' skirts, and so on, does not in fact mean entrapment since it is now a matter of choice rather than obligation. This new masquerade refers to its own artifice and its adoption by women is done so as a statement, with the woman in the masquerade making the point that this is a freely chosen look. In addition, the post-feminist masquerade is all the more effective on the grounds that it seems not to fear male retribution.

Instead, it is the reprimanding structure of its substitute – the fashion and beauty system which acts as a substitute authority. (Hence the seeming disregard for male approval, especially if the outfit and look are widely admired by those within the fashion milieu.[9]) The masquerade creates a habitus for women who have now found themselves ensconced within the fields of work, employment and public life, all of which have hitherto been marked out as masculine domains. The masquerade disavows the spectral, powerful and castrating figures of the lesbian and the feminist with whom they might conceivably be linked. It rescues women from the threat posed by these figures by triumphantly re-instating the spectacle of excessive femininity (on the basis of the independently earned wage), while also shoring up hegemonic masculinity by endorsing this public femininity which appears to undermine, or at least unsettle, the new power accruing to women on the basis of this economic capacity. In practice it can be read as a nervous girlish gesture on the part of young women (think of Bridget Jones's flirty presence in the workplace and her 'oh silly me' self-reprimands) who remain somewhat fearful that their coming forward and competing on the labour market with men as their equals will jeopardize their sexual desirability. The young woman adopts this new masquerade (assuming, for example, the air of being 'foolish and bewildered': see Riviere, 1986[1929]: 29) in fear of retribution now that she is actually and legitimately inside the institutional world of work, from which she was once barred or had only limited access to. The new masquerade draws attention self-consciously to its own crafting and performance, and this space of reflexivity is also suggestive of a deep ambivalence.[10] The post-feminist masquerade is a knowing strategy which emphasizes its non-coercive status; it is a highly-styled disguise of womanliness now adopted as a matter of personal choice. But the theatricality of the masquerade – the silly hat, the too short skirt – are once again a means of emphasizing, as they did in classic Hollywood comedies, female vulnerability, fragility, uncertainty, and the little girl's 'desire to be desired'.

Both Riviere and Butler refer to the sublimated aggression directed towards masculinity and male dominance in the form of the masquerade. Riviere uses words like triumph, supremacy and hostility to describe the female anger which underpins the façade of excessive feminine adornment, and she pinpoints the fury of the professional woman who perceives her own subjugation in the dismissive behaviour of her male peers. All of this anger gets transmogrified into the mask of make-up and the crafting of a highly-styled mode of personal appearance. This strategy re-appears today in very different circumstances. Women now routinely inhabit these masculine spheres, and now find themselves in competition with men on a daily basis. They take their place alongside men thanks to the existence of non-discriminatory policies, and more recently to systems of meritocratic reward as advocated by New Labour. The woman in masquerade wishes to have a position as a 'subject in language' (i.e., to participate in public life) rather than existing merely as 'women as sign' (Butler, 1999). It is precisely because women are now able to function as subjects in language (i.e., they participate in working life) that the new masquerade exists to manage the field of sexual antagonisms and to re-instate women as sign. The successful young woman must now get herself endlessly and repetitively done up (dragged up), so as to mask her rivalry with men in the world of work (i.e., her wish for masculinity) and to conceal the competition she now poses because only by these tactics of re-assurance can she be sure that she will remain sexually desirable.

The need for such a masquerade in a post-feminist context remains a source of sublimated anger. The private voices of the heroines of popular 'chick lit' fiction regularly give vent to their anger and outrage that they have to make themselves submissive to avoid giving out the wrong signals to men. But by abiding 'The Rules' as laid down for them by the new experts in sexual decorum means they can no longer risk being seen as too powerful women for fear of jeopardizing their chances in marriage and family life, hence the thin line between coercion and consent. The message to the post-feminist young woman is that if she is going to opt for marriage and motherhood (and play it straight) then she must adopt this mask of feminine submissiveness. What is required of the young woman inside the heterosexual matrix and in search of a male partner with whom she can have children is the dramatic enactment, performed with some degree of knowing calculation, of seductive femininity. The masquerade functions to re-assure male structures of power by defusing the presence and the aggressive and competitive actions of women as they come to inhabit positions of authority. It re-stabilizes gender relations and the heterosexual matrix (as defined by Butler) by interpellating women repeatedly and ritualistically into the knowing and self-reflexive terms of highly-stylized femininity. The masquerade works on behalf of the Symbolic pre-emptively in light of the possible disruptions posed by the new gender regime. It operates with a double movement; its voluntaristic structure works to conceal that patriarchy is still in place, while the requirements of the fashion and beauty system ensure that women are still fearful subjects, driven by the need for 'complete perfection' (Riviere 1986[1929]: 42).

Education and employment as sites of capacity

Thus far I have examined some of the terms and conditions which permit young women to emerge as subjects of capacity. This marks something other than their designation as subjects in language for the reason that the processes which attribute capacity bear the traces of prior feminist antagonisms and the threats posed by feminism to patriarchal authority which has consequently had to adapt and respond. The female subject of capacity is not merely the outcome of this re-adjustment on the part of the Symbolic, which if we follow Butler's argument (as I do here) is not so much a transhistorical deity as a socio-historical horizon of authority (Butler, 2000). The designation of 'girl' or 'young woman' in these capacious terms also emerges from the contemporary logic of the global political economy, the needs of which have fortuitously overlapped in timing with the feminist demand for justice, participation, equality, and so on. Women have always been wage labourers but the effectivity of the women's movement, and the adjustment to this on the part of national governments as well as international corporations, has been to promote and enhance this working identity so that it marks out a new horizon of recognizable agency. Within the framing of the UK government's modernizing project, I argue that this process in actuality ensures the re-stabilization of gender hierarchies and in the pages that follow I consider some of the ways in which education and employment play a key role in this re-designation of young women. In this context the attribution of capacity contributes, I would suggest, to the re-making of social divisions along a more emphatic axis of gender.

As they emerge through the education system young women, more so now than their male peers, come to be associated with the gaining of qualifications. Although of course class and ethnic disadvantages still account for the wide disparities in the gaining of school qualifications for both sexes, the success in recent years of young women in both school and university is a key feature of the process of coming forward into visibility. The education system looks favourably towards young women and rewards them for their effort. The result is that the young woman comes to be widely understood as a bearer of qualifications, she is an active and aspirational subject of the education system, and she embodies the success of the new meritocratic values which New Labour has sought to implement in schools. Such re-positioning does not of course mean that we can make any assumptions about female success in the school system, other than that this is a site of intense governmental activity. Various studies from the USA, the UK, Australia and Europe provide detailed accounts of the various inequities which are newly generated by these very same practices of government; changes to welfare regimes, the decline in state funding of education and the emergence of competitive meritocratic systems of reward, all of which impact negatively on the educational achievements of young women from low income families. This evidence suggests that middle-class white girls and those from well off, or privileged Asian and black families, become part of the new competitive elite; that lower middle-class girls and some of their working-class counterparts are now expected to gain degree level qualifications so as to position themselves at certain levels of competence and capacity within the flexible labour market; that those 10 per cent of girls who leave school with no qualifications are now singled out more forcefully as educational failures and for them there are now fewer routes back into formal education, as post-school learning is now based on fees, loans and parental support.

The acquisition of qualifications comes to function then as a gendered axis of social division. Young women are in effect graded and marked according to their ability to gain qualifications, which in turn provides them with an identity as female subjects of capacity. The young woman now is normatively in possession of a distinct occupational identity. The principles that underscore the new gender regime require willingness, motivation and aptitude on the part of young women that if instilled within the school system will also be sustained and further developed in the workplace (Walby, 2002). In singling out young women for this special attention, New Labour and other governments are here displacing the role and legitimacy of feminist interventions in the politics of education, while also orchestrating this opportunity to instill new values of competitive individualism on the basis of emerging gender divisions intersecting in novel ways with class and ethnicity so as to produce re-configured entanglements seemingly characterized by openness and opportunity rather than the older structural rigidities. The girl thus comes forward or appears to make herself available as a subject of social change who has the capacity and the determination to transcend the barriers of the older class system. She will also step forward as an exemplary black or Asian young woman, on the basis of an enthusiasm for hard work and the pursuit of material reward.

The question then arises – to what extent can it be claimed that inside schooling and education processes of gender retrenchment or re-stabilization are also being secured within these overarching terms of female capacity? Arnot, Davis and Weiner offer the most comprehensive account of how feminist initiatives inside schooling were forced, over a period of time, to fold into and eventually become submerged by the more aggressively competitive values promulgated first by Mrs Thatcher and then by New Labour (Arnot et al., 1999). They point to how feminist practice was officially supplanted by a more target-oriented and accountability-directed regime. However, unofficially embedded feminist pedagogic principles found ways of negotiating this transition to a meritocratic logic so that young women might be able to reap some of the benefits from both old feminist and New Labour policies. Arnot et al. describe the way in which the attack by the new right on educational practices associated with the left and feminism forced teachers to abandon the vocabulary that had been in place in regard to girls and schooling in favour of one which emphasized results, targets and external ratings. The high achieving girl, who could be seen as the success-ful outcome of feminist pedagogy, now came to embody the seeming improvements and changes in the educational system as a whole.

Notwithstanding the perpetuation within secondary education of glaring inequities, the authors say 'successive generations of girls have been chal-lenged by economic and social change and by feminism' (Arnot et al., 1999: 150). However, this notion of challenge remains rather vague. Could it not be argued that the new educational vocabulary, haunted as it is by the impact of feminist initiatives in this terrain, takes it upon itself to eradicate the traces of feminism by itself championing the cause of young women, so that femi-nist pedagogy becomes a thing of the past, frozen in educational history as marking out a moment of now outmoded radicalism? This process of sup-planting and re-placing feminist pedagogy, with those of the new meritocracy in which young women nonetheless play a leading role, needs to be more fully documented. Such an analysis would also need to incorporate the way in which the 'global girl' also comes to be understood as a subject worthy of educational opportunities. Within practices of US governmentality, for instance, Spivak has raised the question of the forms of pedagogy which are (intermittently) made available within Western aid programmes. She asks, are these not compliant rather than critical pedagogies and are they not about gender training to the long-term benefit of the global corporations (Spivak, 2000)? Is the global girl, who is a deserving subject of international aid in the form of education, and is also the archetypal subject of gender mainstreaming initiatives, not also the ideal active and energetic, rather than docile, subject of the new international division of labour now interested in more than just her nimble fingers (Mohanty, 2002; Spivak, 2000)?[11]

If education remains the privileged space within the countries of the affluent West for overseeing and ensuring appropriate modalities of female economic participation, recent attempts on the part of the UK's govern-ment to create more direct links between education and employment by emphasizing work experience, employability, and enterprise culture have particular resonance for young women also. Recent research points to the apparent success of these initiatives. Interviewees, across the boundaries of class and ethnicity, self-present in the context of the research as motivated and ambitious; they have clear plans about what direction they might hope to follow from a young age and they frequently refer to the support they receive from their parents, especially mothers (Budgeon, 2001; Harris, 2004; Roche, 2005). Having a well-planned life emerges then as a social norm of contemporary femininity. The question then is how does this transpose into the workplace? Are there grounds for arguing that here too gender retrench-ment is being pursued through a vocabulary of female capacity and by means of the various attentions which produce public visibilities around the figure of the working girl or the young career woman?

The forces which come into play in enforcing the new sexual contract and which set sharp limits on patterns of participation and gender equality in the workplace (as forms of retrenchment) are inevitably both complex and various, but for the purposes of this chapter I propose that they can be at least partially understood, first within the terms of what Crompton describes as the social compromise and second within those of the new flexible economy (Crompton, 2002). Rosemary Crompton argues that the significant rates of retention in employment and return to work shortly after having children by UK women are based on a social compromise which requires that (heterosexual) women play a dual role – active in the workplace and primarily responsible for both children and domestic life (labour). The element of compromise reflects the rejection of the critique of hegemonic masculinity in the home (suggestive as this is of feminism) and the reliance by women on government to support working mothers (or hardworking families, to use government terminology) within the terms of the work-life balance agenda.

Once again the government substitutes for the feminist, displaces her vocabulary, and intervenes to assist women and to avert the legitimacy of critique by women of the injustice of their double responsibilities and hence of masculine privilege.[12] In effect, government acts to protect masculinity by supporting women in their double responsibilities. The social compromise (more narrowly defined by Crompton) is then a key element of the new sexual contract, which is premised on the management of gender and sexuality by a wide range of biopolitical strategies which subvert the possibilities of renewed feminist challenges to patriarchal authority. At the same time, this settlement (e.g., then Chancellor of the Exchequer Gordon Brown's commitment to nursery provision and support to low income families) also means that success in the workplace on the part of women with children is also reduced, as a result of the sheer inevitability of this double load of work and domestic responsibility. With the onset of maternity the social compromise applies both in the home and in the workplace. Jobs which are compatible with the demands of the home are preferred over those which might have more advantageous career ladders. New Labour also appears to benefit from the concern it shows for women's dual role. With such attention and commitment as this, what need might there be for an analysis which would suggest that such a settlement re-confirms rather than undermines male privilege? Nancy Fraser has argued that men must again become more accountable to gender inequities in the household, while what I have attempted to demonstrate here are the forces which prevail against this kind of expectation re-emerging as a possibility (Fraser, 1997).

Nancy Fraser also argues that the Universal Breadwinner Model increasingly takes precedence over the Caregiver Model which was associated with the older welfare regime that took into account women's role as caregivers and the limits that role put on possibilities for economic activity (Fraser, 1997). This care role was heavily criticized by feminists from the mid-1970s onwards on the grounds of its maternalist essentialism. What the social compromise now suggests is that the currently dominant Universal Breadwinner Model remains deeply inegalitarian in that it normatively assumes that women are active in the labour market while also primarily responsible for providing care in the home. The logic of the new flexible capitalism in the affluent West and the decline of the welfarist underpinning of the so-called family wage means that everyone who can work must do so. The coming forward of women into the workforce on a more sustained basis than ever before is clearly advantageous to both government and the economy. It promises degrees of wealth and prosperity. Armed with good qualifications and having been encouraged to display an enthusiasm and willingness to pursue careers as a mark of new and independent sexual identities, this female participation becomes an important feature of the success of the new economy. Labour market participation over a lifetime reduces the cost of welfare to women as traditionally low paid earners, and it also brings down the high rate of female poverty in old age. And in addition, this immersion in work also creates a thriving and re-energized consumer culture directed towards women.

It is for these reasons that we can make the claim that young women are the privileged subjects of economic capacity and it is on this basis that we can also expect degrees of social mobility to be more marked among women without children. But under these circumstances of seeming freedom and independence (i.e., without children or family responsibilities) can a case be made for the re-subjugation of young women within the terms of the Universal Breadwinner Model? Scott Lash remarks *en passant* that women are indeed 'reflexivity losers' in the context of the information society (Lash, in Beck et al., 1994). And Lisa Adkins has explored in much more detail the way in which what she labels as re-traditionalized gender relations re-emerge in the de-regulated workplace and with the return to small-scale, family-run enterprises that are integral to the production processes which underlie global consumer culture (Adkins, 2002).[13] Clearly what is required is a more thorough sectoral analysis of the specific of employment into which young women are moving, and an examination of the way in which they find themselves positioned in regard to the macro-transformations of work (as investigated by Castells, Sennett and Beck among others). For the purposes of this truncated account here, it is perhaps sufficient to point to the paradoxical situation which emerges with young women flowing into the labour market just at that point at which the social-democratic conditions which were recently propitious to their arrival are being dismantled.

'Fertility Tests For Career Women' (*London Evening Standard* headline, 25 January 2006)

I have argued that the elements which comprise the new sexual contract include participation on the part of young women in the consumer culture (i.e., the post-feminist masquerade), and access to educational opportunities with young women emerging as the subjects of educational capacity, with this then connecting inexorably with the normative expectation of (possibly lifelong) female employment. The final feature of this sexual contract is the provision of an entitlement to sexuality and the control of fertility. However, as various feminist sociologists in the USA have shown, this attention to young women's reproductive capacity frequently takes place within a discourse which is underpinned by normative assumptions about race and cultural difference with punitive outcomes for those young women whose sexual activities are construed, for reasons of their poverty and ethnicity, as pathological. Young motherhood, across the boundaries of class and ethnicity, now carries a whole range of vilified meanings associated with failed femininity and with a disregard for the wellbeing of the child. A respectable middle-class status requires the refusal of early motherhood and much effort is invested in ensuring that this norm is adhered to. If the young woman is now envisaged as an assemblage of productivity, then she is also now more harshly judged for inappropriate reproductive activity. The concept of planned parenthood emerges in Western liberal democracies as an address to young women so that they may postpone early maternity to accrue the economic advantages of employment and occupational identity and thus contribute to the solving of the crisis of welfare. Single mothers are seen as feckless or are accused in the press and in other moralistic discourses of depriving a child of his or her human right to a father. Despite or rather because of the proliferations of different modes of kinship in increasingly multi-cultural and sexually diverse cultures, nonetheless the marital couple re-emerges as the favoured form for family life. Interventions to ensure that help is given to those who abide by the rules of responsible and economically viable parenthood, as the headline quoted above from the London Evening Standard indicates, mean that those young career women who have followed the advice of New Labour and have postponed childbirth until they have secured wage earning capacity become the deserving subjects of investment.[14]

On condition that she does not reproduce outside marriage or civil partnership, or become the single mother of several children, the young woman is now granted a prominence as a pleasure-seeking subject in possession of a healthy sexual appetite and identity. Consumer culture negotiates this complicated terrain by inviting young women to overturn the old sexual double standard and emulate the assertive and hedonistic styles of sexuality associated with young men, particularly in holiday locations and also within the confines of licensed transgression (i.e., the weekend heavy drinking culture). The assumption of phallicism on the part of young women requires detailed attention. While this is by no means the first time the phallic girl has occupied a position of prominence within popular culture, the modalities of the current visibilities around this figure of the phallic girl are I would claim distinctive on the basis of 'equality', with male counterparts assumed as having been achieved and hence no longer in question (see Bennett and Woollacott, 1987). However, I would also argue that this space of assumed or imagined equality is the site of intense and obviously unresolved sexual antagonisms within contemporary heterosexuality. The taking up of the position of phallic girl bears the superficial marks of boldness, confidence, aggression, and even transgression (in that it refuses the feminine deference of the post-feminist masquerade). Yet this is a licensed and temporary form of phallicism. And like the post-feminist masquerade, it is predicated on the renunciation of the possibility of a critique of hegemonic masculinity, for fear of the slur of feminism or lesbianism. Indeed lesbianism is re-configured as a popular (rather than pornographic) space of activity for phallic girls within circumscribed scenarios for male pleasure.

This playful female phallicism is also underpinned by a range of possible punishments, which give rise to a spiralling of female anxiety and pain for those who misread the rules.[15] The phallic girl seeks to emulate male behaviour as a post-feminist gesture. She appears to have gained equality in that she can play them at their own game; she expresses a distaste for feminism, and on the basis of having assumed some male privileges finds no reason to challenge masculinity per se. Like young women in the post-feminist masquerade, the phallic girl (or ladette) is suggestive of novelty and change in their inhabiting of femininity as a mark of gender equality now gained, without this providing the occasion for the critique of masculinity. Indeed the position of phallic girl can be understood as made available by the logic of the consumer culture, which in this case confirms and consolidates patriarchal privilege and masculine hegemony by apportioning some limited features of this privilege to young women, within specified conditions that they withhold critique of their male counterparts and that they are complicit with the norms of the new leisure culture where sexuality is re-defined within the tabloid language of masculinist pleasures. However, the regulatory dynamics of this sexualized field of leisure and entertainment are disguised by the prevalence of the language of personal choice.

To sum up, the duality of sexual difference is re-confirmed anew and gender norms are re-consolidated and re-stabilized within an overarching framework of change, freedom and equality. Within this constellation of attention, these terms and conditions of visibility for young women are defined primarily by the commercial domain. The post-feminist masquerade and the phallic girl each offer possibilities for reconciling the forms of power now available to young women on the basis of the attribution of capacity, with the demands for the re-instatement of hierarchy by the Symbolic (or patriarchal authority). There is also compatibility between free market discourses of consumer culture (phallic girls, post-feminist masquerade) with those emerging from the offices of the state. And in these circumstances where female sexuality is so well provided for by the administrations of both state and consumer culture, the prospect of a more autonomous sexual politics re-emerging is slight. The new sexual contract designates young women, in a post-feminist move, as the subjects of capacity, and in doing so it appears to respond energetically to their every need. In all of its dimensions, the new sexual contract is appealing to its female constituency because it appears to take them on board and is apparently more than willing to listen to their needs; in this respect the UK's New Labour excels itself in its good habits of everyday governmentality.[16]

New Labour also endorses access to specific forms of youthful feminine consumer citizenship, and this becomes a figuration of contemporary girl-hood for wider international circulation. The global girl, like her Western counterpart the career girl, is independent, hardworking, motivated, ambi-tious, and able to enjoy at least some of the rewards of the feminine con-sumer culture which in turn becomes a defining feature of her citizenship and identity. These re-configurations of normative femininity re-stabilize sexual identities which might otherwise be disrupted as a result of these new occupational positions, educational achievements and control of fertil-ity available to young women, and of course the spectral presence, or the lingering aftermath, of feminist politics. This gender re-stabilization simul-taneously entails the re-colonization of Third World young women who now also find themselves mobilized within the discourses of neo-imperialism and corporate multi-culturalism. Consumer global citizenship, predicated on the hyper-activity, enthusiastic capacity and visible luminosity of youth-ful female subjects, marks the contours of the new dangers for women.[17] By these means of containment in the landscape of spectacular femininity women are removed once again from public life, the political sphere, and from the possibility of feminism.

While the question of how feminism might become again imaginable is open, and would of course necessarily be a different species of feminism from that which has informed this current discussion, and while it is also imperative to understand the spectral as an effectivity without nostalgia, the account provided here of pervasive practices of biopolitical activity operates to diminish activity in the sphere of formal politics as well as in civic society. As social theorists including Mouffe (1999), Hall (1999), and Brown (2002) have all argued, the political rationality of these neo-liberal strategies is to grant dominance to economic life. For young women the opportunities for fulfilling this are compelling, since access to the world of work permits specific modalities of much sought-after independence. But the means by which such a role in economic life is being made available substitute notional ideas of consumer citizenship in place of political identity, and elevate the choices made available by consumer culture so that these might be extended into social as well as political fields. The new sexual contract for young women inscribes such features within its over-arching terms, and we could read this as a feminist tragedy, the 'fall of public woman'.

Notes

Thanks to my PhD students Kim Allen and Hatty Oliver for their insights and extensive knowledge of tabloid culture. Thanks also to Sarah Banet-Weiser for inviting me to give a version of this chapter at USC in February 2006.

1   My use of the term sexual contract in this context is cultural rather than legalistic, and to be understood as a provision to young women on behalf of government including education, employment, and the control of fertility within specific conditions. In this respect my use of the term is therefore quite different from the more contractual language of Pateman. (1988).
2   The term sexual contract is of course associated with the influential work of Carole Pateman (1988).
3   I use the term patriarchy with caution, aware that in its previous usage it has been deployed as a universalizing strategy, a means of proposing that women across the world share what are in fact particularistic modes of subjugation. Despite this, I re-employ the term here while taking into account Mohanty's terminology and her use of the word patriachies.
4   Both Harris (2004) and myself have pursued similar examinations in regard to the emerging categories of girlhood, and Harris's book *Future Girl* is outstanding for its comprehensive account. My aim however is to connect these changes with processes of retrenchment and re-stabilization.
5   The *Daily Mail* provides many different illustrations of racialized configurations of the capable young woman. For example, the archetypal Asian girl who has struggled to make a break with traditional family pressures, has got to university and is embarked on a successful career, but is still estranged from her parents. This of course is a re-run of the old 'between two cultures' notion, now updated to incorporate young women's more assertive identities and career aspirations.
6   The Rt Hon Tessa Jowell made comments to this effect in 2000 when she launched the government's Body Image Summit.
7   Returned to by feminists who must, however, have been dismayed by Riviere's uncritical use of racist stereotypes to describe the intersection of fear and desire in the (white) woman's fantasy of finding herself attacked by a 'negro'.
8   The totalizing attention to the female body, feminine image, appearance and adornment apparent in the vastly increased volume of TV programmes given over to this topic, as well as the rising circulations for women's and girls' magazines across class, race and age boundaries, mark out the contours of the pervasiveness of the post-feminist masquerade.

95

9 This is a regular theme in *Sex in the City*. Carrie's date does not care for her silly hat, which she knows only fashion experts would appreciate. Thus the wearing of the hat provokes much self-reflexivity, 'should she, shouldn't she'? Carrie tends to cling onto these 'ridiculous' items, as a mark of her own independent identity. But both we and she know that in the end these items work to her feminine advantage. They make her endearing to men. Their 'over the top' quality shows her vulnerability, her childish enjoyment of dressing up. If she gets it wrong and she looks a little foolish, it is because she is still a girl, unsure of herself as she takes on this mask of womanliness.

10 This style of self-mockery in regard to the adoption of the post-feminist masquerade is clearly in evidence in the fashion journalism found in the quality press in the UK, especially in the *Guardian* and the *Independent*. There is both an adamant attachment to the expansive range of feminine looks and products, and at the same time, an awareness that this is indeed a shallow set of 'girlish' pursuits.

11 Bob Geldolf on *BBC Newsnight* (31/5/05) said that the best way to secure US aid for Africa was to focus on the education of girls as this was a favourite concern of George W. and Laura Bush.

12 This same transposition appears in recent debates about women and work. Male privilege, patriarchal authority and sex discrimination are not in any way responsible for pay gaps and wage discrepancies between men and women. According to the Women and Work Commission (Feb, 2006), instead this is the result of young women's poor choices of careers; they continue it seems to opt for low pay occupations (see www.womenandequalityunit.gov.uk/women_work_commission, March 2006.)

13 There are also fields of employment like advertising which might be expected to be more liberal in their attitudes towards a female workforce but which are in fact (as Nixon describes) exceptionally dominated by the masculine and overtly discriminatory against women (see Nixon, 2003).

14 Within a day or so of this headline appearing in the press, daytime TV shows were trying out the aforesaid fertility tests on female participants from the public on these shows.

15 The new genre of young men's magazines operate as a source of aggressive judgement and punishment. Amidst the pin-ups, the centrefolds and the many girls who are 'up for posing' emerges a voice of triumphant masculinism, what Beck calls 'constructed certitude' i.e., re-assuring men once again of their privilege. This is a mark of gender retrenchment and resurgent patriarchalism (Jackson et al., 2001).

16 New Labour Minister Tessa Jowell was also charged with the responsibility of setting up focus groups up and down the country in 2004 to ask what women wanted in relation to the work-life balance (see www.dfes.gov.uk/work-lifebalance).

17 This notion of capacity is mindful of recent work by both Sen and Nussbaum on 'capabilities' (see Sen, 1995; and Nussbaum, 2003).

References

Adkins, L. (2002) *Revisions: Gender and Sexuality in Late Modernity*. Buckinghamshire: Open University Press.

Arnot, M., David, M. and Weiner, G. (1999) *Closing The Gender Gap*. Cambridge: Polity.

Beck, U., Giddens, A. and Lash, S. (1994) *Reflexive Modernization*. Cambridge: Polity.

Bennett, T. and Woollacott, J. (1987) *Bond and Beyond: The Political Career of a Popular Hero*. Basingstoke: Macmillan.

Budgeon, S. (2001) 'Emergent feminist (?) identities', *European Journal of Womens Studies*, 8 (1): 7–28.

Butler, J. (1999) *Gender Trouble: Feminisam and the Subversion of Identity*. London and New York: Routledge.

Butler, J. (2000) *Antigone's Claim: Kinship Between Life and Death*. New York: Columbia University Press.

Butler, J. (2005) *Undoing Gender*. New York: Routledge.

Crompton, R. (2002) 'Employment, flexible working and the family', *British Journal of Sociology*, 53 (4): 537–58.

Foucault, M. (1984) *The Foucault Reader*, (ed. P. Rainbow). London: Penguin.

Fraser, N. (1997) *Justice Interruptus*. London: Routledge.

Harris, A. (2004) *Future Girl*. London: Routledge.

Jackson, P., Stevenson, N. and Brooks, K. (2001) *Making Sense of Men's Magazines*. Cambridge: Polity.

McRobbie, A. (2004) 'Post-feminist popular culture', *Feminist Media Studies*, 4 (3): 255–65.

Mohanty, C. T. (2002) '"Under western eyes" revisited: feminist solidarity through anticapitalist struggles', *Signs: Journal of Women in Culture and Society*, 28 (2): 499–535.

Mouffe, C. (1999) *The Democratic Paradox*. London: Verso.

Nixon, S. (2003) *Advertising Cultures*. London: Sage.

Nussbaum, M. (2003) 'Capabilities as fundamental entitlements', *Feminist Economics*, 9 (2–3): 33–59.

Pateman, C. (1988) *The Sexual Contract*. Stanford, CA: Stanford University Press.

Probyn, E. (1997) 'New traditionalism and post feminism', in C. Brunsdon et al. (eds), *Feminist Television Criticism*. Oxford: Clarendon, pp. 126–37.

Riviere, J. (1986[1929]) 'Womanliness as masquerade', in V. Burgin et al. (eds), *Formations of Fantasy*. London: Methuen, pp. 35–44.

Roche, C. (2005) 'Celtic cubs'. PhD Thesis, University of Limerick, Ireland.

Rose, N. (1999) 'Inventiveness in politics', *Economy and Society*, 28 (3): 467–93.

Sen, A. (1995) 'Gender, inequality and theories of justice', in M. Nussbaum and J. Glover (eds), *Women, Culture and Development*. Oxford: Clarendon, pp. 259–73.

Spivak, G.-C. (2000) Unpublished lecture, Goldsmiths College, London.

Walby, S. (1997) *Gender Transformations*. London: Routledge.

Walby, S. (2002) 'From community to coalition', *Theory, Culture and Society*, 18 (2–3): 1–23.

6

The Identities of Self-Interest: Performitivity, History, Ethics

Paul du Gay

Introduction

If specific concepts and comportments of the person can be seen to perform quite different functions in different contexts, then it is important not to underdescribe them. If we do, it is more than probable that we won't be able to see the job that each is doing, how each has its own history and distribution, has fashioned its own ethos, and is directed by its own techniques to its own ends.

In this Chapter, I seek to live up to this injunction by unpacking 'the' concept of 'self-interest'. This concept has frequently functioned as a unifying device. 'Self-Interest' is regularly viewed, by its friends as well as its foes, as one of those concepts that, in Rorty's (1988: 45) words seeks 'to pull one rabbit out of several hats', by providing a transcendental unity of the concept of the person. All the better then to show how historically there have been quite discontinuous changes in the characterization of the 'self' deemed to be 'self-interested'. 'Self-Interest', I will argue, refers to a number of historically distinct conceptions and behaviours. There is, in other words, no such thing as *the* concept of 'self-interest', just as there is no such thing as *the* concept of a person 'whose various components form a harmonious structure that could provide adjudication among competing normative claims about what does or does not fall within the domain of the rights and obligations of persons' (Rorty, 1988: 31).

Above all, perhaps, it is neo-classical economics that has accustomed us to the image of human beings as 'rational maximizers' of their own 'self-interest'. As many economists would hasten to point out, though, this idea of rational self-interest is not intended to function as a complete description of human conduct. Rather, it is a theory. A deliberate, reductive move designed to construct mathematically tractable models of human behaviour that, in turn, will yield testable predictions. This is an important point. Yet, under the sway of such economic modelling, a not insignificant number of social scientists have come to see such maximizing behaviour everywhere, and to install self-interest as the central generating mechanism of all social relations; in effect, to establish 'self-interest' as the hard rock on which all of social life is founded (Becker, 1981, 1986; Buchanan,1978; Niskanen, 1971; Schotter, 1981).[1]

As Callon (1998), for instance, has argued, such reductionism has been regularly denounced by sociological commentators, who, in pointing to the poverty, atomism and basic fictiveness of this conception of humanity, seek, instead, to reassert the primacy of 'the social' in 'man's' complex constitution: 'the sociologist denounces this *(economic)* reductionism in order to disqualify economic theory and propose replacing it by another theory, a sociology of real man, one taken in a bundle of links which constitute his sociality and hence his humanity' (Callon, 1998: 51).

In what follows, I seek to side-step the issue of whether individual human beings are radically 'socially' embedded creatures, or essentially rational maximizers of their own interests, and to focus, instead, on how, historically, particular 'self-interested' conducts were programmed. I argue that 'self-interested' conduct does indeed exist, but is not an unchanging human essence. I then attempt to show how, at a certain historical period, and in relation to specific purposes, a particular version of self-interested personhood was made up.

I begin by exploring the historical context in which this version of 'self-interest' emerged as a normative doctrine whose dissemination, far from engendering society's ruin, as much post-romantic sociology would have it, was represented as a viable means to its salvation. In so doing, I seek to highlight the distinctive understanding of 'self' that this doctrine promoted and its performative role as a device designed to secure social pacification. In historicizing self-interest in this manner, and treating its theorization as culturally performative, rather than as simply empirically descriptive, a more sympathetic understanding of the historical plurality of self-interested conducts can, perhaps, be developed.

Persons and contexts

For as long as sociology has been practised, capitalism, or markets, or rational self-interested conducts, have been the target of considerable critical opprobrium/denunciation. The mode of critique has varied with the theoretical position favoured, from Marx's theory of alienation, Durkheim's *anomie*, or Freud's thesis of libidinal repression, up to, and including, more recent visions of contemporary economic conducts as destructive of morality (Sayer, 1997). In these, and other, implicit or explicit critiques of capitalism, the stress, more often than not, is on the repressive, alienating, or

The Identities of Self-Interest

otherwise inhibiting aspects of economic conducts on the development of, what we might term, 'the full human personality'. Without wishing to dispute, or indeed interrogate, the veracity of these critiques, it is nonetheless worth pointing out that rather than being an unforeseen side-effect of commercially 'self-interested' conduct, one to be denounced and eradicated at the earliest opportunity, the one-sided, predictable, rational and in some senses 'repressed' personality it produced was exactly what its advocates trusted that it would accomplish. And this was for good reasons, as Albert Hirschman has indicated.

> This position, which seems so strange today, arose from extreme anguish over the clear and present dangers of a certain historical period, from concern over the destructive forces unleashed by the human passions with the only exception, so it seemed at the time, of 'innocuous' avarice. *In sum, capitalism was supposed to accomplish exactly what was soon to be denounced as its worst feature.* (Hirschman, 1977: 132)

In other words, commercially directed forms of 'rational' self-interest were viewed, in context, as possible solutions to the disastrous conflicts besetting early modern Europe, particularly those associated with religious war and aristocratic adventurism. From this perspective, the focus on interest governed conduct, commercial or otherwise, was a product of an urgent quest 'for a new way of *avoiding society's ruin*, permanently threatening at the time because of precarious arrangements for internal and external order' (Hirschman, 1977: 130). For its early modern advocates, 'self-interested' conduct appeared as a potential cultural counterweight to the menace posed by the world of the 'full human personality', replete with its destructive passions. From the perspective of the present, such a belief in the efficacy of 'self-interest' can appear remarkably naive or just plain monstrous. The ravages of contemporary economic globalization, for instance, are regularly held up as exemplars of the full horrors of unbridled self-interest. And yet, if we exercise our historical imaginations just a little, we might also wonder at contemporary critics' forgetfulness of the dire consequences of a time when social and political existence was dominated by rival religious zealotries and the search for 'glory'.

Passions, interests and persons

In *The Passions and the Interests* (1977), subtitled 'arguments for capitalism before its triumph', Albert Hirschman explored why and how certain, frequently commercial, ideas of self-interest were popularized, and particular self-interested conducts endorsed, by a wide variety of seventeenth and eighteenth century thinkers. The latter, many of whom were personally antithetical to money making and commerce, came to look favourably upon commercial self-interest, he argues, because they saw it as a relatively peaceful and harmless alternative to the violent passions that had fuelled the European wars of religion and inspired military and aristocratic adventurism. Weary of the destruction caused by the unbridled passions, and bent on reform, a number of these thinkers were hopeful that the 'mild' passion for money making and calculation, 'although admittedly ignoble and uncouth, could defeat and bury the violent passions that so ruinously stoked the endless cycles of civil butchery' (Holmes, 1995: 54). These attempts to harness the moderating effects of enlightened self-interest were therefore driven by a need to counteract and neutralize what were seen as the destructive consequences of mobilizing passion in the service of a religious cause and aristocratic ideals.

The idea that self-interest was a relatively harmless and even beneficial form of human conduct was, according to Hirschman, a novel idea, contradicting the old association of avarice with sin. Its relative novelty and contrariety with the prevailing cultural norms suggested that its advocates would have their work cut out in establishing its standing as a prestigious doctrine (Johnston, 1986). And yet, as Hirschman (1977: 31–48) argues, such was the desperation to find a way out of 'perpetual war', and such was the impotence of the two established categories that had 'dominated the analysis of human motivation since Plato', namely 'passions', on the one hand, and 'reason', on the other, in promoting that endeavour, that the emergence of a 'third way', the category of 'interest', that could potentially counteract the weaknesses of the first two, was received with remarkable enthusiasm, given its established (negative) connotations.

> Once passion was deemed destructive and reason ineffectual, the view that human action could be exhaustively described by attribution to either one or the other meant an exceedingly sober outlook for humanity. A message of hope was therefore conveyed by the wedging of interest in between the two traditional categories of human motivation. Interest was seen to partake in effect of the better nature of each, as the passion of self-love upgraded and contained by reason, and as reason given direction and force by that passion. The resulting hybrid form of human action was considered exempt from both the destructiveness of passion and the ineffectuality of reason. No wonder that the doctrine of interest was received at the time as a veritable message of salvation! (Hirschman, 1977: 43–4)

Given this context, it seems unsurprising that 'interest' could come to assume a 'curative' connotation that its prehistory and established meanings would otherwise have rendered unthinkable. And, that, in turn, the association of 'interest' with a more enlightened idea of governing human affairs and attenuating some of the latter's more destructive propensities helped to bestow upon certain practices of 'interest' governed conduct a similarly positive and 'curative' set of meanings. Commerce, for instance, might be low,

The Identities of Self-Interest

but in contrast to the bloody and destructive consequences of the pursuit of glory or religious fanaticism, it might be a more civilized and less unpredictable form of life. Interests might be base, but they could also be seen to 'raise the comfort level of social interaction' (Holmes, 1995: 54).

Self-interested agents, whether commercially motivated or not, were regarded as acting with a certain coolness and deliberation, cultivating a particular approach to human affairs which appeared the very antithesis of that expected from a 'full human personality'. Interest thus assumed a certain standing because it seemed to offer a counterweight to pre-eminent – dangerous and unpredictable – human motivations. Here lies the heart of Hirschman's argument. By failing to discern the implicit contrast with the violent passions, and continuing, therefore, to conceive of interest as fundamentally inhumane, we may be at a loss to explain the positive and curative attitude towards 'interest' and 'interests' displayed by a wide range of thinkers in seventeenth and eighteenth century Europe. Moreover, by ignoring the irrational and destructive antonyms of self-interest, we might fall into the sort of error popularized by R.H. Tawney (1926) and C.B. Macpherson (1964), for instance, and continuing today in the work of critical intellectuals such as Jürgen Habermas (1996), where affirmations of calculating self-interest end up being represented as a mean spirited repudiation of the common good.[2]

The 'self' in self-interest

If, then, we continue to view self-interest as either a hard-wired, and unvarying, human capacity, the 'rock' upon which all of social life is built, or, alternatively, we consider it as always and already the enemy of the common good, we may fail to appreciate the ways in which 'self-interested' conduct varies conceptually and materially over time, and the distinctive purposes particular forms of 'self-interest' are designed to meet. This becomes evident when attention is focused on the kind of person deemed capable of acting in a 'self-interested' fashion.

It has become a common place in contemporary sociological debates about personal identity to argue that individual human beings are not essentially 'free' or 'self-interested' agents, directed by a sovereign and integral consciousness. What is, or should be, at issue here, though, is not the *status* of 'free agent', or 'subject of right', but rather the claimed or assumed ontological foundations of that status (Hirst and Woolley, 1982: 132). In other words, the idea that individuals are 'free agents' is not an illusion. As Paul Hirst and Penny Woolley (1982: 132) argued some time ago, while categories of person such as 'the free agent' are correctly described as fictional, in the sense that they are artificial and not natural kinds, they are not illusions in the sense of having no practical basis in cultural life. The idea of the 'free agent', for instance, could not be understood as 'imaginary' in this sense precisely because it is implicated, to a greater or lesser extent, in our legal systems, in our conceptions of contract and the employment relationship and many of our assumptions about education (Hirst and Woolley, 1982: 132). It exists, not in a natural or, indeed, singular state, but in many conceptual and material forms. It is differentially 'formatted, framed and equipped', to use Callon's (1998: 51) phrase.

With regard to 'self-interested' personae, then, we can say that for individuals to take an interest in their own conduct as its ethical subject requires the elaboration and transmission of specific ethical disciplines and practices. In other words, before an individual can act on the basis of their own 'interests' they must first become the sort of person disposed to and capable of relating to themselves as the responsible agents of their own conduct. In seventeenth and eighteenth century Europe, as we shall shortly see, an enormous amount of work went into supplying the cultural 'equipment', the norms and mechanisms necessary for cultivating such capacities among elite populations culturally habituated to other, frequently antithetical, ideals and forms of conduct (Hirschman, 1977; Pocock, 1985; Tully, 1988).

In contrast to those who would seek to explain all forms of behaviour through the prism of rational self-interest (in the singular), and, equally to those who would only view self-interest (again, in the singular) as the harbinger of the destruction of social relations, thinkers such as Hobbes and Hume, for example, had a very different agenda. First, their respective works are characterized by an acute awareness of human irrationality and the diversity of destructive human motivations, rather than the monochrome psychological reductionism levelled at them by critics (and a number of supporters) alike. In other words, they do not assume that 'human beings' are essentially, or even frequently, self-interested creatures. Quite the contrary, they continually point to the massive historical importance of self-destructive human irrationality and impulsiveness and the socially ruinous consequences of the uncontrollable passions (Holmes, 1995). By focusing upon the passions and their deleterious social consequences, their respective anthropologies set up 'the full human personality' as a dangerous creature in need of civil restraint. They also position 'interest', albeit in non-reducible terms, as a beneficial mechanism by which such restraint was to be engendered.

It is precisely such an ethico-cultural intent which underlies the prescriptive and performative aims of Hobbes's so-called 'egoistic' model in *Leviathan*, for instance, as I seek to indicate at greater length later in the chapter. Rather than assuming that human beings are by nature self-interested, rational maximizers of their own utility, the purpose of Hobbes's philosophical anthropology was rather to promote a 'cultural transformation' in their ethical make up. Only when the lives of human beings were invested less in religious passions and more in 'caring for necessary things' would they begin to possess those characteristics required of political subjects in the sovereign state, which Hobbes represented as necessary conditions for the securing of civil peace (Johnston, 1986: 215–16; Minson, 1993: 167; Tuck, 1993: see Chapter 7) Self-interest here functions as an element in a philosophical anthropology designed to counteract destructive human passions, not as an imperialistic attempt to explain all forms of behaviour through the prism of one human capacity.

For Hobbes, Hume and, indeed, Adam Smith, 'interest' – while differentially formatted to suit their respective purposes – would be a useless category if it were not reserved for one motive vying with others. Representing it as the primary, or natural, human motivation robs 'calculating self-interest' of the specificity it acquires when seen against the backdrop of selfless urges and thoughtless acts. For these thinkers, as Holmes (1995: 57) has put it, 'the rational pursuit of utility, far from being universal, is a rare moral achievement, possible only for those who undergo an arduous dispositional training'.

So what exactly is this 'self' that is deemed to be 'self-interested', if it approximates neither to the always already rational maximizer of much economically influenced social science, nor to the unbridled egoist invoked in much critical sociology? An answer to this question begins to present itself when we focus on the philosophical anthropologies through which particular seventeenth and eighteenth century versions of 'self-interest' were constituted. In seeking to redescribe 'self-interest' as a comportment of the person derived from a distinctive philosophical anthropology, I will have recourse to a particular approach which investigates philosophies in terms of the 'ascetic' relation to self that they impose, and the 'spiritual exercises' they require (Foucault, 1984, 1986; Oestreich, 1982; Gaukroger, 1995; Hadot, 1995; Hunter, 2001).[3] Characteristically, histories of philosophy conducted in this manner

> focus on the anthropologies, psychologies and cosmologies through which members of specific intellectual elites acquire the capacity to take up a particular relation to themselves and their world. This is typically a relation that imbues such individuals with a conviction of their deviation from an ideal way of thought or life – a relation of self-problematisation. In this way, they are inducted into a particular intellectual regimen or practice of self-cultivation, through which they may reshape themselves in the image of this ideal. (Hunter, 2001: 23)

Despite some significant differences in method and emphasis, studies framed by this historiographic and anthropological approach treat their respective philosophical objects as reflexive ethical instruments – that is, as means by which 'individuals are inducted into new existential relations to themselves' (Hunter, 2001: 23). As such, they approach the 'self' not as a subjectivity transcendentally presupposed by experience, but in terms of 'one historically cultivated to meet the purposes of a particular way of life' (Hunter, 2001: 23–4).

We have already seen that certain seventeenth and eighteenth century conceptions of 'self-interest' were promulgated with specific purposes in mind – to act as an ethical and cultural counterweight to religious ideals of conscience and aristocratic ideals of glory. Hume (1998: 38–43), for instance, viewed Christianity as an almost intolerable moral provocation. He certainly conceived of commercially directed, self-interested conduct as a relatively peaceful alternative to sectarian zealotry. He also viewed enthusiasm as socially undesirable, and just as alien to a calculating mindset as the nobility's addiction to glorious adventurism. As Holmes (1995) has put it, the principal aim of those who wrote favourably of self-interest at this time was

> to bridle destructive and self-destructive passions, to reduce the social prestige of mindless male violence, to induce people, so far as possible, to act rationally, instead of hot bloodedly or deferentially, and to focus on material goals such as economic wealth, instead of spiritual goals such as avenging a perceived slight or compelling neighbours to attend church. (Homes, 1995: 4)

In so doing, as a number of commentators have pointed out, they had recourse to the certain tenets of Hellenistic philosophy, most notably Stoicism and Epicureanism (Brown, 1994; Hirschman, 1977; Hunter, 2001; Oakeshott, 1975: 154–8; Oestreich, 1982; Tuck, 1993).

Brown (1994) and Force (2003), for instance, are simply among the latest scholars to point to neo-stoicism as the primary influence on Adam Smith's ethical thought. As is well known, the Stoics were centrally concerned with perturbations and disorders of the soul. A passionate person, they believed, was unable to pursue their own best interests in a coherent fashion being ungoverned by reason. Thus, rational choice was impossible until the individual had achieved a state of 'apathy'[4] or emotional serenity. Equanimity or tranquillity of mind, in turn, presupposed a strenuous process of self-discipline, a mental therapy in which the unruly passions were not simply moderated but extirpated (Nussbaum, 1994).

According to Brown (1994: 217), it is extremely difficult to code 'the overall structure of Smith's discourse' through the tropes of unbridled egoism, the embrace of crass materialism and the repudiation of the common good, for instance, precisely because the stoic moral hierarchy underpinning his *oeuvre* suggests a rather different interpretation of key concepts such as 'self', 'interest' and 'liberty'. The self-love praised by Smith in *The Theory of Moral Sentiments*, for instance, is the very antithesis of the celebration of 'unbridled egoism' frequently ascribed to him by his critics. As Brown (1994: 94) argues such assumptions about the status of 'self-love' and other related concepts overlook their Stoic pedigree. As she makes clear, here 'self-love is akin to *amour de soi*, a caring for the self that is entirely consistent with moral behaviour' (1994: 94). Stoic self-love cannot be seen as a synonym for selfishness in the modern sense of the term. Rather, it refers to the command of one's faculties and the control of one's impulses. By being in control of oneself – an unrelaxing vigilance for the Stoics – one is fundamentally being attentive to oneself, caring for oneself in that one is seeking to ensure progress towards an ideal of wisdom (Hadot, 1995: 87). The wise person will take an interest in their own health and choose to live a healthy life not because a healthy life is an end in itself, but because it is reasonable for a person to do this; such a person, however, will be indifferent to the outcome in a moral sense in that s/he will accept ill health or good health with equanimity (Brown, 1994: 77; Long, 2001).

Similar issues arise when the 'concept' of liberty is invoked. Once again the neo-stoic underpinning of Smith's conception of 'liberty' entirely disappears in much modern interpretation of Smith's *oeuvre*. As Brown (1994: 219–20) argues, with regard to the current paradigmatic status accorded the *Wealth Of Nations* as the founding text of free market economics, 'freedom came to be seen as negative freedom and an end in itself, an ultimate moral and political good against which other claims would appear subordinate, whereas the Stoic concept of freedom was bounded by an insistence on the ultimate moral indifference of worldly outcomes'. Liberty of action then, is not about freedom to do whatever the individual desires so to do, precisely because freedom for the Stoics 'is not acquired by satisfying yourself with what you desire but by destroying your desire' (Epictetus, quoted in Brown, 1994: 218). This state of freedom, then, is not a natural state of being as it has to be fastidiously worked at (Nussbaum, 1994). Nor is it state of self-indulgence or self-obsession – a celebration of unbridled egoism. Quite the contrary. It offers up a view of freedom as a kind of ethical *askesis* – the work one performs to turn oneself into an ethical subject capable of shaping one's own nature.

Given this, it seems implausible to assume that seventeenth and eighteenth century advocates of self-interest were simple motivational reductionists. There is little here to support the view of rational self-interest either as an inherent element of human personality or as the harbinger of a corrupted humanity. For neo-stoics, self-interest was a rare moral ideal. It could only be achieved after a strenuous process of moral (self)disciplining (Oestreich, 1982; Tuck, 1993).[5]

'Caring for necessary things': Hobbes and the politics of cultural transformation

As I argued above, early modern formulations of self-interest may be better understood as normative projects, framed by particular neo-hellenistic philosophical anthropologies, rather than as descriptive claims about human motivation. We can see this most clearly, perhaps, by focusing in more detail on the works of Thomas Hobbes.

Hobbes is frequently represented as the first important political theorist to conceptualize human beings as essentially rational animals devoted solely or primarily to self-preservation and, in effect, as the great proto-theorist of bourgeois society (Macpherson, 1964). However, Hobbes held no such reductionist view and, as a consequence, could not have bequeathed it to his contemporary social scientific successors (Holmes, 1995: see Chapter 3). Indeed, he held directly the opposite view. He emphatically denied that human beings are essentially rational animals who by nature are driven to pursue their own self-interest. Instead, according to Hobbes, mankind appears throughout history to have been driven by self-destructive passions and urges. Put bluntly, 'human beings dread dishonour and damnation more acutely than they fear death' (Holmes, 1995: 3). The arguments in *Leviathan* and *Behemoth*, for instance, reinforce this insight. Both explicitly reject the rational-actor model as an accurate description of actually existing humanity even if, at the same time, they partly seek to reconstruct human conduct in its image.

According to David Johnston (1986: 215), for example, 'Hobbes's new view of man' as a rational agent driven by self-interest was not a representation of reality as he saw it. 'On the contrary, it was a carefully constructed model of man as Hobbes believed it would have to be in order to live in a peaceful and lasting political community'. In this reading, Hobbes's work is viewed as a political act of 'cultural transformation', an attempt to bring a world into being rather than simply reporting on the world as it is. After all, if most human beings, most of the time, were rational pursuers of their own self-interest, Hobbes suggests, history might not be a perpetual chronicle of slaughter and destruction. Civil wars are so frequent, instead, precisely because at least some people are prepared to risk death for the sake of 'higher' ideals such as 'glory' or 'salvation' (Holmes, 1995: 72).

To help put a stop to the destructive violence of civil war, it was therefore crucial for Hobbes to discredit those ideals that tempt human beings to defy death. According to Johnston (1986) this is the main aim of Hobbes's project of 'cultural transformation'. In a reformed polity – a commonwealth – people will, for the most part, rationally pursue their self-preservation, oblivious to the siren songs of aristocratic glory and religious redemption. As I suggested earlier, only when people's lives were invested less in religious imaginings and more in 'caring for necessary things' would they possess 'those characteristics required of political subjects in a Commonwealth or Sovereign State (especially constancy and a fear of death and insecurity) which Hobbes regarded as essential to the securing of civil peace' (Minson, 1993: 167–8).

In order to discredit his chosen targets Hobbes had recourse to a particular philosophical anthropology, in this instance Epicureanism (Oakeshott, 1975: 154–8). In attacking his rivals – both religious and civic republican – Hobbes relied upon an Epicurean anthropology in which man was represented as a dangerous creature, a passion-driven and self-destructive being, in desperate need of civil re-education and political and legal restraint (Johnston, 1986; Hunter, 2001; Skinner, 2002). *Elements of Law* and *Leviathan*, for instance, both begin with a lengthy treatise on human nature in which this Epicurean anthropology looms large. In both texts, human beings are represented, by nature, as remarkably self-destructive entities. Left to their own devices they will inevitably come into conflict with one another. Hobbes cites a number of causes of the 'offensiveness of man's nature one to another'. In *Elements of Law* he highlights, on the one hand, the insatiability of people's appetites and, on the other, their desire for glory, which is 'that passion which proceedth from the imagination or conception of our own power, above the power of him that contendenth with us' (1994: I.9.1). Taken together, these explain why men are always in conflict with one another. For 'some are vainly glorious, and hope for precedency and superiority above their fellows, not only when they are equal in power, but also when they are inferior' (1994: I.14.3). His hope for superiority makes even those who are moderate and ask for nothing more than recognition of their equal standing with other people 'obnoxious to the force of others, that will attempt to subdue them' (1994: I.14.3). Even if people's appetites were not insatiable, their vanity would lead them into conflict with one another, and it would do so even if there were some men who were neither vain nor immoderate of appetite.

A similar coding of human motivation is to be found in the first part of *Leviathan*. Here, '[N]ature hath made men so equall' in both 'ability' and 'right' (1991: I.XIII. 60) that 'from this ... there ariseth equality of hope in the attaining of our Ends. And therefore if any two men desire the same thing, which nevertheless they cannot both enjoy, they become enemies; and in the way to their End ... endeavour to destroy or subdue one an other' (1991: I.XIII. 61). In the state of nature, therefore, 'they are in that condition which is called Warre; and such a warre, as is of every man, against every man' (1991: I.XIII. 62). In 'such condition, there is no place for Industry; because the fruit thereof is uncertain ... and which is worst of all, continual feare, and danger of violent death' (1991: I.XIII. 62). Both texts represent a view of humanity that is far from rational and prudent; instead, they paint a picture of human beings as compulsive and impulsive creatures, frequently unreflective and prone to torrid emotional outbursts.

The destructive consequences of this 'natural offensiveness' would be inevitable were it not for the existence of countervailing elements in human nature. The most important of these is fear of death. In *Elements of Law*,

Hobbes argues that 'necessity of nature maketh men to will and desire *bonum sibi*, that which is good for themselves, and to avoid that which is hurtful; but most of all that terrible enemy of nature, death' (1994: I.14.6). Similarly, in *Leviathan* Hobbes states that 'Feare of Death' is a crucial feature of human nature that can help 'encline men to peace' (1991: I.XIII. 63). The second is the potential of Reason. In *Elements of Law*, Hobbes argues that the capacity to reason provides human beings with the potential means required to avoid the greatest of all evils: death. It is therefore 'reason' which 'dictateth to every man for his own good, to seek after peace ... and to strengthen himself ...' (1994: I.15.1; I.14.6; I.14.14). This contention is repeated in *Leviathan* where Hobbes states, for instance, that 'Reason suggesteth Articles of Peace, upon which men may be drawn to agreement' (1991: I.XIII. 63). If the consequence of natural appetite is pride and fear, then the 'suggestion' of Reason is peace. But how can this 'suggestion' be translated into a concrete solution? The answer to this question is contained in what Oakshott called Hobbes's 'hypothetical efficient cause of civil association' (1975: 43). It is an account that owes not a little to neo-stoicism as well as to Epicureanism (Oestreich, 1982; Tuck, 1993: see Chapters 2 and 7).

For Hobbes, as Oakeshott (1975: 38) has it, 'the precondition of deliverance is the recognition of the predicament. Just as for Christians, the repentance of the sinner forms a crucial first step towards salvation', so for Hobbes, humanity must first control its violent passions. So long as human beings are in the grip of these passions they will continue in a state of 'Warre'. The controlling counter-emotion is, as we have seen, fear of death. This fear illuminates prudence, and what begins in prudence is continued in reasoning. For while reasoning may well help guide individuals 'in the pursuit of their own private felicity, it is also capable of illuminating certain axioms in respect of their competitive endeavours to satisfy their wants' (Oakshott, 1975: 38). As Oakeshott continues, 'since what threatens to defeat every attempt to procure felicity in these circumstances is the unconditionally competitive character of the pursuit (or in a word, war), these truths found out by reason for avoiding this defeat of all by all may be properly called the articles of Peace' (1975: 39). Such reasons are practically fruitless, however, unless they can be translated into maxims of human conduct and from maxims into laws; that is until they are recognized as 'valid rules of known jurisdiction, to be subscribed to by all who fall within that jurisdiction and to which penalties for nonsubscription have been annexed and power to enforce them provided' (Oakeshott, 1975: 39).

At first sight, it might appear that the operation of 'right Reason' itself is capable of doing this job, and thereby of securing 'lasting peace'. This would be a mistaken conclusion, however. Inspired by the fear of death, Reason 'suggesth' the means by which 'Warre' might be ended by articulating the

The Identities of Self-Interest

'convenient articles of Peace'. But reason in and of itself is incapable of securing such peace precisely because it is already part of the problem it seeks to remedy. In *Elements of Law*, Hobbes indicates why. He argues that 'right Reason' is not a singular but a multiple. 'Commonly, they that call for right reason to decide any controversie do mean their owne'. The invocation of 'Right Reason' thus returns us instantly to the dead end of natural equality and freedom and the crucial question: Who is to decide what is reasonable and what is right?.[6]

The articles of Peace that 'Reason suggesth' are summed up by Hobbes in one phrase: '*Do not that to another, which thou wouldest not have done to thy selfe*' (1991: I:XV: 79). Here, rather than commanding them to honour and cherish the inherent worth of their fellow humans (who are to be treated as ends, not means), Hobbes invites people to join in a defensive compact based on mutual mistrust. Rather than calling people to the higher perfection of charity and universal love, Hobbes preaches instead the universality of self-interest. Moved by fear of death, instructed by the conclusions of reasoning about how the disasters of 'perpetual Warre' might be mitigated, and endowed with the ability to set these conclusions to work, human beings have at their disposal the means of escaping from the horror of their 'natural state'. The solution is elegant and simple. The mechanism by which a transformation from 'natural person' to a 'civil person' is to be effected requires the establishment of a neutral arbiter: an artificial, unitary person whose judgements must be accepted in advance as beyond appeal. This is the 'Sovereign'. It is in every individual's self-interest to submit to the power and authority of the Sovereign, Hobbes argues, because the consequences of refusing allegiance to the only body capable of protecting them will always be worse, individually and collectively, namely 'the miseries and horrible calamities' that accompany 'Warre' (1991: II:XVIII: 128). As Hobbes puts it in *Elements of Law*, the person who occupies the place of 'Right Reason' must be 'he, or they, that hath the Soveraigne power', from which it follows that 'the civil Lawes are to all subjects the measures of their Actions, whereby to determine, whether they be right or wronge, profittable or unprofittable, vertuous or vitious; and by them the use, and definition of all names not agreed upon, and tending to Controversie, shall be established' (1994: 188–9).

A 'constant and lasting Peace' is therefore dependent upon settled and known rules of conduct, embodied in Laws, and a power sufficient to coerce those who fall within their jurisdiction to observe them. The nature of mankind being such that 'during the time that men live without a Common Power to keep them all in awe', they will be 'in that condition which is called Warre; and such a warre, as is every man against every man', it is in every individual's self-interest, their very hope of pursuing their own 'felicity', that they surrender their 'natural rights' to such a common power. By giving up their 'Right to self-government' to a sovereign authority endowed with 'the use of so much power and strength' they thereby ensure that peace is enforced equally on everyone (1991: II:XVII: 120). Human beings who are equal in power and desire are now equal in subjection; each surrenders their natural freedom and liberty on the condition that their fellows do the same, and in this way peace and security are established for everyone. By surrendering a potential liberty to everything – and equally the potential loss of everything – people are establishing the most viable means for securing their own self-interest.

Self-interest, liberty and necessity

It is in this discussion of liberty and self-interest that Hobbes's debt to neo-stoicism is, perhaps, most apparent. Hobbes's conception of liberty revolves around the compatibility of freedom and necessity (e.g., liberty and coercion, liberty and absolute authority), which many critics have taken to be at best inconsistent and at worst a category error (even sympathetic critics, such as Ryan, 1996: 235ff). For the Stoics, however, determinism and freedom were not merely compatible, they actually presupposed one another (Long and Sedley, 1987: I: 392; Oestreich, 1982: 7), and it is this Stoic vision that Hobbes mines in his discussion of the relationship between 'natural liberty' and the 'liberty of subjects', the cardinal distinction framing his discussion of the topic in *Leviathan*. As I indicated earlier, nature and artifice are viewed by Hobbes as two separate 'conditions of mankind' and *Leviathan* is, in effect, a cultural and political roadmap aimed at aiding the transition from the former to the latter 'condition'.

It is in relation to this duality between 'nature' and 'artifice' that we need to assess the coherence of Hobbes's views about the capacity of laws to abrogate freedom and hence about the relationship between necessity and liberty (Skinner, 2002). For Hobbes, liberty, in the proper sense of the term, is always marked by the absence of something, most explicitly by 'the absence of externall impediments' (1991: I:XIV: 91). 'A FREE-MAN' is therefore one 'that in those things which by his strength and wit he is able to do, is not hindered to doe what he has a will to' (1991: II:XXI: 146). A free man is one who in respect of his powers and capacities 'can do if he will and forbear if he will' (Hobbes, quoted in Skinner, 2002: 211).

Now, in one sense, as Hobbes makes clear, the institution of civil law does appear to limit 'naturall liberty' in that the force of the law definitely limits our freedom as subjects. For subjects are by definition human beings who have given up the condition in which everyone is naturally placed, where 'every man holdeth this Right, of doing anything he liketh' (Hobbes, 1991: I:XIV: 92).

The Identities of Self-Interest

For *Right* is *Liberty*, namely that Liberty which the Civil Law leaves us: But *Civill Law* is an *Obligation*; and takes from us the Liberty which the Law of Nature gave us. Nature gave a Right to every man to secure himselfe by his own strength, and to invade a suspected neighbour, by way of prevention: but the Civill Law takes away that Liberty, in all cases where the protection of the Law may be safely stayd for. (Hobbes, 1991: II: XXVI: 200)

However, for Hobbes, such 'naturall' freedom isn't really a freedom worth having as it is so arbitrary and uncertain. While the institution of civil law means that subjects must relinquish their potential right to everything, they also gain from the fact that no individual has the potential right to take away their life or property simply because they happen to be more powerful. 'Naturall liberty' as 'exemption from laws' is, in effect, a form of servitude since it is a condition in 'which all other men may be masters' of our lives and our goods (1991: II:XX: 141).[7] Hence the emphasis Hobbes places on 'that misery that accompanies the Liberty of particular men' (1991: I:XIII: 90). Nonetheless, despite this, Hobbes is insistent that to speak of the liberty of a Subject is to speak first and foremost of the 'Silence of the Law' (1991: II:XXI: 152). If there are 'cases where the Soveraign has prescribed no rule, there the Subject hath the Liberty to do, or forebeare, according to his own discretion' (1991: II:XXI: 152). Where the law demands or forbids a certain action, there the subject is required to act or forbear to act as the law and hence the sovereign command. However, as Skinner (2002: 221) correctly notes, 'the main point on which Hobbes wishes to insist is that, even in those cases where the freedom on the state of nature is undoubtedly abridged by our obligation to obey the civil laws, this does nothing to limit our liberty in the proper signification of the word'. In other words, the presence of the laws does not fundamentally effect the capacity of a human being to 'do if he will and forbear if he will' and thus to be free in Hobbes's 'proper' sense of the term.

At first sight this seems a category error of the highest order and yet, for Hobbes it is of the utmost importance. To understand why this is the case, it is necessary first to explicate the account that Hobbes gives of the distinctive ways in which any system of civil law operates to ensure the obedience of its subjects. Hobbes delineates two routes by which this can be achieved. First, he argues, as we saw earlier, that because the basic aim of the law is to establish and maintain civil peace by protecting life and liberty, all reasonable people will agree to obey the law because they will see it is in their own interests so to do. 'So the liberty of such agents to act as their judgement and reason dictate will not in the least be infringed by their obligation to obey the law. The dictates of their reason and the requirements of the law will prove to be one and the same' (Skinner, 2002: 221–2). In submitting to the law, people therefore express rather than restrict their liberty. As Hobbes puts it, 'The use of the Lawes is not to bind the People from all Voluntary actions; but to direct and keep them in such a motion, as not to hurt themselves by their own impetuous desires, rashnesse, or indiscretion; as Hedges are set, not to stop Travellers, but to keep them in the way' (1991: III:XXX: 239–40).

Secondly, however, Hobbes is aware that this is not the main reason that human beings obey the law, moved as they are, he believes, by unruly passions. Ultimately, they can only be brought to obey because the fear of not doing so is so enormous. Only if there is a 'common power to keep them all in awe' with overwhelming force at its disposal, can human beings be made to obey the law and thus to forbear from acting as partiality, pride, revenge and so forth would otherwise dictate (Hobbes, 1991: II: XVII: 117). Hobbes's point here is that liberty and coercion are not antithetical. For the presence of such a common power does not in and of itself deprive a subject of his or her capacity to act as their will and desires dictate. As he puts it, 'generally, all actions which men doe in Common-wealths, for feare of the law, are actions, which the doers had liberty to omit' (Hobbes, 1991: II:XXI: 146).

According to Skinner (echoing Bishop Bramhall), Hobbes is here reviving a quintessentially 'Stoic vision of the compatibility between liberty and necessity' (2002: 226). Vitally, absolute sovereignty, regardless of form, 'so far from being inimical to liberty, is a necessary condition for it. Liberty of the natural state is intolerable and, in its proper signification, almost meaningless as a ubiquitous feature of existence' (Condren, 2002: 71). Rather than being a designed destruction of individual liberty, as many have argued, the sovereign state is, in fact, 'the minimum condition of any settled association among individuals' (Oakeshott, 1975: 66). It furnishes individuals with a secure basis for the exercise of their liberty and the pursuit of their interests in a way that the state of nature, where everyone is potentially free to do anything and hence free to be enslaved, simply cannot.

Hobbes thus grants nothing to 'natural sociability'. To do so would be to open the door to the very demons his work was striving to extirpate. For Hobbes, the classical republican theory of liberty espoused by so many of his contemporaries, and trading on the idea of the liberty to self-government as a 'natural birthright', was a provocation to 'warre', fuelling rather than controlling the 'licentious passions' (1996; II: XXI: 149–50). Such a formulation posed a direct challenge, in his view, to the liberty of subjects properly understood as founded in the laws of the sovereign civil power. Demanding a right to opinions about justice and natural law independent of the sovereign is, for Hobbes, to invite a sort of anarchy. The appeal to 'nature' is, in effect, 'a mechanism for returning us to it' (Condren, 2002: 72).

This is why it would be 'absurd' to see Hobbes as the progenitor of an image of humanity as 'naturally equipped' with the capacity to rationally maximize its own self-interest. The capacity for 'self-interested' conduct is a

The Identities of Self-Interest

product of entry into the civil state. It is not a natural faculty, but a politically and culturally superimposed mode of conducting civil life. To argue for such a natural capacity would, in Hobbes's schema, be to support the forms of passionate egoism and partiality found in the state of nature, the worst features of which the institution of the civil state was designed to allay.

That 'self-interest' is not a 'natural' faculty, for Hobbes should give no succour to those who, by contrast, decry the inhumanity and reductionism of rational (civil) 'self-interest' by stressing the damage it does to the 'full human personality' seen as 'the person' embedded in her or his full social context. Again, to talk of the 'full human personality' in this way is immediately to return us to the state of nature and to a problem not a solution. As Hobbes was only too aware, the world of the full human personality with its diverse passions needed to be exorcised to the greatest degree possible. It was a social menace, not a social good. True 'sociality' could only be produced in the civil state, it was not something that existed as a 'moral good' in its own right, independent of the *civitas*. If it were granted such autonomy, it would allow, by default, a re-specification of 'natural law' independent of sovereignty and in effect a re-introduction of tyranny in the form of the 'warre of all against all'.

From all this we can adduce that, for Hobbes, the pursuit of one's self-interest cannot be equated with unbridled egoism, for such conduct is akin to a natural rather than an artificial condition. Similarly, true self-interested conduct, that which is caring of necessary things within the bosom of the sovereign state, is indeed antithetical to the development of the 'full human personality'. For the latter too, in Hobbesian logic, is simply the product of a natural rather than artificial condition. Hobbes's self-interested person is therefore only produced and suited to existence in the *civitas*.

As we have already seen, Hobbes indicates that those who 'clamour for liberty and call it their birthright' always make a fundamental error. For if they demand 'liberty' in the proper signification of the term, then they already manifestly possess it. In other words, the presence of the sovereign state does nothing to undermine 'corporall liberty' or 'freedome from chains and prison'. Such liberty already exists. But if they demand 'exemption from the laws' – if they do not want to be subjects – then this really is mad. For asking for such freedom is, in effect, to call for your own servitude – that form of unrestricted liberty 'by which all other men may be masters' of your being and possessions. Far from outlining the conditions in which human individuality and self-interest are undermined, Hobbes is, in effect, seeking to delineate the only secure forms in which individuality and self-interest could be pursued peacefully and effectively. The proper liberty of subjects to pursue their self-interest thus derives from their giving up the right to govern themselves according to their own desires. It is instituted through their absolute obedience to the civil laws and the commands of a sovereign.

Here Hobbes's neo-stoicism is evident. As Tuck (1993: 346) points out, Hobbes's human beings 'find peace and security by denying themselves individual judgement: by subordinating their own wills and desires to those of the sovereign, not because the sovereign knows better, but because the disciplining of an individual psychology is necessary for one's well being'.

Concluding comments

What can we take away with us from this brief and rather perfunctory discussion of 'self-interest'? If nothing else, perhaps, a somewhat sceptical attitude both to the routinely ahistorical and censorious critical sociological association of the 'self' of self-interest with unbridled egoism, crass materialism and a repudiation of the common good, and the similarly ahistoric, preponderantly economistic, conception of persons as naturally rational maximizers of their own utility. Historically, as I have sought to suggest, there have been quite discontinuous changes in the characterization of the 'self' deemed to be 'self-interested'. 'Self-Interest' thus refers to a number of historically distinct conceptions and behaviours. There is, in other words, no such thing as *the* concept of 'self-interest', just as there is no such thing as *the* concept of a person 'whose various components form a harmonious structure that could provide adjudication among competing normative claims about what does or does not fall within the domain of the rights and obligations of persons' (Rorty, 1988: 31). As I indicated earlier, Hirst and Woolley (1982: 131–3) pointed out some time ago that the temptation to unity in relationship to 'persona', for sociologists, as for other social and human scientists, represents an elementary error: 'a metaphysical fiction'. The error in question lies in a failure to recognize that specific conceptions and comportments of the person perform quite different functions in different socio-cultural circumstances and contexts. Given their context specificity, forms of personhood, and their definite but limited settings, must not be under-described. If they are, the danger is that we will fail to see the job that each is doing, that each has its own history and distribution, has fashioned its own ethos, and is directed by its own techniques to its own ends.

In this chapter I have therefore attempted to approach the 'self' of predominantly early modern conceptions of self-interest, not as a subjectivity transcendentally presupposed by experience, but as one historically cultivated to counter the exigencies of particular circumstances – the disaster of perpetual 'warre' in seventeenth century Europe – and to meet the purposes of a particular way of life – existence in the *civitas*. It has been my contention that the homogenisation of the term 'self-interest' – in sociological and economic discourse – has resulted in many misconceptions about what particular doctrines of 'self-interest', and the practices with which they

The Identities of Self-Interest

were associated, were instituted to achieve at certain historical periods and in specific cultural milieux. At its worst, I have suggested, this has led to a misunderstanding of the import of particular doctrines of self-interest which are read in terms of general tradition – such as that which views self-interested conduct as a natural faculty – rather than in terms of the context specific aims of those advocating them.

In so far as such homogenisation is successful – and the standing accorded to 'rational actor' modelling in the social sciences suggests it has been remarkably successful – it inevitably brings in its wake another abstraction, the demand for enrichment. Here, as I argued earlier, the presumed poverty and atomism of (homogenised) 'self-interest' are taken as the occasion for the 'return' of that which it is held to repress: passion, emotion, desire, culture, spontaneity, morality, virtue (the list is as long and varied as the basic premise is misguided). An obsession (particularly among critical sociologies) with the social, moral and cultural 'negativities' of 'narrowly' self-interested conduct (seen as the apogee of 'pure' calculation, whatever that might be), fuels the demand for a more complete conception of humanity; a return, in effect to 'the full human personality'. What we are confronted with here, it would seem, are two abstractions feeding off one another in a seemingly neverending dialectical frenzy. Interest begets passion begets interest and so on and so forth *ad infinitum*. What is lost though is the contextual specificity of particular doctrines of self-interest, the problems which they were designed to address, and the conceptions of persons they gave rise to in so doing. As Hirschman (1977: 132) points out, only by forgetting the desperate conditions that had fostered the emergence of early modern doctrines of 'self-interest' could the Romantic critique, for example, represent 'self-interested conduct' as incredibly impoverished in relation to an earlier age of nobility, freedom and passion.

Hobbes also knew only too well that 'self-interested' conduct, as he envisaged it, would always be a remarkably fragile achievement. In *Leviathan*, he argues that the experience of the English Civil war provided a unique opportunity to alter the terms of debate, and the terrain, of political, cultural and ethical life. However, he thought that this window would only stay open as long as the memory of the horrors of that conflict remained vivid in people's minds.

> There be few now (in England), that do not see, that these Rights [of sovereignty] are inseparable, and will be so generally acknowledged, at the next return of Peace; and so continue, till their miseries are forgotten; and no longer, except the vulgar be better taught than they have hetherto been. (Hobbes, 1996: II:XVIII: 93)

If the neo-stoical vision of 'self-interest' that Hobbes proposes seems hostile to many current sociological and political hobbyhorses, such as the contemporary revival of interest in popular conceptions of political community, for instance, we may do well to recognize that many of the problems to which he was attempting to respond are still real enough, and should be approached by us, today, only with great circumspection. In other words, we should remind ourselves, occasionally, of the ills which Hobbes's conception of 'self-interest' was attempting to escape or at least mitigate. Only by turning Hobbes's specific creation into a travesty of itself can the demand for enrichment make any sense at all.

As Hobbes was only too aware, though, it was a mistake to count out the ideals of the unity of personality, or of 'natural liberty', by assuming they were permanently 'driven from the field' (Pocock, 1985: 122).[8] The appeal of siren voices, religious and metaphysical, he argued, 'can never be so abolished from human nature' (1991: I:XII: 58). Self-interest, as a 'singularly cool and deliberate passion' (Holmes, 1995: 67) was, for Hobbes, always one impulse vying with many others. Instead of continually homogenising its multiple conceptions and behaviours into a simplified 'tradition', thus exaggerating the paradigmatic control of only one version of 'self-interest', we might do better to exercise our historical imaginations a little more and learn to appreciate early modern conceptions of self-interest as remarkable human achievements, especially given the incredibly fallow earth in which they were expected to grow.

Notes

1   As Becker (1986: 112), for instance, has it, 'the economic approach is a comprehensive one that is applicable to all human behavior, be it behavior involving money prices or imputed shadow prices, repeated or infrequent decisions, large or minor decisions, emotional or mechanical ends, rich or poor persons, men or women, adults or children, brilliant or stupid persons, patients or therapists, businessmen or politicians, teachers or students'.

2   According to Habermas (1996: 27), for example, '[F]or self-interested actors, all situational features are transformed into facts they evaluate in the light of their own preferences, whereas actors oriented toward understanding rely on a jointly negotiated understanding of the situation and interpret the relevant facts in the light of intersubjectively recognized validity claims'.

3   *Askesis*, here, does not refer simply to the interdictions we place upon ourselves, but rather to the work one does to turn oneself into a particular ethical subject.

4   Stoic 'apathy' is not complete impassivity or insensibility, but rather the absence of uncontrollable and irrational impulses (Holmes, 1995: 282 n.67).

5   As Oestreich (1982: 7) puts it, 'neostoicism ... demanded self-discipline and the extension of the duties of the ruler and the moral education of the army, the officials, and indeed the whole people, to a life of work, frugality, dutifulness and obedience. The result was a general enhancement of social discipline in all spheres of life, and this enhancement produced, in its turn, a change in the ethos of the individual and his self-perception'.

6   As Hobbes makes clear in *Leviathan*, all reasoning depends on naming; but in moral reasoning all naming depends upon individual passion and prejudice. The

implication is that those who champion the settlement of moral disputes by 'reason' are in effect calling for 'every of the passions, as it comes to bear sway in them, to be taken for right Reason, and that in their own controversies: bewraying their want of right Reason, by the claym they lay to it' (I:V: 33). As Skinner (2002: 139 n.322) argues, Hobbes's contention is thus that moral consensus can only be created politically.

7 As Oakeshott (1975: 66–7) argues in this respect, 'Hobbes conceives the sovereign as law-maker and his rule, not arbitrary, but the rule of law ... [T]hat law as the command of the Sovereign holds within itself a freedom absent from law as custom or law as reason: it is Reason, not Authority that is destructive of individuality. And of course, the silence of the law is a further freedom; when the law does not speak the individual is sovereign over himself. What is indeed, excluded from Hobbes's *civitas* is not the freedom of the individual but the independent rights of spurious authorities and of the collections of individuals such as churches, which he saw as the source of the "civil strife of his time"'.

8 Hirschman (1977: 135) suggests that Cardinal de Retz got it right when he insisted that the passions are not to be discounted in situations where interest-motivated behaviour is assumed to be the norm. Or, as Hobbes (1996: I:XII: 58) himself remarked 'Powers invisible, and supernaturall ... can never be so abolished out of humane nature'. Recent corporate scandals give credence to this view. In time, the distinctive role of 'the full human personality', 'natural liberty' and other metaphysical ideals in these developments may be more fully discerned.

References

Becker, G. (1981) *A Treatise on the Family*. Cambridge, MA: Harvard University Press.

Becker, G. (1986) 'The economic approach to human behaviour', in J. Elster (ed.), *Rational Choice*. New York: New York University Press.

Brown, V. (1994) *Adam Smith's Discourse*. London: Routledge.

Buchanan, J. (1978) 'From private preferences to public philosophy: the development of public choice', in J. Buchanan (ed.), *The Economics of Politics*. London: Institute of Economic Affairs.

Callon, M. (1998) 'Introduction: the embeddedness of economic markets in economics', in M. Callon (ed.), *The Laws of the Markets*. Oxford: Blackwell.

Condren, C. (2002) '*Natura Naturans*: Natural law and the sovereign in the writings of Thomas Hobbes', in I. Hunter and D. Saunders (eds), *Natural Law and Civil Sovereignty*. Basingstoke: Palgrave.

Force, P. (2003) *Self-Interest Before Adam Smith: A Geneaology of Economic Science*. Cambridge: Cambridge University Press.

Foucault, M. (1984) *The Use of Pleasure: The History of Sexuality Volume II*. Harmondsworth: Penguin.

Foucault, M. (1986) *The Care of the Self: The History of Sexuality Volume III*. Harmondsworth: Penguin.

Gaukroger, S. (1995) *Descartes*. Oxford: Oxford University Press.

Habermas, J. (1996) *Between Facts and Norms: Contributions to a Discourse Theory of Law and Democracy*. Cambridge: Polity.

Hadot, P. (1995) *Philosophy as a Way of Life*. Oxford: Blackwell.

Hirschman, A. (1977) *The Passions and the Interests*. Princeton, NJ: Princeton University Press.

Hirst, P. and Woolley, P. (1982) *Social Relations and Human Attributes*. London: Tavistock.

Hobbes, T. (1991) *Leviathan*. Cambridge: Cambridge University Press.

Hobbes, T. (1994) *The Elements of Law Natural and Politic*. Oxford: Oxford University Press.

Holmes, S. (1995) *Passions and Constraint*. Chicago: Chicago University Press.

Hont, I. and Ignatieff, M. (1983) *Wealth and Virtue*. Cambridge: Cambridge University Press.

Hume, D. (1998) *Selected Essays*. Oxford: Oxford University Press.

Hunter, I. (2001) *Rival Enlightenments*. Cambridge: Cambridge University Press.

Johnston, D. (1986) *The Rhetoric of Leviathan*. Princeton, NJ: Princeton University Press.

Long, A.A. (2001) *Stoic Studies*. Los Angeles, CA: University of California Press.

Long, A.A. and Sedley, D.N. (1987) *The Hellenistic Philosophers (Vol. 1)*. Cambridge: Cambridge University Press.

Macpherson, C.B. (1964) *The Political Theory of Possessive Individualism*. Oxford: Oxford University Press.

Minson, J. (1993) *Questions of Conduct*. Basingstoke: Macmillan.

Niskanen, W. (1971) *Bureaucracy and Representative Government*. Chicago, IL: Aldine-Atherton.

Nussbaum, M. (1994) *The Therapy of Desire*. Princeton, NJ: Princeton University Press.

Oakeshott, M. (1975) *Hobbes and Civil Association*. Indianapolis, IL: Liberty Fund.

Oestreich, G. (1982) *Neostoicism and the Early Modern State*. Cambridge: Cambridge University Press.

Pocock, J.D. (1985) *Virtue, Commerce and History*. Cambridge: Cambridge University Press.

Rorty, A-O (1988) *Mind in Action*. Boston: Beacon.

Ryan, A. (1996) 'Hobbes's political philosophy', in T. Sorrell (ed.), *The Cambridge Companion to Hobbes*. Cambridge: Cambridge University Press.

Sayer, A. (1997) 'The dialectic of culture and economy', in R. Lee and J. Wills (eds), *Geographies of Economies*. London: Edward Arnold.

Schotter, A. (1981) *The Economic Theory of Institutions*. Cambridge: Cambridge University Press.

Skinner, Q. (2002) *Visions of Politics Volume III: Hobbes and Civil Science*. Cambridge: Cambridge University Press.

Tawney, R.H. (1926) *Religion and the Rise of Capitalism*. New York: Harcourt, Brace and World.

Tuck, R. (1993) *Philosophy and Government 1572–1651*. Cambridge: Cambridge University Press.

Tully, J. (1988) 'Governing conduct', in E. Leites (ed.), *Conscience and Casuistry in Early Modern Europe*. Cambridge: Cambridge University Press.

7

The Constitution of Identity: Primary Repression After Kristeva and Laplanche

Anthony Elliott

In recent years several psychoanalytic authors working within the European tradition of contemporary critical thought have addressed anew the problem of the constitution of the human subject (see, amongst others, Anzieu, 1989; Castoriadis, 1987, 1997; Green, 1985; Kristeva, 1989, 1993; Laplanche, 1987; in addition, for a comprehensive synthesis of these trends see Elliott, 2004). Essential to all such recastings of subjectivity is a shift away from an Oedipal-centred to a pre-Oedipal perspective, from a Lacanian-inspired theory of the linguistifaction of the subject to a post-Lacanian theory of pre-verbal, imaginary significations. Moreover, these far-reaching investigations have raised afresh the question of human creation, the question of representation and fantasy, and the question of the imaginary constitution of the socio-symbolic world. In doing so they offer alternative perspectives on the very nature of representation and repression in the structuration of social action and thus potentially contribute to a reconsideration of social theory more generally.

The essential value of such a reappraisal of the constitution of the subject for critical social theory lies in its stress on the unconscious aspects of social reproduction – that is, on the ways in which a society's structures are reproduced through a redoublement of a primary, if inaccessible, field of the subject's imaginary productions. This stress on the irreducibly creative, imaginary fabrications of the subject is particularly suggestive for social theorists seeking to grasp the potential reach of contemporary recursive theories of the structured features of human action – without which there could be no reflexivity in personal life and thus no recursivity in society (see, for example, Bourdieu, 1977, 1993; Giddens, 1984, 1990). In today's recursive theories, structured features of action are conceptualized as unregulated but regular with reference to more preconscious than conscious dispositions. In conceptualizing the mysteries of such recursive dispositions, however, most theorists make recourse only to limited notions of the unconscious (as, say, a reservoir of memory traces) or to pre-psychoanalytic understandings of tacit assumptions or shared dispositions. By contrast, what post-Lacanian perspectives indicate must be grasped is not how dispositions or memory traces are pressed into structured action with reference to preconscious or even unconscious figurations, but rather how structured action is structured at each and every moment with reference to primitive identificatory processes, the pre-verbal sensory experience of others and objects, as well as the ongoing impact of a primary protorepresentation or instituting fantasy. For a critical social theory that addressed recursive dispositions in this way would provide a framework within which other concerns, such as the imaginary constitution of bodily and sensory experience, could be recast.

This chapter seeks to address and critique some of the claims of post-Lacanian conceptualizations of the human subject. I shall do so by focusing in particular on the recent psychoanalytic departures of Julia Kristeva and Jean Laplanche on the status of primary repression as a condition for the constitution of the subject. The chapter goes on to suggest ways in which the analyses set out by Kristeva and Laplanche can be further refined and developed, partly through a reconsideration of the intertwining of unconscious representation and repression as developed in the writings of Cornelius Castoriadis, Thomas Ogden and others. The final sections of the chapter are reconstructive and innovative in character. For existing psychoanalytical accounts I suggest we should substitute the concept of *rolling identification*, the psychical basis of the shift from self-referential representational activity to an elementary form of intersubjectivity. Rolling identifications are defined as a representational flux that permits human subjects to create a relation to the self-as-object and pre-object relations. Such primal identification, it is suggested, operates through a *representational wrapping of self and others*. The chapter concludes with a consideration of the significance of primary repression, and the politicization of identification.

Freud on the unconscious, representation and repression

In classical Freudian theory, the creation of the human subject occurs in and through repression. Primary repression, Freud wrote, 'consists in the psychical (ideational) representative of the drive being denied entrance into the conscious' (1915: 148). The outcome of primary repression, which arises from the non-satisfaction of infantile needs, is the bonding or fixing of drives to representations. But Freud stops short of spelling out the precise implications of primary repression for the structuration of subjectivity.

Instead, his own theoretical and clinical accounts of the development of subjectivity centre upon the concept of secondary repression, or 'repression proper', as formulated in the Oedipus and castration complexes. In Freud's scheme, it is the paternal break-up of the imaginary child/mother dyad which initiates 'repression proper', and constitutes the development of identity and culture.

However, Freud's construction of Oedipal repression as constitutive of identity obscures as much as it illuminates. The view that the small infant (re)presents or discovers *itself* through Oedipal identifications implies that subjectivity is a given, and not a phenomenon to be explicated. The inconsistency here is that the infant surely cannot identify with Oedipal presentations unless it already has a more rudimentary sense of subjectivity. Moreover, it seems that this problem is only compounded if we reverse the logic in operation here, as Lacan does, and trace the imaginary ego as modelling and misrecognizing itself in specular images. For, as various commentators have noted (Castoriadis, 1987; Elliott, 1999), the specular relation is only constituted as a *relation* to the extent that it is shaped by psychic space itself. And in Lacan's account, this (mis)copying is linked to further alienation through the constitution of the subject via a phallocentrically organized structure of language and culture.

By contrast, the psychoanalytic direction of contemporary theory involves a renewed emphasis upon primary repression and identification. Kristeva (1987, 1989) and Laplanche (1987, (in Fletcher and Stanton) 1992) provide detailed treatments of the topic. Here it is suggested that the dynamics of primary repression and identification involve an elementary gap between self and other, a gap which is the very condition for the arising of the subject. Primary repression is thus not merely a preparatory step for the constitution of Oedipal identity. Rather, primary repression is considered as elementary to the establishment of subjectivity itself. In what follows, I shall critically examine some of the central theoretical issues on primary repression as discussed by Kristeva and Laplanche. Following this, I shall attempt to sketch an alternative account of primary repression as linked to the dynamics of subjectivity and intersubjectivity.

Primary repression and the loss of the thing: Kristeva's exploration of the imaginary father

For several decades, Kristeva has focused on recasting the relations between subjectivity and society in a series of works situated at the intersection of psychoanalysis, feminism and modern European thought, including *Tales of Love* (1987), *In the Beginning was Love* (1988), *Strangers to Ourselves* (1991), and *New Maladies of the Soul* (1993). Her work blends linguistic and psychoanalytical theory to advance a novel account of how pre-verbal experience – maternal, infantile, poetic – enters into, shapes, distorts and disrupts language through processes of art, literature and psychoanalysis. The result has been a radical opening of the intersections between psychoanalysis and critical social theory, which in turn has provided a transformative political and feminist dimension to Freudian thought and an enhanced psychoanalytical dimension to critical social theory.

Kristeva's various discussions of the constitution of repressed desire demonstrate a persistent concern with human imagination and the creativity of action. In order to adequately grasp Kristeva's contribution to the development of a theory of the human subject, it is necessary now to situate her work in the context of Lacan's 'return to Freud'. Having undertaken her psychoanalytic training with Lacan, it is perhaps not surprising that Kristeva's early writings should emphasize the ordering power of the Symbolic, of language as such. In Lacan's rewriting of Freud, the human subject comes to language, and adopts a position of speaker, from a devastating primordial loss. The pain of this loss leads to a repression that at once buries memories of fulfilment experienced through contact with the phallic mother on the one hand, and catapults the subject-to-be into a Symbolic order of individuation, differentiation and cultural signification on the other. In her early work Kristeva accepts these basic tenets of Lacanian theory, but she contrasts Lacan's account of the Symbolic order with a revaluation of the persistence and force of repressed libidinal desires, somatic dispositions and affects – a kind of unconscious rhythm that Kristeva terms 'the semiotic'. Prose and poetry are symbolic forms that Kristeva has psychoanalytically deconstructed to try to capture something of 'the semiotic' or 'maternal body' that remains truly inexpressible. She finds in acts of artistic expression that press language to its limits – that is, in the ruins of the symbolic – a zone, by definition incommunicable, in which desire bursts forth. Is this zone a set of organized subjective meanings, a language, or is it prelinguistic, and hence indescribable? Not so much prelinguisitic according Kristeva, as an expression of the prolinguistic: affects, bodily dispositions, silences, rhythms.

In her recent work, Kristeva has become especially interested in Kleinian psychoanalysis, or more specifically Klein's elaboration of Freud's theory of representation or the proto-fantasy. A close reading of Klein, argues Kristeva, demonstrates that the child, from the very beginning of life, is consumed with anxiety. 'No matter how far back Klein reaches into childhood', writes Kristeva (2001: 137), 'she always discovers a fantasizing ego. A sundry entity made up of verbal and non-verbal representations, sensations, affects, emotions, movements, actions and even concretizations, the Kleinian phantasy is a wholly impure theoretical construct that defies the purists as much as it fascinates clinicians, particularly those who specialise in children,

The Constitution of Identity

psychosis, or the psychosomatic disorders'. Moreover, the fantasy-like omnipotent construction of the primary object – the breast – is first and foremost a construction from within, that is, of unstable representational distinctions between *inside* and *outside*, between *inner* and *outer*. From the outset', writes Kristeva (2001: 63) 'the primal object of the paranoid-schizoid position emerges, in Klein's view, if and only if it is an *internal object* constructed through a fantasy of omnipotence'. As Kristeva notes, rightly in my view, Klein's notion of the internal object is entirely distinct from Lacan's order of the imaginary, for Lacan primarily stressed the visual side of fantasy. Lacan's account of spectral distortion – that narcissism is constituted through the intermediary of the object as a function of the subject's absorption in a reflecting surface – underscores the role of the scopic function in the structuration of the ego and the object. Yet what of transverbal representations, affects, emotions, sensations? Here – and make no mistake about it – Kristeva, a 'post-Lacanian', speaks up for Klein's understanding of the internal object, primarily since the Kleinian approach offers a fruitful conceptual map for grasping heterogeneous psychic representations that are altogether missing in Lacan's 'return to Freud'.

As with her previous work, especially *Tales of Love* (1987), *Black Sun* (1989) and *New Maladies* (1993), Kristeva repositions Klein's clinical and conceptual approach to ask: what is psychic representation? Here Kristeva applauds Klein for uncovering *diverse domains of representation* – not only verbal or symbolic representations, but affects, sensations, gestures, and even 'concretizations' to which fantasies are sometimes reduced in psychotic suffering. In Klein's theory, says Kristeva, the centrality of wish and fantasy to human subjectivity is borne of sensation and affect. The movement of the Kleinian investigation, rooted in clinical experience with children and which contributes significantly to our understanding of both psychosis and autism, is fundamental for grasping the richness and multi-layered creativity of the psyche. In exploring the transverbal archaic realm, a realm that belies visual representation, Klein went beyond the 'secondary imagination' which runs throughout the whole tradition of Western thought to the primary fantasy or constitutive imagination. Kristeva makes an interesting case for the contemporary relevance of Klein's hypothesis of a proto-fantasy, or the instituting fantasy. The correctness of Klein's psychoanalytic theory is confirmed, she argues, by more recent studies that portray the psyche, lodged between anxiety and language, in the form of 'pre-narrative envelopes' (Daniel Stern), 'nameless dreads' (Wilfred Bion) and 'life narcissisms' (Andre Green). Such a focus on the psychic representative prior to representation also connects strongly with Kristeva's own theoretical account of semiotic articulations, defined as a heterogeneous play of unconscious forces – of drives and desires – which exert a pulsional pressure within language itself, and which may be discerned in the rhythm, tone and disruption of speech.

This brings us to an important aspect of Kristeva's interpretation of Freud, an aspect I want to concentrate on in some detail. In her recent writing, Kristeva connects the constitution of subjectivity to the imaginary tribulations of the pre-Oedipal phase rather than to the Oedipal symbolic process alone. According to Kristeva, the primary identifications of narcissism already represent an advancement over the affective, representational flux of auto-eroticism. She describes primary identification as the 'zero degree' that shapes psychic space itself, and links this arising of the subject to Freud's notion of a 'father in individual prehistory'. In this 'prehistory', the child forges an initial identification, prior to sexual division, with a maternal-paternal container. As Kristeva explains this *pre-Oedipal* identification:

> Freud has described the One with whom I fulfil the identification (this 'most primitive aspect of affective binding to an object') as a Father. Although he did not elaborate what he meant by 'primary identification', he made it clear that this father is a 'father in individual prehistory' ... Identification with that 'father in prehistory', that Imaginary Father, is called 'immediate', 'direct', and Freud emphasizes again, 'previous to any concentration on any object whatsoever ... The whole symbolic matrix sheltering emptiness is thus set in place in an elaboration that precedes the Oedipus complex. (Kristeva, 1987: 267)

And again, on the sexual indistinction of primary identification:

> The archaeology of such an identifying possibility with an other is provided by the huge place taken up within narcissistic structure by the vortex of primary identification with what Freud called a 'father of personal prehistory'. Endowed with the sexual attributes of both parents, and by that very token a totalizing, phallic figure, it provides satisfactions that are already psychic and not simply immediate, existential requests; that archaic vortex of idealization is immediately an other who gives rise to a powerful, already psychic transference of the previous semiotic body in the process of becoming a narcissistic Ego. (Kristeva, 1987: 33)

Note here that the reference to an *other* ties the emergence of identity to the intersubjective field. Note too that this identification with the imaginary father (which is less a partial object than a pre-object) *constitutes* primary repression; it 'bends the drive toward the symbolic of the other' (Kristeva, 1987: 31).

Kristeva argues that primary identification arises, not from the child's desire for the pre-Oedipal mother, but from an affective tie with the *mother's desire for the phallus*. Echoing Lacan, she contends that the child comes to realize that the mother herself is lacking, incomplete. In this connection, the child encounters the desire of the other: that the mother's desire is invested elsewhere, in the imaginary phallus. For Kristeva, identification with the imaginary father functions as support for the loss of the maternal object, and provides an imaginary lining to subjectivity which guards against depression and melancholia. Yet, because the investment in this imaginary father comes from the inside, the emergence of identity is itself a precarious, fragile process.

Enigmatic messages: Laplanche

Like Kristeva, Laplanche is also concerned with reconceptualizing the conditions of primal identification and repression, with the purpose of mapping the inaccessible, unconscious significations between the individual subject and the intersubjective realm. Laplanche suggests that an elementary form of subjectivity is constituted when the small infant enters into an identification with certain 'enigmatic signifiers' in the pre-Oedipal phase, a phase which initiates the binding of unconscious drives through primal repression. Though highly technical in formulation, what Laplanche means by the notion of an enigmatic signifier, roughly speaking, is the uncanny decentring influence of the Other upon our psychical life. This process of decentring, says Laplanche, occurs at the crossroads of language, body and desire – wherever another's 'message' (Laplanche's term) implants itself as a perplexing question or foreign body in the human subject's psyche. Subjectively speaking, the role of enigmatic signifiers is one that is always at work in the emotional life of the subject, and yet the sort of specific enigmas or perplexing messages that tend to dominate a person's experience of self derive, by and large, from childhood. According to Laplanche, enigmatic messages conveyed by parents (at first by the mother) are especially consequential for the development of subjectivity, since such implantations arise prior to the establishment proper of the signifying character of the symbolic order.

If the enigmatic message is integral to the psychic origins of the unconscious, it is equally central to human subjectivity itself, so that Laplanche is able to develop a neo-Lacanian critique of the trajectory of both psychosexuality and identity. He outlines the foundational force of an opaque, impossibly paradoxical Otherness – the result of intrusive and exciting adult enigmas – so that the human subject can never get to the heart of family secrets or sexual researches, but must live nevertheless with these enigmas through the continual emotional work of translation, reconstruction and binding. In any case, this is so since adult messages always-already outstrip the small infant's capacity for emotional processing and affective response. Laplanche calls this the 'fundamental anthropological situation' of humans, the fact that the infant wouldn't survive without the care and nurturance provided by the adult, a situation that locates the infant as struggling to comprehend the adult's expressions of feeling, gestures of care and conveyances of relatedness. For try as the infant might to comprehend elements of the adult's communication – attempting a kind of 'proto-understanding' through the primitive translation and binding of adult enigmas – there is always a left-over or residue, which for Laplanche constitutes the unconscious and primal repressions.

More than merely perplexing, however, enigmatic messages are completely mysterious. For the enigmatic message is itself, in an uncanny sort of way, always scrambled, overloaded with signification, impenetrable. Laplanche's account of all this might perhaps be likened to the sense of strangeness an adult might feel when, having entered a room, he or she discovered people talking a highly specialised language, like the jargon of nuclear physics, nanotechnology, or deconstruction. For Laplanche, messages are enigmatic because they are compromised by the repressed unconscious lodged inside us: a contradictory condensation of unconscious desires invades the enigmatic signifiers, such that the adult does not know what it wants of the infant in any case. This is a version of the classic psychoanalytic doctrine that the small infant's unconscious is formed with reference to the parental unconscious.

Laplanche's favourite stage of infant development appears to lie with the earliest transactions between mother and child, the pre-Oedipal realm where floating needs and appetites meet with scrambled and mysterious adult messages, which he uses to illustrate the paradox of primal seduction. Returning the Freud's discussion of maternal care and devotion as central to the origins of the infant's psychic life, Laplanche argues that the breast is a carrier of maternal fantasy which transmits opaque sexual significations within the mother-child relation. The child, says Laplanche, receives a sexually distorted, overloaded message from the mother, a message which the child is emotionally unable to process or translate.

Primary repression rethought: rolling identifications and representational wrappings of self and other

There is, I believe, much that is of interest in Kristeva and Laplanche on the constitution of the unconscious through primary repression. Both Kristeva and Laplanche, in differing theoretical ways, underline the importance of primary repression as a support for the arising of an elementary form of subjectivity, which is subsequently secured through the Oedipus and castration complexes. However, there are also serious theoretical difficulties arising from their work. Kristeva has been much criticized, in both psychoanalytic and feminist circles, for linking the moment of identification with the imaginary father. For feminists such as Cornell (1991: 68–71), this has the effect of reinscribing gender stereotypes within the pre-Oedipal phase, resulting in a denial of woman's imaginary. Cornell's critique of Kristeva interestingly stresses that it is from a reading of the desire of desire, the desire of the Other, that primary identification arises and grants the subject's assent to identity in the symbolic order. From a feminist angle, Cornell is especially attuned to the abjection of the mother that this moment of identification involves, though she is also to some degree aware of the positioning of desire as an external, impersonal force (the desire of desire) rather than as emanating from the child's desire *for* the mother. From a related but distinct perspective, Laplanche's work has also been criticized for its neglect of the more creative dimensions of sexual subjectivity. As Jacqueline Rose has pointed out, Laplanche's reinterpretation of primary repression means that the 'child receives everything from the outside' (cited in Fletcher and Stanton, 1993) desire being inscribed within the repressed unconscious via the deformations of parental sexuality itself (Fletcher and Stanton, 1992: 61). In my view, these criticisms are indeed valid. The standpoints of Kristeva and Laplanche are flawed in respect of the power accorded to the other (imaginary father/seduction) over psychic interiority, or the outside as constitutive of desire itself. By contrast, I suggest that we must develop a psychoanalytic account of subjectivity and intersubjectivity which breaks with this inside/outside boundary.

For these accounts I suggest we should substitute the delineation of an elementary dimension of subjectivity formed in and through primary intersubjectivity – a mode dependent upon the fixation of primal repression and identification. In the constitution of primary intersubjectivity, the small infant actively enters into the push-and-pull of object – or, more accurately, pre-object – relations. This is less a phenomenon of the other 'breaking in' from the outside than one of ordering psychic interiority within the intersubjective boundaries of shared, unconscious experience. The organizing of shared, unconscious experience occurs through a process that I call *rolling identification*. Derived from the representational flux of the unconscious, rolling identifications provide for the insertion of subjectivity into a complex interplay between self-as-object and pre-object relations. Rolling identifications literally spill out across libidinal space, with a representational flux passing into objects, and objects into psychical life, in a ceaseless exchange. Here the rudimentary beginnings of pre-self experience arise from factors such as sensory impressions of autistic shapes and objects (Ogden, 1989; Tustin, 1980, 1984), which form feelings of warmth, hardness, coldness, texture and the like; a primitive relation to bounded surfaces (Ogden, 1989), such as the child's own body and the body of the mother, as well as non-human substances; and from maternal rhythmicity (Kristeva, 1984), including tone, breath and silences.

There is a proto-symbolic as well as a sensory poetics at work here. Persons and things may not yet be objects, but the small infant constantly invests and assimilates what is outside itself – though, once again, it must be stressed that the monadic core of the subject as it functions during this elemental form of intersubjective experience is, in fact, diametrically opposed to all that we understand by the terms 'inside' and 'outside'. 'Here', as Castoriadis (1987: 294) says, 'there is no way of separating representation and "perception" or "sensation". The maternal breast or what takes its place, is a part without being a distinct part, of what will later become the "own body" and which is, obviously, not yet a "body"'. There is thus something of an infinite regress operating here, such that a primitive psychological organization of experience is constituted by identificatory incorporations of the (m)other that structure relations to self, others and the object-world in an ongoing way. Does the other, in some way, transport the infant to the heart of reality, a mix of proto-subject and proto-world? How can the libidinal articulations of the babbling child become somehow 'organized' within the uncontrollability that otherness necessarily brings?

Now as regards the psychoanalytic notion of primary repression, it can be said that all individuals develop a framework for reworkings of psychical organization, based on sensory modes of organizing experience which remain undivided at the level of psychic reality. The analysis of the sensory core of the primal subject worked out by Thomas Ogden, rather than that of Castoriadis himself, is very useful here. Reaching back to the earliest days of the pre-Oedipal, Ogden theorizes what he terms an 'autistic-contiguous position', described by him (1989: 31) as 'a sensory-dominated mode in which the most inchoate sense of self is built upon the rhythm of sensation, particularly the sensations of the skin surface'. Such autistic-contiguous experience is not a biological or prepsychological phase of development, but rather is psychodynamically operative from birth and functions in the life of the subject in large part from connections and relations of a sensory kind. Like Castoriadis, Ogden stresses that the infant's earliest relations with objects come from contact with the caretaking other in a presymbolic, sensory-dominated mode. Theorizing the autistic or undivided nature of such experience in neo-Kleinian terms, Ogden notes that the infant's relationship to the object is quite different to the depressive position (where there is a relationship between subjects) and also to the paranoid-schizoid position (where both self and other are treated as objects). Rather, the nascent subject's undivided or autistic 'experience' or 'state' is that of non-reflective sensory Being, the first imaginative elaboration of bodily needs.

In one sense, Ogden aestheticizes imagination, so that – thanks to the autistic-contiguous valorization of bodily experience – subject and object, sensation and representation pass fluently into each other so as to ensure the possibility of a presymbolic break-up of the psychical monad. The neo-Kleinian Ogden thus adds particular insight and intriguing depth to Castoriadis's paradoxical claim that the 'autism is undivided', in the sense

The Constitution of Identity

that he details the small infant's or proto-subject's relationship to the object in the autistic-contiguous position. As Ogden (1989: 32) writes, 'It is a relationship of shape to the feeling of enclosure, of beat to the feeling of rhythm, of hardness to the feeling of edgedness. Sequences, symmetries, periodicity, skin-to-skin "moulding" are all examples of contiguities that are the ingredients out of which the beginnings of rudimentary self-experience arise'.

Ogden, together with Castoriadis, stand out among psychoanalysts who have preserved certain universal elements of Freud's original account of the psychic origins of the human subject, while at the same time expanding and refining it in a systematic manner to account for the primary force of representation and repression in the constitution of the unconscious. In what follows, I shall draw – albeit selectively and critically – upon their ideas. On the basis of both his clinical work and the reconstruction of diverse traditions in contemporary psychoanalysis, Ogden has identified the forms of object-relation – or, more accurately, relations to the pre-object – that derive from autistic-contiguous modes of experience. The nursing experience, the experience of being held, of being rocked to sleep, sung to as well as caressed by the mother: Ogden's discussion of rhythmicity and experiences of sensory contiguity that make up a person's earliest relations with objects is highly persuasive. But I do not think that he unearths sufficiently the essential nature of such primary, autistic or what I term rolling identifications as a constructive process, one in which the internalized attributes of pre-objects and part-objects are employed in the service of a transformation or working through of the psyche.

Ogden sees us all as permanently producing and reproducing primitive representations of pre-objects or proto-objects in our dealings with things and other people, drawing upon elementary identifications from the autistic-contiguous mode to bolster the shape and content of our more mature, multiple identifications with self and others in daily life. Yet what does this radically imaginary positing of elementary identifications consist of? Ogden posits the existence of basic mechanisms whereby external experiences are taken in, of primitive identificatory processes by which a contiguity of surfaces may be introjected. But he does not provide a satisfactory account of the imaginary constitution of sensory surfaces, the elements of creation in the subject's constitution of a sensory world, nor the initial unmediated identity of the infant, sensation, affect and representational flux. Ogden says that autistic identifications provide a kind of 'sensory floor' to psychic experience. And yet if we reflect on the pre-Oedipal tie of infant (proto-subject) and breast (proto-object), it can be said that the making of fluid identifications from experiences of rhythmic rocking or sucking involves more than the constitution of the breast as an object, as separate or different from the subject. From the angle of the monadic core of the psyche, what is important about rhythm, texture, boundedness, warmth, coldness and the like is the undifferentiated, unmediated quality of identification as a process. Before experiences of hardness or softness are located as representations of what the proto-subject finds in interpersonal contact, the proto-subject just *is* hardness or softness. But, *pace* Ogden, I argue that there must be some minimal representational colouring involved here – which I seek to delineate with reference to Freud's concept of primary repression and also the representative prior to representation, of which more shortly.

Rolling identifications veer away in erratic directions, and their elaboration is plural, multiple, discontinuous. The elementary form of identification, the pre-identification presupposed by internalisation, saturates libidinal space. The mode of identification flows, continually *rolls* out anew. Before the differentiation proper of self and other, this modality of psychic organization is basic to the wealth of images, fantasies and feelings that circulate within intersubjective communication. To capture the nature of rolling identification, we must connect the auto-erotic indistinction between the self and the non-self of which Castoriadis speaks with the concept of primary identification and repression. Now primary identification 'does not wait upon an object-relationship proper' (Laplanche and Pontalis,1985: 336). It is constituted, rather, through a process of incorporating a pre-object; or, as Kristeva says, primary identification 'bends the drive toward the symbolic of the other' (1987: 31). But how, exactly, is the drive 'bent' in the direction of the other? How does the subject make this shift from self-referential representational fulfilment to primary intersubjectivity? How, in any case, does the presentation of otherness enter into the construction of the psyche? Several factors suggest themselves on the basis of the foregoing observations. To begin with, the infant's subjectivity – marked by representational flux – can be thought of as becoming *internally split* once the emergent relation to the pre-object is established. Primary identification, and the general narcissism which it ushers in, are therefore closely bound up with loss. Loss here is understood as a result of the preliminary dissolution of basic representational self-sufficiency. As Castoriadis expresses this:

> Once the psyche has suffered the break up of its monadic 'state' imposed upon it by the 'object', the other and its own body, it is forever thrown off-centre in relation to itself, orientated in terms of that which it is no longer and can no longer be. *The psyche is its own lost object.* (Castoriadis, 1987: 296–7)

The subject, simply, suffers the loss of self-referential representational fulfilment, and it substitutes a relation to pre-objects and self-as-object as the basis for creating 'a place where one lives' (Winnicott, 1971).

To be sure, the possible adaptive reactions must register basic relational connections. Indeed, this is the outlook described by Kristeva and Laplanche – the subject is referred beyond itself via an imaginary anchor in parental significations. This standpoint, while more sophisticated than most, is still inadequate however, since its conception of the subject and the unconscious is too simple. In my view, the relation between the rudimentary beginnings of subjectivity and primary intersubjectivity – the psychical registration of self-as-object and pre-object relations – cannot be understood outside of the representational dynamics of desire itself. Now in Freud's account of the nascent subject's fall from pre-Oedipal Eden, basic relational connections are established in the psyche through the arising of the affect of unpleasure associated with hunger. The nascent subject creates an hallucinatory representation of the breast in an attempt to avoid the terrors of reality, which in Freud's theorization involves a primordial wound incurred by the absence of the mother. Through hallucinatory wish fulfilment, the nascent subject imagines the mother present in fantasy, even though she is in fact missing in actuality. Originary fantasmatic representation for Freud is thus the prototype of all further representations, fantasy and dream formation in the psyche. The 'original representation' is what cannot be included within any self-grasping or self-reflexivity of the subject's imaginary productions, but whose very absence marks the stratified and intercommunicating elaborations of our imaginary worlds, as a kind of vortex around which desire circulates.

As far as a foundational myth of the psychic constitution of the subject goes, Freud's narrative is, one might claim, at once too subject-centred and not focused enough on the imaginary domain. His treatment of how unpleasurable affect, drawing on traces of reality, triggers the creation of the hallucinated breast contains rich insight, with its subtle examination of the origins of imaginary creation. Certainly when Freud speaks of the pre-Oedipal infant as having 'created an object out of the mother' (1926: 170) he captures with original insight the breathtakingly innovative and creative dimensions of the imaginary domain. For the most part, however, Freud's speculations here fail to do justice to the lucidity of his concepts. For what allows the nascent subject's originary representation to become the prototype of all further representations is conceptualized by Freud only at the level of the hallucinated breast as 'object'. Yet, as Castoriadis notes, this supposedly 'original' hallucination is, in fact, a secondary formation – based on the elaboration of quite complex connections between subjectivity, part-objects and objects. As Castoriadis sees it, it is not hallucinatory wish fulfilment (a secondary figuration) which shapes the paradox of representation. For Castoriadis, the roots of our unconscious lives develop out of the creation of an 'Ur-Vorstellung', an instituting fantasy or protorepresentation which must be absent from the unconscious if, paradoxically, we are to function as 'subjects of the unconscious'.

Just as Castoriadis would have us concentrate on the monadic core of the psyche (the nascent subject as 'unitary subjective circuit') and accordingly refashions the psychoanalytic doctrine of *anaclisis* ('leaning-on') to elucidate how the psyche 'lends itself to socialisation', Ogden would have us concentrate on the presymbolic, sensory mode in which surface contiguity cements a person's earliest relations with objects. As Ogden (1989: 33) puts this: 'These sensory experiences with "objects" (which only an outside observer would be aware of as objects) are the media through which the earliest forms of organised and organising experience are created'. But even if we recognize that radically imaginary processes and experiences of sensory contiguity contribute to the earliest 'structure' of psychological organization, we are still confronted with the dilemma of how the nascent subject encounters shared experience. There is also the further problem of determining exactly what facilitating factors are necessary for primary or rolling identification to unfold.

Now contemporary research concerning human subjectivity suggests that the psyche's capacity to produce unconscious representations from the earliest days of life is not separated off from the time/space environments of other persons in the manner that classical Freudian theory supposes, and for which Castoriadis (and in some senses Ogden too) provides a challenging justification. In recent research, work has focused on the earliest and most primitive phases of psychic functioning, emphasizing the role of the mother in a very different manner from Freud and Castoriadis. The relation between the nascent subject (infant) and other (mother) is revalued as essentially creative, and the constitution of psychic structure is held to depend upon various affective exchanges and communicative dialogues. Feminist psychoanalysts, in particular, have stressed that the maternal body plays a constitutive role in emotional life and the structuring of the psyche. From this perspective, the use of the symbolic father or phallus to conceptualise the emergence of individuation in the Freudian and Lacanian standpoints is shown to rest on a masculinist inability to envision the mother as both a containing and a sexual subject within the child's psychic world. As Irigaray has argued, the failure to represent the umbilicus – in psychoanalytic theory as well as in cultural life more generally – as a symbol of connection with, and separation from, the mother has led to the continuing dominance of the phallus in contemporary theory.

This revaluing of the intersubjective sphere as it concerns the development of the psyche also incorporates a recognition that the creative play of subjectivities structures a potential space within which a web of psychic and sociosymbolic identifications can unfold. Various theorists emphasize how psychic space and the location of otherness are interwoven in the constitution of subjectivity and the frame of intersubjectivity. In the work of Irigaray, this investigation emerges as part of an attempt to rework the psychoanalytic conceptualisation of the child/mother dyad, giving special attention to bodily flows and to experiences of fluidity as itself other.

133

Anzieu (1989) discusses the archaeology of a 'skin ego', a preverbal writing made up of traces upon the skin. Helene Cixous similarly seeks to explore the repudiation of the body in the nascent subject's imaginary relationship to the phallic mother. There is also research in psychology suggesting that interaction between the psyche and its environment starts in the womb, and that from the moment of birth the infant is engaged in creative and active communications with the world (see Chamberlain, 1987; Stern, 1985).

The general characteristics I outlined in the forgoing discussion regarding primary or rolling identification, if they are valid, are also relevant for describing how the psyche opens up to externality (otherness, difference) in a predominantly imaginary mode. Now Odgen's account of the earliest experiences of sensory contiguity, I have suggested, comes close to filling out in detail Castoriadis's philosophical construction of the radically imaginary as genuine psychic creation. Yet if we return to Odgen and his discussion of how the earliest sensory experiences with 'objects' are the media through which psychical production is created, we see that, although his discussion is subtle and intricate, he does not in fact specify the facilitating conditions necessary for the structuration of such primitive psychic organization. Indeed, there is a passage in Ogden where he appears to rule out the necessity of considerations of representation in the autistic-contiguous mode altogether. 'The rudiments of the sensory experience itself in an autistic-contiguous mode', writes Ogden (1989: 35), 'have nothing to do with the representation of one's affective states, either idiographically or symbolically'.

However, and here I return to the threads of my argument concerning primary or rolling identification, Ogden's assertion cannot stand without some explanation of the status of the *representative prior to representation*. According to the view I am proposing, there is a *representational wrapping of self and other* achieved through primary repression and identification. By this I mean that the subject establishes a preliminary ordering, to use a kind of shorthand, of pre-self experience, otherness and difference as the basis for the elaboration of psychic space itself. Such representational wrapping does not just 'register' other persons and the object world, but is the central mechanism which makes their humanization possible. Representational wrapping spirals in and out of intersubjective life, ordering and reordering both psychical imagination and the social process of which it is part. What I am suggesting is that the status of the representative prior to representation, though never explicity theorized by Freud as such, is turned from the outset towards otherness and sociality. I say 'turned towards' in the sense not of a representational incorporation of difference (as the psyche functions here in a presymbolic mode), but rather as the minimal capacity for the registration of pre-self and pre-object experience in the productive imagination.

The significance of primary repression, and the politicization of identification

How far do the concepts of primary repression, rolling identification and representational wrapping lead us to rethink the constitution and/or positioning of the subject in terms of socio-symbolic signification? The insights of Freud, and of contemporary psychoanalysis more generally, should of course lead us to caution in this respect. Whatever the radicalizing possibilities of this more differentiated rendering of repression and identification that I've presented, identity requires meaning, and therefore symbolic law, which constitutes subjectivity in its socio-cultural dimensions. The transition from a fantasy world of representation to socio-symbolic signification refers the individual subject beyond itself. The break-up of the psychical monad, and crucially the socialization of the psyche, are the medium through which a relation to the Other is established, and therefore to broader cultural, historical and political chains of signification.

However, none of this means that human subjects can be reduced to mere 'supports' of symbolic law. Contrary to Lacanian and related deterministic theories, 'history' is not fixed once and for all, and offers no guarantees with regard to the organization of power. Thus the connection between law and desire, ideology and the affective, is not a fixed reality instituted by the symbolic. Freud's account of Oedipus, as Kristeva comments, 'was not, as he has been too easily accused of, to respect the paternal law of taboos that sketch our social interplay ... [but rather] to sort out the types of representations of which a subject is capable' (1987: 9–10). In this respect, representational forms, I have suggested, are shaped to their core in and through pre-Oedipal processes of repression and identification. As an elementary elaboration of pre-self experience and pre-object relations, primal repression permits the *representational splitting of the subject*, which is bound up with the pleasures and traumas of the intersubjective network itself. This elementary organization of psychical space will be repressed with entry to the socio-symbolic order, thus cementing the reproduction of 'social imaginary significations'. However, these elementary, representational wrappings of self and other are never entirely repressed. Pre-Oedipal representations, at the outer limit of our symbolism and discourse, cannot be shut off from identity and culture, and continually burst forth anew within any of our symbolic systems.

The argument I am developing here is closely linked to that of Kristeva, who sees us all as permanently swept along by semiotic forces, bearing at the very core of our identity something intrinsically resistant to symbolic articulation yet always-already derailing or overriding our interpersonal dialogue. Kristeva, who is very much taken with Freud's notion of a 'father in prehistory', is divided in her more recent work as to the possibilities for transforming the symbolic order through the semiotic on the one hand, and the necessity of identification with the imaginary father for the production of individual identity on the other. Some critics, such as Cornell (1991, 1993), interpret this as a turn from the semiotic to an idealised relation to the paternal function. Even if this is so, however, it is surely possible to step back from Kristeva's inflation of the paternal function and instead stress, as I try to do, more creative possibilities arising from the fluid, rolling and multiple identifications stemming from the imaginary constitution of sensory experience. From this angle, then, what is the socio-cultural significance of primary repression and rolling identification? What is at issue here is the interlacing of representational wrapping of pre-self and pre-object connections on the one hand and socially instituted representations on the other hand. If we understand that social significations are taken up and invested by subjects within the matrix of former pre-Oedipal modes of generating experience, we can see that there is a wealth of fantasies, identifications, contiguities and rhythmicities available to the subject as she or he creatively engages with cultural forms. Such early, pre-Oedipal modes of generating experience provide not only a support for identity, but also the identificatory basis from which to re-imagine our world. Representational wrappings of self and other – constituted in and through primal repression – infuse the power of the radical imagination and help to contest, question and destabilize our relation to the symbolic order.

Applied to the field of social difference and sexual identity, recognition of the imaginary valorisation of sensory experience becomes a vision of alternative meanings and desires positioned against closure in the name of socio-symbolic reproduction. Developing upon the work of Castoriadis, Kristeva, Laplanche and Ogden, I argue that the autistic-sensory forms the imaginary basis for the constitution of the subject. In the pursuit of radical imagination, there are meanings and values embedded in this domain of the pre-Oedipal which are of vital importance. Representational wrappings of pre-self and pre-object connections, as an ongoing unconscious process of identification, are resilient enough to always threaten or destabilise the hierarchical closure imposed on meaning and language in the socio-symbolic order. The dream of radical imagination is thus, in part, the dream of retracing the shared representational and affective modes of generating experience which link us ineluctably together.

The politics of difference require creativity, innovation, reflectiveness, in order to enact the different itself. In pursuit of the new, the different, beyond the constraint and domination of the current social order, there are values and affects embedded in the subject's relation to primal identification which are of vital importance. Primal identification, and the repression which consolidates it, open a preliminary distance between the self and others, and are thus a foundation for personal and collective autonomy. For this link to the other, prior to mirror asymmetry and the imprint of social significations, can offer a prefigurative image of a cultural condition in which relatedness, fulfilment and creativity are more fully realized. The role of unconscious representation in dreaming the new lies precisely in this connection to the other, primary intersubjectivity, a condition from which we might imagine self, society, politics and ethics anew.

References

Anzieu, D. (1989) *The Skin Ego*. New Haven, CT: Yale University Press.

Bourdieu, P. (1977) *Outline of a Theory of Practice*. Cambridge: Cambridge University Press.

Bourdieu, P. (1993) *The Field of Cultural Production*. Cambridge: Polity Press.

Castoriadis, C. (1987) *The Imaginary Institution of Society*. Cambridge: Polity.

Castoriadis, C. (1997) *World in Fragments*. Stanford, CA: Stanford University Press.

Chamberlain, D. (1987) 'The cognitive newborn: a scientific update', *British Journal of Psychotherapy*, 4: 30–71.

Cornell, D. (1991) *Beyond Accommodation*. New York: Routledge.

Cornell, D. (1993) *Transformations*. New York: Routledge.

Delrieu, A. (1977) *Sigmund Freud: Index Thématique*. Paris: Editions Anthropos.

Elliott, A. (1999) *Social Theory and Psychoanalysis in Transition: Self and Society from Freud to Kristeva*. London: Free Association.

Elliott, A. (2004) *Subject to Ourselves: Social Theory, Psychoanalysis and Postmodernity*. Boulder, CO: Paradigm.

Fletcher, J. and Stanton, M. (eds) (1992) *Jean Laplanche: Seduction, Translation and the Drives*. London: ICA.

Freud, S. (1911) 'Formulations on the two principles of mental functioning'. S.E.12.

Freud, S. (1915) 'Repression'. S.E.14.

Freud, S. (1921) 'Group psychology and the analysis of the ego'. S.E.18, pp. 69–143.

Freud, S. (1926) *Inhibitions, Symptoms and Anxiety*. S.E.20.

Freud, S. (1926) *Psycho-Analysis*. S.E.20

Giddens, A. (1984) *The Constitution of Society*. Cambridge: Polity.

Giddens, A. (1990) *The Consequences of Modernity*. Cambridge: Polity.

Green, A. (1985) 'Réflexions libres sur la représentation de l'affect', in *Propédeutique. La métapsychologie revistée*, Éditions Champvallon, 1995.

Kristeva, J. (1984) *Revolution in Poetic Language*. New York: Columbia University Press.

Kristeva, J. (1987) *Tales of Love*. New York: Columbia University Press.

Kristeva, J. (1988) *In the Beginning was Love*. New York: Columbia University Press.

Kristeva, J. (1989) *Black Sun: Depression and Melancholia*. New York: Columbia University Press.

Kristeva, J. (1991) *Strangers to Ourselves*. London: Harvester.

Kristeva, J. (1993) *New Maladies of the Soul*. New York: Columbia University Press.

Kristeva, J. (2000) *The Sense and Non-Sense of Revolt: The Powers and Limits of Psychoanalysis*. New York: Columbia University Press.

Kristeva, J. (2001) *Melanie Klein*. New York: Columbia University Press.

Laplanche, J. (1987) *New Foundations for Psychoanalysis*. Oxford: Blackwell.

Laplanche, J. and Pontalis, J.B. (1985) *The Language of Psychoanalysis*. London: Hogarth.

Ogden, T. (1989) *The Primitive Edge of Experience*. Northvale, New Jersey: Jason Aronson.

Stern, D. (1985) *The Interpersonal World of the Infant*. New York: Basic.

Tustin, E. (1980) 'Autistic objects', *International Review of Psycho-Analysis*, 7: 27–40.

Tustin, E. (1984) 'Autistic shapes', *International Review of Psycho-Analysis*, 11: 279–90.

Winnicott, D. (1971) *Playing and Reality*. New York: Basic.

8

Melancholic Identities: Post-traumatic Loss, Memory and Identity Formation[1]

Jeffrey Prager

Introduction: On trauma, loss, and afterwardness

This past century has been especially violent and destructive. World history knows no parallel both for the scale of horrors inflicted and for the awareness by humans of their own potential for destruction. Contemporary thinkers have struggled to capture the depth and enormity of this reality, especially the effect on human beings of the knowledge of their own capacity to destroy. In describing a century-long production of violent assaults on human populations (e.g., world wars, genocides, massive dislocations and nuclear threat and destruction), writers underscore the pervasiveness of a 'sense of trauma' (Agamben, 1999; LaCapra, 2001; Levinas, 2001). Focusing on the experience of those living through these events, both their being overwhelmed by its enormity and incapable of fully absorbing its impact, many suggest that human experience itself has been transformed by the unique scale of events and the potential for danger to which people are aware and to which they have been subjected.

Trauma – a psychologically-inflected term implying an order of experience to which individuals are incapable of fully assimilating – has entered the lexicon to explain the damage to humankind caught up in the vortex of its capacity to destroy. This pervasive sense of trauma describes the distinctiveness of this past century and the perhaps irreparable toll it has taken on the individuals living under its shadow. It is invoked to capture events so monumental as to be beyond the capacity of individuals either to fully absorb, comprehend or control. This language, originating with Freud, now dominates the contemporary imagination, extending beyond an individual's narrative of traumatic personal experience to now include an account of socio-political events of great magnitude that have swept up whole populations and that continue to exert influence.

Trauma, too, has come to orient many contemporary nations' efforts to reconcile today's population to their brutal pasts. It not only acknowledges the range of atrocities that have been inflicted on human beings over the past century, but also their characterization as traumatic reflects keener attention to the short- and long-term suffering incurred by its victims. Traumatic histories of nations have generated interest in a new set of social questions, no less relevant to collectivities as to individual persons: whether it is either possible or desirable for survivors of trauma to forget the various horrors they have lived through, of trauma's legacy over time, of social memory, and of the quest for reconciliation and the possibility of forgiveness.

Now, early on in this new century, understanding *the causes* of war, genocide, plague and terror – scholarship that brackets out from consideration its impact on those individuals who find themselves at the centre of trauma's path – is being overshadowed by an interest in how people within nations, both victims and perpetrators alike, comprise themselves in the aftermath of death and destruction. What has emerged, case by case, is greater attention on how best to reconstitute community in the face of these overwhelming experiences, how to engineer reconciliation. The intellectual landscape concerned with political and social conflict, now charged with these sets of moral quandaries, is dominated by both empirical studies and philosophical and theoretical examinations detailing the ways in which various agencies representing their collectivities attempt to respond to their pasts and to deal with their particular history of violence and trauma (see, for example, Barkan, 2000; Cohen, 2001; Minow, 1998; Thompson, 2002; Torpey, 2006).

The aftermath of the Holocaust probably continues as the paradigmatic case to explore these outer edges of political, social and moral dilemmas defining both the limits of the representation of evil and the enduring traumatic legacy both for survivors and their descendants. Yet there is no dearth of examples through which the problem of traumatic pasts has come to preoccupy scholars: the AIDS epidemic and the question of mourning; the ethnic and religious wars in Eastern and Central Europe and the emergence of international tribunals of human rights; post-apartheid South Africa and the implementation of The Truth and Reconciliation Commission and debates over reparations; the killing fields of Cambodia, Peru, Columbia and civil wars in Central America and efforts there at social repair; dictatorships in the Southern Cone of Latin America and various policies of official forgetting, memorializing, and publicly remembering the disappeared, imprisoned and exiled.

Before this recent turn to issues of trauma and its aftermath, identity, whose interest emerged from the politics of the 1960s, had been thought of almost exclusively along a horizontal axis, where social actors, often willfully and willingly, define themselves or are defined by others in relation to others co-existing in time and space. Individuals have tended to group themselves, to identify, topographically as belonging to one group, existing in relation to others. In the United States, Italian-Americans co-exist with, say, Irish-Americans and African-Americans, each standing in relation to White Anglo-Saxon Protestants (those who lay claim to no specific ethnic identity), or Catholics distinguish themselves from Protestants and Jews and together comprise the vast majority of American citizens. Similarly, those who identify themselves as gay understand themselves as living together in a world of others who define their sexual orientation as straight, together more-or-less making up the sexual population of the nation. Identities such as 'Asian American' or 'West Indian', or 'Hispanic' reveal clearly this contingent character of identity – where the temporal plane of a nation divides populations into socially-constructed categories that come to be adopted by those so designated. To be an Asian or a West Indian in the USA or in the United Kingdom may reflect the social organization of ethnicity in these countries – a mapping across a plane of artifactual ethnicities more than it captures common affective links between, say, Japanese, Koreans, and Chinese, for example, or Bermudans, Guyanese, and Trinidadians. 'Asianness' or 'West Indianness' of course are realities only in a political-cultural environment where finer distinctions between groups are of no consequence. Nonetheless, these designations over time have produced those who identify themselves (especially by second and third generation immigrants) vis-à-vis others as Asian Americans, and both in the USA and in the UK as West Indians.

Up to this point, interest in identity has focused largely on describing the intense affective attachments created between self and others, where common ties of kin, blood, political and sexual orientations, religious beliefs and other categories implying 'likenesses' are imagined or constructed to crystallize, to demarcate, and to oppose other groups. In the USA, especially, but elsewhere as well, identity has become a basis and rationale for collective action – what Brubaker and Cooper (2002: 4) have called 'categories of practice', 'used by "lay" actors in some ... everyday settings to make sense of themselves, of their activities, of what they share with, and how they differ from others'. Identities and memories, as J.R. Gillis (1994: 5) notes, are not things we think *about*, but things we think *with*. Movements toward 'ethnic cleansing', whether in Serbia, in Rwanda, or in India express at their extreme their disastrous potential to mobilize action, oftentimes of a brutal kind.

'Identity politics', in sum, has served as a cognitive map for actors to orient themselves toward others and for commentators to explore conflict at home and across the globe (see Calhoun, 1994). It is what Axel Honneth (1996) characterizes as 'the struggle for recognition', providing, again both to actors and scholars, a new grammar to explain the intersection of social identity and social conflict. Charles Taylor in *The Sources of the Self, The*

Making of Modern Identity (1997)underscores identity's synchronicity – the in-the-present division of the world by identity groups – when he defines identity as 'the self in moral space' in which individuals more or less con- sciously situate themselves in the present, thereby to orient themselves to an ideal future. Taylor demonstrates the significance of modern identity for persons orienting their actions vis-à-vis other 'identity groups' co-existing with one another, each defining social action with respect to a particular moral vision of a world-in-the making.

Our contemporary preoccupation with what I refer to as the condition of 'afterwardness', or the challenges posed to reconstitution in the face of both personal and social tragedy, also implicates considerations of selfhood and identity. But it has done so in a decidedly different fashion. In addition to identifying trauma as an experience whose consequences persist through time, Freud (1954d: 356) alerts us to the imprecise and constructed charac- ter of its remembering, the impossibility of the 'pure' retrieval of experience. He employs the term *nachtraglichkeit*, sometimes translated as 'deferred action', to describe how traumatic experience comes to be remembered later, after the fact, and, as a result, is necessarily subject to the distortions that inhere both from memory and desire: the imprecision of our capacity to recollect and our own psychological investments in what about the past we want to believe (see also Green, 2002; Thoma and Cheshire, 1991). 'Afterwardness' has posed for social actors and commentators alike different questions of identity, ones that are now decidedly more historical and psy- chological. There is now far greater interest in identity's diachronic relation to its past, less to its contingent in-the-present character, (i.e., the social con- struction of identity), and more to the ways in which past experiences appear to 'hard-wire' or determine categories of identity. The genealogy of identity – the process by which individuals vertically place or imagine themselves into ongoing social categories of experience and construct their own understanding of themselves in relation to these categories – has taken the topic in some ways full circle back to its origins, to the work of Erik Erikson (1985 [1950]) who first named identity as a stage in an individual's psycho-cultural development and, ultimately, back to Freud himself who, while never referring directly to identity, at times was keenly aware of the mechanisms of identification.

Freud explicitly links identification – and ultimately identity – to the experience of loss. A child's early experience of fusion between self and other necessarily gives way both to individual differentiation or separation and an emotionally persistent yearning for a return to a sense of oneness with others: the life-long dialectical search for a balance between autonomy, differentiation and independence, on the one side, in the midst of impulses for connection, fusion, and dependence with others, on the other. What Freud describes is a process, one which largely operates below the surface of awareness, in which, to ward off feelings of abject loss and abandonment, individuals internalize these lost others – in the first instance, our parents from whom emotional separation becomes required – into a sense of who we are as individuals. In this regard, gender identity, sexual identity, and ethnic identity, for example, derive from similar interpersonal processes of loss and differentiation, though gender and sexual identity develop earlier in personality development and operate deeper beneath the conscious surface than other forms of self-representations such as religious, regional, and racial identity. Individuals take for themselves aspects of those they feel most attached to and from whom it is necessary to separate. Identity therefore constitutes a largely unconscious mechanism of recording and retaining in-the-present, after-the-fact aspects of those who are loved but, from the perspective of once having been enveloped by them, who no longer survive in the same way. This process of internalization/identification allows for the loosening of an eroticized attachment to these people and enables us to direct that emotional focus outward and toward others. Internalization and identification occur, of course, only over time as the individual registers and processes the experience of loss. Afterwardness, framed by both memory and desire, describes the basis upon which self-formation and character development, contending with the crisis of an all-encompassing world giving way to the painfulness and difficulties of individuation, occur.

Identity and internalization thus require an understanding of the processes by which individuals psychologically respond over time to loss: how is identity related to past experience and in what ways are individuals capable of altering identity? Are some identities malleable? Or does the history of loss become the source for timeless identifications in the present? Can history be freed of its obligation to provide the basis for living presently? Moreover, because of the prevalence of traumatic loss – experiences in which the world as it had been known is violently extruded from the self – are some losses incapable of being overcome, where a sense of trauma defines a person's relationship to his or her past, where mourning loss can never overcome a melancholic holding on to it? This 'backward-looking' interest in identity formation has generated new interest in a distinctive form of identity, a melancholic one, and it has placed Freud's *Mourning and Melancholia* (1954c [1917]) and his *The Ego and the Id* (1954a [1923]) centre stage in theorizing the relation between losses experienced (ones that might include terror and trauma) and identity-formation. In *Mourning and Melancholia*, Freud writes 'mourning is regularly the reaction to the loss of a loved person, or to the loss of some abstraction which has taken the place of one, such as one's country, liberty, an ideal, and so on' (1954c [1917]: 243). Now in today's political cultural milieu preoccupied with the sense of trauma and social repair, the concept of loss and its role in identity-formation, especially as it refers to the loss of 'country, liberty, an ideal' serves as a companion concept to that of trauma and its aftermath: remembering losses melancholically, those incurred in the past through traumatic violations of the self, becomes the foundation for identity-formation in the present.

Melancholia has emerged as a key category not only in the analysis of individuals but also of whole communities and nations as well. Yet as I will argue, there is danger in conflating melancholic community – a social category describing a collectivity defined in some sense by its history of traumatic losses – with an individual suffering melancholia – a clinical description of an individual who suffers a form of psychological distress as Freud defines it. As melancholia has increasingly been invoked to describe members of groups who live with a memory of their traumatic origins, there has been a concomitant tendency to treat as acceptable (even desirable) personal identities forever bound to their communal pasts. Too often personal identity reduces exclusively to the nature of the community that spawns it and, as a result, treats both the self and the question of identity as an extension of the current narrative of the social conditions that generated the collectivity. Identity is both thoroughly historicized and narrativized, even politicized: the individual tends not to be treated as more than the social conditions under which he or she was produced. In spite of a heavy reliance upon Freud's melancholia, there is ironically a propensity to overlook the psychological life of individuals, influenced by the world but not identical to it and, moreover, to overlook the debilitating effects that, as Freud explained it, melancholia holds for an individual's capacity to engage life.

Melancholy has both been invoked to introduce subjective states into social analysis, 'the sense of trauma', and defended, *contra* Freud, as an embodied form of remembering. As David Lloyd (2003, 217) writes in *The Memory of Hunger*, a study of the memory of the Irish Famine among contemporary Irish, the modern postcolonial subject ought to develop a 'nontherapeutic relation to the past, structured around the notion of survival or living on rather than recovery'. For Lloyd, a nontherapeutic relation to the past means that an overcoming of the past – its erasure or supercession – ought not be the aim of present day living. Instead, 'damage itself becomes the locus of survival, the pained trajectory of what lives on' (2003: 216). Melancholia is synonymous with remembering, and traumatic loss rightly becomes a more-or-less conscious feature of contemporary identity.

This new interest in melancholia, and the claim that it is constitutively linked to identity in this age of trauma and ought to be in some fashion preserved, differs dramatically from its more conventional usage in social analysis, one forged most famously by the German psychoanalysts Alexander and Margarete Mitscherlich in *The Inability to Mourn* (1975). In this influential book, published originally in German in 1967, the Mitscherlichs sought to understand the enduring impact of the Second World War on the post-war

German population. Based largely on a reading of Freud's *Mourning and Melancholia*, they argued that Germany, struggling with a deep sense of collective responsibility, guilt and shame, sought to break all 'affective bridges to the immediate past' (1975: 26). Thus, the powerful love and hope that most Germans had invested for a time in their Nazi leaders and the 'fantasies of omnipotence' (1975: 23) that were mobilized in support of the war effort were powerfully dashed. The loss and disappointment marked by Germany's defeat had gone largely unacknowledged and, therefore, unmourned. Forgetting the past, the Mitscherlichs argued, was a defensive strategy by the German people to prevent a melancholic holding-on to their shameful past but which served, as well, to make impossible mourning the losses experienced at the hands of the Allied powers. Melancholia, characterized by a profound devaluation of oneself, was averted by this refusal to mourn. But – and this was the central thrust of the Mitscherlichs' analysis – the result was a 'psychic immobilism' (1975: 27) in which Germans felt incapable of confronting the many serious social and political problems that were then confronting them. Both melancholia and mourning were consciously staved off, but only by those members of German society who were denying historical continuity with their past. Defensive denial, on the other hand, sapped the German population's capacity to invest necessary energy to solve the problems of post-war German society.[2]

In *Postcolonial Melancholia* (2005), Paul Gilroy builds upon this tradition of social analysis pioneered by the Mitscherlichs. Employing Freud's concepts of mourning and melancholia, he describes how members of contemporary Western societies have succeeded in repressing the brutalities of colonial rule that were 'enacted in their name and to their benefit'. The result has been the creation of a pathological political culture dominated by fear of the immigrant, anxiety over multiculturalism, and a yearning for a romanticized past when the nation putatively was culturally 'pure'. As the real past of colonial violence has been denied and the end of empire insured, in its place has been produced a 'postimperial melancholia'. Melancholia for Gilroy describes contemporary Western political cultures, results from a process of denial of brutality and a severing of the present from the past, and, similar to the argument in *The Inability to Mourn*, undercuts the capacity of a current generation from engaging the world fully – what Gilroy describes with respect to racial and ethnic diversity as multicultural conviviality – and with enthusiasm. It hypostatizes identities based upon race and immigration, preserving in place categories of affiliation based upon past histories of those who occupied the centre, and those from the periphery.

Both in the analysis of the Mitscherlichs' and of Gilroy's, following Freud's seminal essay, melancholia is a pathological condition, one from which recovery is possible, albeit difficult. Remembering, and acknowledging one's own relation to the past – recognizing the psychologically-fraught experience of loss – promises the possibility of no longer being wholly constrained by it. Melancholia may be avoided, self-devaluation prevented, and creativity and enthusiasm engaged with the overcoming of defensive denial and the capacity developed to acknowledge and to accept responsibility, in these cases, for the crimes of the past. Contemporary identities need not be forever determined by past social affiliations: loosening the hold of melancholic attachments to the past describes the political projects for both the Mitscherlichs' and for Paul Gilroy. Only by recovering the past and knowing one's personal relationship to it, they imply, will this generate the possibility for a less unencumbered future. Both in the case of post-war Germany and in postcolonial Western societies, the authors offer a cultural and political critique, insisting that melancholia is a psychological condition that might be avoided. Each of their social analyses is intended to describe the societal mechanisms necessary to achieve personal and cultural healthiness. The Mitscherlichs and Gilroy each argue that for members of a society to know and remember loss and to overcome a defensive denial of the painful experiences that encourage not knowing (i.e., to make the unconscious conscious) are keys to melancholy's prevention. They hold out the possibility that despite the traumas of the past the present need not remain forever its victim.[3]

In contrast, there has recently emerged a new assessment of melancholy and the possibility, even the advisability, of it being avoided as a permanent condition of individuals in the contemporary world. In the Afterword to a recent collection of essays entitled *Loss: The Politics of Mourning*, that included David Lloyd's essay discussed above, Judith Butler (2003: 468) writes 'loss becomes condition and necessity for a certain sense of community, where community does not overcome the loss, where community *cannot* overcome the loss without losing the very sense of itself as community'. Butler's claim here adumbrates the larger project of the collection of articles of which her contribution is a part; namely, an assertion of both the reality of a 'melancholic identity' and a valorization of 'melancholic history'. The editors of *Loss* (Eng and Kazanjian, 2003: ix) reacting against conventional Freudian and neo-Freudian readings, write 'instead of imputing to loss a purely negative quality, the essays in this collection apprehend it as productive rather than pathological, abundant rather than lacking, social rather than solipsistic, militant rather than reactionary ... the pervasive losses of the twentieth century are laden with creative, political potential'. In 'A dialogue on racial melancholia', David Eng and Shinhee Han (2003: 353) recast Freud's insistence on the debilitating effects of melancholy and seek to 'depathologize' its understanding. Rather than portraying it as a damaging psychic feature, they suggest that it expresses rather a productive conflict within the individual. In the case of Asian Americans, the subject of their essay, melancholia describes the healthy tension between efforts toward assimilation and the preservation of racialized difference within the American body politic. This new valorization of melancholia as a form of preserving lovingly a connection to one's traumatic past generates a different understanding of Freud's essay *Mourning and Melancholia* (1954c [1917]). No longer interpreting Freud as offering an analysis of two discrete psychic processes – mourning and melancholia – Eng and Han suggest instead that the two exist on a continuum, and a healthy postcolonial identity consists in the capacity to live with the tension between the two. 'The material and psychic negotiations of these various issues', they write, 'are conflicts with which Asian Americans struggle on an everyday basis. This struggle does not necessarily result in damage but is finally a productive and a necessary process' (2003: 364). Eng and Han situate their argument (2003: 366) within a larger political project of 'living melancholia', and, invoking the writings of the gay activist Douglas Crimp who, in the face of the AIDS epidemic, writes of 'mourning *and* militancy', conclude their essay with a call for 'mourning *and* melancholia'. Not only do they misread Crimp, an argument that I will develop shortly, but in so doing they distort Freud and underestimate melancholia's capacity to paralyze.

The essays in *Loss* and the more general renewed interest in melancholia as a component of contemporary identity are aimed largely to preserve memory and to insure that traumatic losses in the past are not forgotten. As politics, melancholia is invoked to prevent erasure and supercession, to preserve memory and accountability. Yet in their effort to normalize melancholia, there is a danger of misreading Freud and even to distort contemporary writers who struggle, like Freud, to preserve the difference between the repression of traumatic pasts, on the one hand, that results in it repetitively being recreated in the present and, on the other, mourning the past in service to it being overcome (see also Freud, 1954d [1895]). These authors' celebration of melancholia in which the contemporary subject is forever in the shadow of the lost object and their disinclination to demarcate melancholia from healthy mourning deprive us of one of Freud's most important insights: traumatic loss has the ability to promote in individuals an 'incapacity for living'. Melancholia insures that the present is lived *as if* it were the past, when the present is experienced as less vivid and meaningful than an earlier time, and when the individual is dominated by an 'internal psychical reality' that takes precedence over the reality of the external world (Freud, 1954b [1939]: 76) As Todorov (2001) has argued, mourning is a way of disabling memory, while melancholia disables individuals from living currently. Even in the face of traumatic losses, mourning is (perhaps) nonetheless possible and the past need not be indelibly destined among its survivors to reach the precipice of paralysis.

The significance of these issues, of course, powerfully redounds on efforts at social repair in various settings around the world. By detailing the conditions necessary for mourning to successfully occur and for the circumvention of melancholia, it is possible to consider ways to weaken existing identities too powerfully tied to past loss, too insistent on experiencing the present time-lessly, *as if* it were the past (Prager, 2006b; Prager, 2008).

Identity and loss

In a poignant and courageous essay written in 1989, during a particularly bleak moment of the AIDS epidemic in the United States, gay activist Douglas Crimp published *Mourning and Militancy* (2002). It is an essay about the grief suffered by a whole community of gay men due to the extensive losses suffered to AIDS death and – especially in a society unsym-pathetic to homosexuality – about the difficulties of moving beyond deep sorrow. While Crimp concludes by advocating the need for those who have experienced these losses to both mourn those deaths *and* to be politically militant, the essay in fact is a powerful argument *against* the conflation of mourning and militancy. Ours is a culture that because of its homophobia interrupts the process of mourning, Crimp insists, and the result has been a political militancy inspired by a defensive reaction against this unnatural suppression of personal grief. There are ample grounds for gay activists to be militant in an American society that, certainly in 1989, failed to acknowl-edge gay subjectivity and therefore largely overlooked the devastating losses suffered, Crimp argues. But, nonetheless, the basis for a militant politics needs to be established not defensively but rather freely and unencumbered, independent of a tendency to deny personal grief through politics.

The title of his essay, *Mourning and Militancy*, acknowledges Crimp's debt to Freud's *Mourning and Melancholia*, and it is largely on the basis of Freud's discussion that Crimp developed his arguments. Freud (1954c [1917]: 244) describes grieving as a process in which the loss of a loved object results in 'turning away from any activity that is not connected with thoughts of him', and that only slowly releases the hold that the lost-object has over the survivor. 'It is easy to see', Freud continues, 'that this inhibition and cir-cumscription in the ego is the expression of an exclusive devotion to its mourning, which leaves nothing over for other purposes or other interests'. But as Crimp notes, Freud (1954c [1917]: 243–4) recognizes the debilitat-ing and harmful psychological consequences when mourning the loss of someone is interfered with. When this occurs – as in the case of the preva-lent societal interdiction against homosexuality – pathological mourning may well result. Freud describes this as an inability of the griever to both gradually recognize and acknowledge loss and simultaneously over-time to accept natural and inevitable ambivalent feelings toward the lost object. In the face of this harmful interference with the mourning process, where death by AIDS in a homophobic culture provides no place or space for grieving, gay militancy emerges as a symptom of pathological mourning. Here Crimp reads into the mourning process the formative role of discursive forms and practices (homophobia) that configures the social field and profoundly impacts subjectivity: militancy, in defiance against a rejecting external world, becomes a conscious defense against grief and deference to homophobes. It is a form of acting-out.

Yet Crimp, again following Freud, acknowledges that mourning is also a psychic process, subject to unconscious forces within the griever existing independently of societal interdiction. Militancy may well also serve as a conscious defense against unconscious ambivalences to the death of a loved one, an outcome of one's own antagonism to mourning. 'We must recognize', Crimp writes, 'that our memories and our resolve also entail the more painful feelings of survivor's guilt, often exacerbated by our secret wishes, during our lovers' and friends' protracted illnesses, that they would just die and let us get on with our lives' (2002: 138–9). Like all defense mechanisms, militancy here constitutes an ego function designed to ward off the surfacing of an unconscious ambivalence to the death of others. These ambivalent feelings toward lost objects oftentimes overlay societal prohibitions with purely psychic ones: in identifying the role that defense plays in the mourning process, Crimp offers a more nuanced appreciation of individual psychology independently contributing to pathological mourning.

Crimp's aim, it is clear, is not to condemn militancy but rather, by uncoupling it from defensive reactions to loss, to allow for its full-blown and authentic flourishing. The authentic militant doesn't forget the past, but by engaging politically he or she remembers losses suffered in the name of a better present. Militancy – or, should we say, a gay militant – needs to emerge, to paraphrase Freud, both from the shadow of his dead objects (real loss) and from the guilt of the ambivalences felt at having survived and now permitted to live. 'When the work of mourning is completed', Freud writes, 'the ego becomes free and uninhibited again' (1954c [1917]: 245). Or, as Crimp might say, militancy – an unencumbered one – becomes a possibility when it is not simply in the service of warding off and denying painful affect.

In thinking anew about the question of identity, the significances of Crimp's essay are many. First, and in contrast to many contemporary writers, Crimp resists a tendency to read Freud only as a treatise on the power of the psyche, and the self that emerges only a result of the struggle that occurs between impulse and defense. In the more conventional reading of Freud, external reality exists only as a background to the powerful psychic forces at play in each individual, and identity is viewed largely as an *intrapsychic* achievement. Identity is a product of the internalization of the lost object, a force that unconsciously comes to stand like a garrison army guarding to forever preserve the memory of the loved one. In a homophobic culture unwilling to cooperate in a mourning process for those who died from AIDS, Crimp reminds us that the potential among the mourners for a free and uninhibited ego to emerge is compromised by an external world intent on colluding in forms of defensive denial. Crimp documents how *Mourning and Melancholia* possesses within it a framework to understand the complex relationship between the social world and the psychic one, without reducing one to the other. His analysis demonstrates an important, and underappreciated, feature of identity, applicable to the phenomenon more broadly: identity is *inter-psychic*, resulting from the confrontation between a dynamically structured individual and a social world replete with expectations and pre-figured formulations about the self. The mourning process requires both a mourner who can tolerate the painfulness of grief and an external world that aids and abets in that process. Melancholia expresses a failure to successfully navigate the sometimes-treacherous waters when mourning itself is insufficiently tolerated by social conventions.

Second, by considering the particular potency of the culture of homophobia to disrupt the mourning experience of individuals, Crimp describes the particular ways in which the individual psychically mediates external reality. It is both the premature ending of the grieving process because of its social prohibition, a manic denial of ambivalence, and the acting out of grief through militancy that, for Crimp, result in forms both of inauthentic militancy and pathological mourning. Retaining the distinction insisted upon by Freud between psychic and external reality, Crimp insists that gay identity, as it manifests itself at one point in time or another, is not a product exclusively of a particular discursive or linguistic formation, a form of subjection, to which the individual subordinates him or herself. Identity, in contrast, is an inter-psychic process in which radical subjectivity – impulse, imagination and desire, framed within the ambivalent experiences of love and hate toward its objects – confronts linguistic category and social construction (see Prager, 1998). Sexual identity, in other words, forms simultaneously from the outside in and from the inside out: it is both deeply personal and deeply social. For that reason, identities are not constitutive of the person as much as they are historical in their formation (LaCapra, 1999: 713). Jewish identity changes in relation to the changing character of anti-Semitism, just as racial identity reflects the particular character of racism in a specific historical context. Identities, while originating in relation to personal loss, are nonetheless the products of an intersubjective relation between self and 'society' *at a given time*. At the same time, those who understand language and discursive power as forming the subject – as is often the case in an understanding of homosexual identity as subjected to and thereby shaped by the categories of the external world – homophobia – risk overlooking ways in which self-expression, as the sociologist Jack Katz (1999: 142; see also Prager, 2006a) describes it, are also 'refracted elaborately within' which sometimes requires a person to observe surprisingly his or her own actions, where unconscious impulse, imagination and desire yield behaviours that exceed both social category and cognitive self-understanding. These two domains of irreducible experience (inner and outer, psychic and social) require their own independent understanding. Indeed, a central psychoanalytic tenet is that psychic reality makes its own distinctive contribution to social life, no less transformative of the social world than transformed by it. While ethnic, racial or religious identity is never as deeply inscribed in either the social or personal life as either gender or sexual identity, it is nonetheless true that a psychic and cultural dimension, neither reducible to the other, each plays its independent role in all of identity's formation.

Finally, as an ethical stance, Crimp posits the possibility for social action – engagement in the world – to be free from defensive denial. He holds out the hope, however difficult to achieve, that social critique and an acknowledgement of the psychic impediments to its realization can result in the production of unencumbered selves, informed, even constituted, by past experiences but not dominated by them. This position aligns itself with efforts in various social settings across the globe that attempt both to realize a psychic break with the past, not by forgetting but through remembering, and to loosen the hold of an identity formed by traumatic loss for the present. Here, social repair takes various forms of tribunals, testimonies, commissions, proceedings, legislation and hearings, with each offering specific forms of ritual and performance to demarcate past loss from present actions. Identity, rather than viewed as a kind of eternal reminder of past trauma carried forth into the present, is understood rather as part of a more fluid or mobile self-understanding, in which a sense of self might be finally detached from the dead object (either as victim or as perpetrator) allowing for the possibility of a future not foreclosed by past tragedies.

These then are the contours of a theory of loss and its relation to identity; one, in contrast to those offered by those who endorse the proposition that loss is neither possible nor desirable to overcome, that asserts instead that individuals need not remain melancholically attached to their past. It is a tripartite model in which for the normal mourning process to occur (1) a social world is required tolerant of grief and (2) a griever is capable of experiencing a whole complex of intense ambivalent feelings surrounding the loss of a loved object. When these conditions exist, (3) the lost object can become internalized through identification, setting itself up inside the psyche, but now substantially released from libidinal attachments. Sometimes extraordinary measures to achieve these ends must be undertaken, as in the case of Truth and Reconciliation commissions or other institutions established and framed around a politics of forgiveness and apology, lest the past recur in endless cycles of traumatic repetition.

Mourning or melancholia: loss and healthy ambivalence

Loss, mourning and melancholia were problems that preoccupied Freud largely during the middle part of his career. He consistently sought to understand the common role that losses played in normal mourning (also in pathological mourning) and in melancholia, though the two otherwise were distinctively different from one another. Freud significantly amends his theory between 1917, when *Mourning and Melancholia* was published, written prior to the onset of the wartime experiences of deep loss, and 1923 when *The Ego and the Id* was published, following the experiences of death and destruction of the First World War and subsequent to profound losses he personally suffered. In the 1923 essay, where Freud introduces his structural theory of the mind – a theory of the id, ego, and superego – he also significantly alters his theory of mourning. He offers now a more sober assessment of the capacity to definitively overcome loss and grief.

In *Mourning and Melancholia*, Freud describes normal mourning as a process in which, over time, a detachment of libidinal, or eroticized, energy from the lost object occurs and the narcissistic love, or identification, that had been the fuel of attachment is restored back to the mourner him or herself. Eros now has the opportunity to attach itself to new objects, and mourning ostensibly has come to an end. The melancholic, in contrast, is unable to complete mourning; rather, the lost object does not become psychically detached. Instead, it is incorporated within the self and the ambivalent feeling directed to the lost objects expresses itself as an agent of criticism and judgment (what Freud would later call the super-ego) that mobilizes, in the name of the idealized dead object, a sustained internal attack against the self. Melancholics suffer, Freud argues, from a 'lowering of self-regarding feelings to a degree that finds utterances in self-reproaches and self-revilings, and culminates in a delusional expectation of punishment' (1954c [1917]: 244). Different than for the mourner, the passage of time for the melancholic does not relieve the intense suffering that comes from the trauma of a world disrupted. 'In mourning, it is the world which has become poor and empty', Freud writes, 'in melancholia it is the ego itself' (1954c: 246). Here, Freud suggests that the melancholic has little capacity to have ambivalent feelings 'come into the open', a process that would otherwise aid in the detachment process. Instead, the idealized dead object becomes internalized, and directed inward, forever clouding the freedom of the individual.

In *The Ego and the Id*, Freud reconsiders the problem of identification and loss. He no longer asserts that normal mourners libidinally detach themselves fully from lost objects. He now proposes that common to all is an internalization through identification of those who were lost. Mourning never truly ends. The distinction collapses between mourner and melancholic. He defines the super-ego as 'a special agency of the ego' comprised of 'identifications which take the place of the abandoned cathexes by the id'. The loss of a sexual object, Freud writes, results in the 'setting up of the object inside the ego, *as it occurs in melancholia*', (1954a [1923]: 29, emphasis author's own).

Freud's recognition that the loss of a dead object universally results in its internalization, and is the basis of super-ego formation, becomes the basis for Judith Butler (1997: 134) to assert that all loss is melancholic. Butler suggests that a rigid heterosexual identity, in fact, results from an 'ungrieved and ungrievable loss' (1997: 136) of the same-sex parent and the formation of the gendered character of the ego. Her point is that especially because it goes ungrieved the parent of the same-sex becomes installed as homophobic prohibition, or as melancholic identification. The collusion between 'gendered anxiety' internally – of not being sufficiently feminine, if a woman, in desiring women or not sufficiently masculine, if a man, in desiring men – and a cultural logic of hetero-normative sexuality imposed externally produces a particular psychosexual matrix. For Butler, this matrix requires both men and women melancholically to perform a gendered and heterosexual identity.

For Butler, as for Crimp, identity is forged inter-psychically, the result of an often unconscious, sometimes conscious, struggle between love and hate, dependence and autonomy. The performance of identity describes the ever-present effort to reconcile inner experience (here, sexual desire) and external expectation (socially approved vehicles for desires' expression). But Butler, borrowing from Freud's later formulation of loss as forever present, makes two claims that distinguish her analysis from Crimp's: (1) that melancholia is constitutive in the formation of the subject, since the super-ego is comprised of the residues of the objects of loss, now expressed in the form of ever-present prohibition, and (2) in the face of 'the social regulation of psychic life' constituted intra-psychically (Butler 1997: 167), the capacity for individuals to work-through loss, to defend against powerful life-denying prohibitions and to be able to resist cultural subjection is radically diminished. The human condition is understood as one in which individuals are incapable of simultaneously loving (idealizing or embracing) forms of subjection while also hating (or resisting) prohibitions. In insisting on the constitutive character of melancholia, Butler (and those who have followed her lead either in acknowledging melancholy's omnipresence and/or in valorizing it as a form of identity) conflates a description of the historical subject without acknowledging the capacity for change over time – and the constitutive one where sexuality is a product of the ungrievable loss of the same sex parent (see LaCapra, 1999: 719). The conflation of the historical subject, as Crimp powerfully describes in the AIDS survivor of the late

1980s and 90s, to the constitutive subject, ipso facto bound to loss as decisive to a contemporary identity (for example, the homophobe), freezes history and hypostatizes given identities, as if they are forever unchanging and products of all-powerful mechanisms of subjection.

Butler's analysis and the contemporary endorsement of melancholic identity not only differ from Crimp's framework of understanding identity and its potential, they also resist a still important insight of Freud's. In spite of the shifts in his thought, Freud nonetheless resisted a characterization of melancholia as normative. He continued to treat mourning, even in *The Ego and the Id*, as a normal occurrence and as distinct from the pathological condition of melancholia. Confronted with a whole class of people – a clinical population – plagued with self-hatred and self-doubt, subjected to standards of behaviour to which they could not satisfy and largely incapacitated from acting assertively and decisively, Freud persisted in his effort (despite complications, emendations, reservations in his own thinking) to discover a unique etiology to the condition of melancholia. Toward that end, Freud invoked the decisive role of ambivalence to account for the difference between normal mourning and melancholic loss. The normal mourner, Freud concluded, has the capacity to mobilize ambivalent feelings toward lost objects, what he describes here as positive and negative oedipal positions, in self-defense against their idealized internalizations. In contrast to a melancholic's repudiation of the lost object now installed as a severe and demanding super-ego, the mourner learns to tolerate the ambiguity of his relation to the internalized object. Stated differently, the ego possesses within it an ability to resist unconscious guilt (or, the presence of this capacity of the ego to stand tall against the superego becomes a standard of mental health), to be able to hold conflicting stances toward the internalized object and the abandoned love-relation. The capacity to access hateful as well as loving feelings toward the same object (even as it remains as an idealized internal presence) speaks to the power of a psychic reality, bound by its own logic, language and rules. Resistance by the ego set against the superego ultimately distinguishes, for Freud, these two categories of experience. As Tammy Clewell has argued, 'in recognizing there can be no final severance of attachments without dissolving the ego, Freud's late theory suggests a different alternative: the mourning subject may affirm the endurance of ambivalent bonds to those loved and lost others as a condition of its own existence' (2004: 65). Mourning, rather than diminishing or weakening the individual, enables self-strengthening.

Ambivalence towards the past plays a decisive role in the mourning process: it is what enables the emergence, for example, of a healthy militancy where a politics of anti-homophobia – both culturally and psychically – becomes authentically possible, distinct from a manic defense against grief. It is what makes possible a politics of transitional justice, where new social institutions of reconciliation can be forged, motivated not by reaction and revenge but by the aspiration for a new set of identities no longer steeped in past categories of polarization and division. To acknowledge the difficulties that histories of past loss present for the contemporary individual to move beyond the shadow of the lost object should not, as those who valorize melancholic attachments are wont to do, be confused with the gains that come from an earnest effort to try.

Notes

1   An earlier version of this chapter was presented at the *Identity in Question* conference, St Hugh's College, Oxford, in May, 2005. Thanks especially to Anthony Elliott, Paul du Gay and Jessica Evans and to all the participants at the conference for their comments on an earlier draft; also, to members of the Intersubjectivity Study Group of the New Center for Psychoanalysis, Los Angeles, to members of the University of California Inter-disciplinary Psychoanalytic Consortium, to Alexander Stein and to Douglas Hollan.
2   Germany continues to be deeply engaged with the question of the significance of suppressed histories on contemporary national life and politics. See, especially, Sebald (2003a, 2003b) and Grass (2003). The Nobel Laureate novelist Gunter Grass's recent revelations of his own suppressed history during World War II–his own membership in the elite Nazi Waffen-SS and the controversy and condemnation that resulted from him having kept it secret–reveals how writings about the dangers of unacknowledged pasts for Germans are more than merely a literary convention to explore their own national history. Rather the anger directed at Grass in real life expresses a widely-held conviction there that forgetting or suppressing one's past leaves one ever a victim to it. Remembering, in contrast, insures that new identities become possible and, collectively speaking, new ways of relating to one another are enabled.
3   For other examples of works that treat a nation's incapacity to move out from the shadow of the past as a pathological social condition, interfering with its full-blown capacity to engage the present, yet one that can be overcome, see Schivelbusch (2003), Gobodo-Madikizela (2003), Brooks (2004).

References

Agamben, G. (1999) *Remnants of Auschwitz*. Cambridge, MA: MIT.
Barkan, E. (2000) *The Guilt of Nations: Restitution and Negotiating Historical Injustices*. Baltimore, MD: Johns Hopkins University Press.
Brooks, R. (2004) *Atonement and Forgiveness: A New Model of Black Reparations*. Berkeley and Los Angeles, CA: University of California Press.
Brubaker, R. and Cooper, F. (2002) 'Beyond 'Identity', *Theory and Society*, 29: 1–47.
Butler, J. (1997) *The Psychic Life of Power: Theories in Subjection*. Stanford, CA: Stanford University Press.
Butler, J. (2003) 'Afterword: After loss, what then?', in D. Eng and D. Kazanjian (eds), *Loss: The Politics of Mourning*. Berkeley and Los Angeles, CA: University of California Press, pp. 467–74.

Calhoun, C. (ed.) (1994) *Social Theory and the Politics of Identity*. New York: Blackwell.

Clewell, T. (2004) 'Mourning beyond melancholia: Freud's psychoanalysis of loss', *Journal of the American Psychoanalytic Association*, 52(1): 43–67.

Cohen, S. (2001) *States of Denial: Knowing about Atrocities and Suffering*. Cambridge: Polity.

Crimp, D. (2002) 'Mourning and militancy', in *Melancholia and Moralism: Essays on AIDS and Queer Politics*. Cambridge, MA: MIT. pp. 129–50.

Eng, D. and Kazanjian, D. (eds) (2003) 'Preface', in *Loss: The Politics of Mourning*. Berkeley and Los Angeles, CA: University of California Press. pp. ix–x.

Eng, D. and Han, S. (2003) 'A dialogue on racial melancholia', in D. Eng and D. Kazanjian (eds), *Loss: The Politics of Mourning*. Berkeley and Los Angeles, CA: University of California Press, pp. 343–71.

Erikson, E. (1985 [1950]) *Childhood and Society*. New York: Norton.

Freud, S. (1954a [1923]) 'The ego and the id', *The Standard Edition of the Complete Psychological Works*, XIX. London: Hogarth.

Freud, S. (1954b [1939]) 'Moses and monotheism', *The Standard Edition of the Complete Psychological Works*, XXIII. London: Hogarth.

Freud, S. (1954c [1917]) 'Mourning and melancholia', *The Standard Edition of the Complete Psychological Works*. XIV. London: Hogarth.

Freud, S. (1954d [1895]) 'Project for a scientific psychology', *The Standard Edition of the Complete Psychological Works*, I. London: Hogarth.

Gillis, J. (1994) 'Memory and identity: the history of a relationship', in *Commemorations: The Politics of National Identity*. Princeton, NJ: Princeton University Press, pp. 3–26.

Gilroy, P. (2005) *Postcolonial Melancholia*. New York: Columbia University Press.

Gobodo-Madikizela, P. (2003) *A Human Being Died that Night: A South African Story of Forgiveness*. Boston, MA: Houghton Mifflin.

Green, A. (2002) *Time in Psychoanalysis: Some Contradictory Aspects*. London: Free Association Books.

Grass, G. (2003) *Crabwalk*. San Diego, CA: Harcourt.

Honneth, A. (1996) *The Struggle for Recognition: The Moral Grammar of Social Conflicts*. Cambridge, MA: MIT.

Katz, J. (1999) *How Emotions Work*: Chicago, IL: University of Chicago Press.

LaCapra, D. (1999) 'Trauma, absence, loss', *Critical Inquiry*, 25 (4): 696–727.

LaCapra, D. (2001) *Writing History, Writing Trauma*, Baltimore, MD: Johns Hopkins University Press.

Levinas, E. (2001) *Is it Righteous to Be? Interview with Emmanuel Levinas*. Stanford, CA: Stanford University Press.

Lloyd, D. (2003) 'The memory of hunger', in D. Eng and D. Kazanjian (eds), *Loss: The Politics of Mourning*. Berkeley and Los Angeles, CA: University of California Press, pp. 205–28.

Minow, M. (1998) *Between Vengeance and Forgiveness, Facing History after Genocide and Mass Violence*. Boston, MA: Beacon.

Mitscherlich, A. and Mitscherlich, M. (1975) *The Inability to Mourn: Principles of Collective Behavior*. New York: Grove.

Prager, J. (1998) *Presenting the Past: Psychoanalysis and the Sociology of Misremembering*. Cambridge, MA: Harvard University Press.

Prager, J. (2006a) 'Beneath the surface of the self: psychoanalysis and the unseen known', *American Journal of Sociology*, 112 (1): 276–90.

Prager, J. (2006b) 'Jump-starting timeliness: trauma, temporality, and the redressive community', in J. Parker, M. Crawford and P. Harris (eds), *Time and Memory*. Amsterdam: Koninklijke Brill N.V.

Prager, J. (2008) 'Healing from history: psychoanalytic considerations on traumatic pasts and social repair', *European Journal of Social Theory*, 11(3): 405–420.

Schivelbusch, W. (2003) *The Culture of Defeat, On National Trauma, Mourning and Recovery*. New York: Metropolitan.

Sebald, W.G. (2003a) *Austerlitz*. New York: The Modern Library.

Sebald, W.G. (2003b) *On the Natural History of Destruction*. New York: Random House.

Taylor, C. (1997) *The Sources of the Self: The Making of Modern Identity*. New York: Cambridge University Press.

Thoma, H. and Cheshire, N. (1991) 'Freud's *Nachtraglichkeit* and Strachey's "Deferred Action": trauma, constructions and the direction of causality', *International Review of Psychoanalysis*, 18: 407–27.

Thompson, J. (2002) *Taking Responsibility for the Past: Reparation and Historical Justice*. Cambridge: Polity.

Todorov, T. (2001) *Life in Common: An Essay in General Anthropology*. Lincoln, NB: University of Nebraska Press.

Torpey, J. (2006) *Making Whole what has been Smashed: On Reparation Politics*. Cambridge, MA: Harvard University Press.

9

Goodbye to Identity?

Stephen Frosh and Lisa Baraitser

The displaced subject (again)

The notion that identity might be plural, or indeed, best described as a *process*, is now very familiar within psychoanalysis, as well as in the social sciences. This is despite the way that psychoanalysis continues to display contradictory positions on this issue, perhaps an indication of its own fractured identity. The seemingly stable and achieved nature of identity (the end point of Erikson's (1956) classical psychoanalytic theory) is still visible in the notion that repressed ideas produce stable ways of being that are resistant to change; on the other hand, the vision of identi*ties* as fluid and multiple can be seen in the understanding of unconscious ideas as variable, contradictory and partial. More syncretically, psychoanalysis offers a lens on how multiple and contradictory forces can produce fixedness, and on the permeability of the apparent boundary between 'inside and out'. Well-established notions such as identification, introjection and internalization as well as more contemporary psychoanalytic thinking on recognition (Benjamin, 1998) offer routes to conceptualize the processes whereby human subjects become invested in particular identities, for example through allegiances or emotional connections with specific groups or social fractions. The key intersubjective postulate is perhaps that whilst the original source of identity is based on a relation to body parts, identification with parents and others subsequently leads to more complex and elaborate experiences of identity in a variety of contexts. Identities are constructed through such processes of identification and recognition, and emotional investment by subjects in these processes gives identities their significance – the reason why they can be experienced as constituting psychosocial reality. Because both the constructive processes (such as identification) and the investment are largely or wholly unconscious, identities are lived as if they were 'given' rather than chosen; that is, they are often felt to be fundamental to the subject, as if they have been received whole and constitute the subject's essence. The implication of this is that identities may be lived as real, but are in fact constituted in the flux of contradictory impulses, putting psychoanalysis in line with the generally deconstructive tendency in modern thought that construes identities 'as the place(s) or location(s) where social categories and social relations, symbolic representations and hierarchies of privilege and disadvantage come together and are lived out as forms of subjectivity and community' (Wetherell and Mohanty, forthcoming). More radically, Lacanian and post-Lacanian approaches within psychoanalysis align themselves firmly with those who refute the stability of identities, preferring to track them as modes of what might be thought of as 'masquerade', or as fragile and momentary assemblages of contradictory forces.

So far, so obvious. Yet there is a considerable further challenge to psychoanalytic identity theories that arises from what has been happening outside the clinic and the academy, in the 'real' world of technological change, war and terrorism, in the rising consciousness (but neglect of action) over ecological disaster, in the dissemination of AIDS and the promises of biomedicine and the genome. One might reasonably assume (as do Elliott and Lemert, 2005) that these developments have impacted on people's psychological states and their senses of identity and selfhood, now perhaps more panicked than before, but also more technologically mediated through, amongst other things, the explosive growth of the Internet. Indeed, the argument that we are biotechnical subjects is well established in certain branches of academia, since Donna Haraway's (1991) theorization of 'cyborgs' and Rosi Braidotti's exuberant (1994) evocation of the nomadic subject, fluidly repositioning across a multifarious terrain of non-human life. Social and cultural theory has responded to this by seeking out models of biosocial life that emphasize multiplicity and networked connections, displacing (once again) the human subject and introducing in its place a sense of productive activity that gives rise to sensations and identities. The effects of globalization and technology in particular mean that, according to such theorists, the fragmented and unstable subject of post-modernity has now given way to the 'post-human' subject: a technologically mediated, fluid, ethical, nomadic, simultaneously global and locally produced subject (Braidotti, 2006). This post-human subject is charted as a response to current concerns about diversity and difference, ecology and the 'natural' order, living and dying, safety and terror, location and globalization. Other writers who are not so taken with the idea of the post-human nevertheless concern themselves with the nature of intersubjective ethics in the context of the impingement of 'others', with especial reference to 'liveness' and hence also to death (e.g., Lingis, 1994). Some of this relates to the resurgence of interest in Deleuzian rhizomatic networks of articulated forces (Deleuze and Guattari, 1987), and laying the foundations for a return to an interest in affect as that which gives rise to subjectivity, rather than following on from it. Other writers are beginning to develop a contemporary ethics of 'impersonality', visible for example in Žižek's (2005) critique of Levinas and his 'plea for ethical violence'. As well as being a debate within political philosophy, these perspectives address psychological experiences in a way that is antagonistic to the depth perspective of traditional psychoanalysis, yet which also has resonances with one of its antinomies, Lacanian psychoanalysis, which has left a legacy of interest in the de-narrativizing encounter between a subject who desires and one who is 'supposed to know'. These perspectives give priority to disruption over meaning making, to paradox over order, and most importantly to the criss-crossing of bodily and symbolic networks as they create points of coherence that fade away as one encounters them.

In contrast, there is a movement 'back' towards a kind of humanistic modernism that refuses the deconstructionism of these recent intellectual traditions. This can be seen in the fascination with narrative that pervades much of the social sciences, particularly in their empirical and therapeutic varieties (for critiques, see Frosh, 2007, and Laplanche, 2003), and particularly in the 'relational turn' in psychoanalysis, perhaps most strikingly in the work of Jessica Benjamin (1998, 2004) and the development of a benign conceptualization of 'thirdness' that draws particularly strongly on Winnicott. This work is based in clinical practice, but has been extended to deal with social and political conflicts, including in Israel/Palestine (see Benjamin's contribution to Altman et al., 2006); it focuses on ways of recognizing the other that can bridge without colonizing, that can sustain the other's separateness and difference while allowing links to be built. In a way, perhaps what is happening here is a recognition of the *difficulty* of the postmodern experience of separateness and mistranslation (which is heavily invested in by Lacanian psychoanalysis), and a return to an aspirational mode of writing that seeks to establish relationships, however difficult that task might be. As will be appreciated, there are many problems to be found in what might become a reductive move back to normative models of the human as a source of agency and meaning; in this light, some kind of effort towards an 'impersonal humanism' might be worth pursuing (Frosh, 2008). Nevertheless, the dynamics that have forced the return to a 'depth' model of thinking are worth considering in the light of the continuing appeal of identity and its claims.

In what follows, two rather different approaches to this are discussed: one is that of Benjamin, which is located within psychoanalysis; the other is the highly influential work of Judith Butler, which draws on psychoanalysis from the perspective of social and queer theory. These approaches are often bracketed together, but as is revealed in the exchange between them on the nature of Benjamin's work, focusing especially on the question of destructiveness (Benjamin, 2000; Butler, 2000), they differ radically in their underlying positions. In particular, Benjamin can be seen to be exploring the capacity of subjects to form intersubjective links, and to have been following a path in which these capacities are highlighted in the face of countervailing psycho-analytic and philosophical tendencies that are rather more pessimistic about the prospects for human relating. Butler, on the other hand, has powerfully articulated the fragility of the self and its immersion in networks of force that run through and further fracture it. These writers are not, therefore, being presented here as saying the same things, but rather as providing two exemplary accounts, both of which – one surprisingly, one less so – offer some space for the notion of identity as something more than an alienating fiction.

Relatedness and melancholy

Interestingly, a trend towards the re-establishment of identities can be seen to have overtaken what looked in the early 1990s like one of the most evocative responses to postmodernism, the 'performative' thinking of Judith Butler (1990), which fuelled the rise of queer theory and the more general attempt to 'queer' everything, both specifically in the realm of sexuality and generally as a disruptive, erotic, from-the-margins assault on received wisdoms. This work was phenomenally influential, yet Butler (1997) herself qualified it very quickly by drawing explicitly on psychoanalysis, referencing Freud as a way of examining the place of melancholia in the formation of gender, and moving gradually back into a space of what seems to be deeply felt identity politics, or rather into (Jewish) identity in order to do politics (Butler, 2004). It is no accident in this regard that Žižek's (2005) 'plea for ethical violence', mentioned above, is articulated as a response to Butler's argument 'against ethical violence' (Butler, 2005), in which she draws heavily on non-Lacanian psychoanalysis, especially Winnicott, Bollas and Laplanche. Segal (2007) has recently examined Butler's trajectory, showing that it serves well to reflect a more general retrenchment that may not be backward looking, but rather expresses a willingness to engage politically against oppression and violence with whatever tools it takes, including the tools provided by the concept of identity. Segal lists Butler's moves as

> from primarily semiotic analysis to stressing the significance of the socio-cultural moment; from political abstractions to ethical reasoning; from pivotal concern with gender and sexuality to a general interest in alterity and the face/place of the other; from a Foucauldian engagement with exteriority and performativity to a more psychodynamic interest in interiority and stress upon the formative early years of life; from a rejection of identities into the specific embrace of several very distinct ones, articulated in the form of an identity politics. (Segal, 2007)

One can see here a way in which Butler, perhaps the most iconic figure of queer performativity, has not just sobered up, but has immersed herself in a deeply serious project to contest oppression and abuse from the perspective of ethical engagement: things matter, she says; it is not just some kind of game. (To be fair, she has always taken this position, but the exuberance of her earlier work meant that this theme was consistently overlooked.)

Butler is a central contemporary figure for discussions of the trajectories of psychoanalysis and identities for numerous reasons, not least because she is generally so influential in encouraging, post-9/11 and in the wake of AIDS, a reorientation of attention towards psychoanalytic understandings of loss and melancholy, as if it is becoming possible to consider the impact of deep relationships once again; as if, that is, feelings are being allowed back in as formative elements in the construction of personal identities. Much of this, for instance as referenced in her essay 'Violence, Mourning, and Politics' (in Butler, 2004), revolves around a very moving exploration of the intricate relationships between selves, communities, and otherness, seen through the lens of Freud's thinking on mourning and melancholia. In this account, the experience of loss demonstrates just how much each of us is relationally engaged with others and is dependent on others, however autonomous we might believe ourselves to be. 'What grief displays', she writes (Butler, 2004: 23), 'is the thrall in which our relations with others hold us, in ways that we cannot always recount or explain'. In its often excessive and abysmal effects, its capacity to disrupt identity and to provoke crises of the self, loss shows up the intensity of the relational bond, which can itself often be experienced as excessive and fracturing, as penetrating identity with something external and uncontrollably alien. Deeply felt loss of the kind Butler is writing about thus communicates the dispersal of identities, the way that with every loss something dies inside because our inner world consists of connections with others. The reference here is to something formative, structural even, and hard to reflect upon ('ways that we cannot always recount or explain') and it is suggested that this is endemic to the way our subjectivity is premised on the link with otherness.

Butler takes her appreciation of the core function of this mode of other-directed relationality into the domain of practical, political ethics by asking how what is melancholic and mournful can be turned into an appreciation of the other, of what constitutes the essential humanity of the other person. Reflecting on the way certain others are written out of history, have their humanity decried in the interests, and as a consequence, of violence, she argues that what makes us prone to the other's violence is also what makes us involved with the other – our mutual dependence, our neediness. The 'conception of the human' that she employs here is:

> one in which we are, from the start, even prior to individuation itself, and by virtue of bodily requirements, given over to some set of primary others: this conception means that we are vulnerable to those we are too young to know and to judge and, hence, vulnerable to violence; but also vulnerable to another range of touch, a range that includes the eradication of our being at the one end, and the physical support for our lives at the other. (Butler, 31)

Bodily and psychically – the two are in an important sense one and the same here – the infant is in the hands of the other, with all the potential that situation possesses for love and care, and violence and neglect. This dependence, Butler suggests, establishes a psychic structure that lasts throughout life. It also relates to the idea of the necessary *intrusion* of the other in the formation of selfhood, an intrusion that Žižek (2006: 43) alludes to in his formulation of 'the monstrosity of the neighbour, a monstrosity on account of which Lacan applies to the neighbour the term Thing (*das Ding*)'. That is, an enigmatic demand is made on the self by the other from the start of life, and this enigma resides 'in' unconscious life, or perhaps is better thought of as continually provoking it, once again destabilizing identity at the same moment as it appears to give it shape.

The lyricism of much of Butler's writing here is very noticeable, giving the lie to her famous positioning as an impossibly 'difficult' writer. What she seems to produce is an evocation of a certain kind of appreciation of the place of otherness in identity-formation that gives space not just to recognition, but to love. The other is constantly implicated in the self, not just being carried around as a set of memories and identifications, but absolutely entwined in it in relations of dependence and a kind of passionate embrace, 'another range of touch' that can elide the self by the other, but also sustains existence. Taking this argument on, what is being theorized is a link with an other who can embody internal strangeness and ease the subject out of it, perhaps along the lines of what Laplanche (1999) calls the 'enigmatic signifier', the 'message' put into the infant *unknowingly* by the other/mother, which faces us with a deeply mysterious yet absolutely concrete realization of the other's desire within us. 'Solicit[ing] a becoming', as Butler (2004: 44) puts it, is tied into the other's presence and also the other's relentless strangeness; Žižek, briefly in Levinasian mode, similarly notes the intractability of the mystery of the other as what is essential, arguing that *not* knowing the other is crucial to intersubjectivity itself.

> If I were to 'really know' the mind of my interlocutor, intersubjectivity proper would disappear; he would lose his subjective status and turn – for me – into a transparent machine. In other words, not-being-knowable to others is a crucial feature of subjectivity, of what we mean when we impute to our interlocutors a 'mind': you 'truly have a mind' only insofar as it is opaque to me. (Žižek, 2006: 178)

The solidity of the other comes over in this, its absolute otherness that links both with Winnicott's (1969) ideas on how the other becomes real to the subject by surviving attack, and with the contrary Lacanian emphasis on how all psychoanalytic knowledge is constituted through language, and hence is characterized by 'mis-recognition'. And in this, once again, identities are propped up and slip away; they are lovingly supported yet permeated with something that does not quite fit in.

Recognizing the other – maintaining identity

Recognition of the other, in the strong sense of giving the other ascendancy, is a key element in the maintenance of subjecthood because it brings the internal other to life, holding out the hope that something can be done with it, that the other can name it and give it shape. Butler (2005) explicitly references Levinas here; but this Levinasian take on things contrasts with Jessica Benjamin's attempt to adopt a more reciprocal understanding of how analyst and patient – self and other – construct a third position into which they can project themselves as one. For Benjamin, the intersubjective stance is a specific move within the general domain of relational theorizing, one which holds onto a position in which the other is related *to* but is not appropriated – that is, it is a stance that acknowledges the appeal of omnipotence (in knowing the other we come to colonize her/him) but works against it. Hence it is concerned with processes of identification which allow the other to maintain *separateness in linkage*, and it motions towards a position in which the apparent fixedness of identity allows this other to be, yet also permits an emotional and unconscious connection. The manner in which omnipotence is contested is through 'recognition', denoting a stance towards the other that acknowledges her or him as a source of subjectivity, giving rise (in an echo of the Buberian 'I-thou') to what Benjamin calls a 'subject-subject' psychology. This means that recognition is built out of an understanding of the other's continuing otherness, maintaining the subjecthood of both participants in the exchange who are thus both autonomous and yet also exist in relation to one another, 'cocreating a mutuality that allows for and presumes separateness' (1998: 29). What is being traced here is a particular form of relationship between selves and others, a certain handling of similarity and difference, in which neither is collapsed into the other. Recognition staves off the absorption of self into the other just as it prevents the other being colonized by the self; rather, the possibility is raised of allowing difference yet also appreciating similarity. Benjamin writes, 'The problem of whether or not we are able to recognize the other person as outside, not the sum of, our projections or the mere object of need, and still feel recognized by her or him, is defining for intersubjectivity' (2000: 294) . Recognition of this kind is thus a state of actively reaching-out that makes what it finds, yet also lets the other be; it involves cherishing what is found in the other specifically for its capacity to be different, for its otherness.

If one is adhering to the language of 'identity', what Benjamin's focus on reciprocity does is to position identities as elements of an intersubjective space in which people (selves and others) work together to produce something that is joined and separate at the same time. For example, in relation to mothering (a key site for identity construction in psychoanalytic theory),

Benjamin draws on Winnicott's (1969) ideas about a developmental phase that comes after object relating and involves 'object use', which is made possible through seeing that the (paradigmatically, maternal) object survives unconscious destruction. Attacks on this object – in fantasy, *destruction* of it – support the infant's perception of the existence of an external other so long as the mother survives and is non-retaliatory in her response. That is, what the infant is supposed to discover is that the mother is not subject to the infant's 'internal' experience of having destroyed her, and hence is an object with more than merely imaginary existence. In Benjamin's view there is an ongoing and endless cycle of the establishment of mutual recognition followed by its negation, constituting a never ending tension between complementarity and mutuality, between relating to the other as object or like subject (Baraitser, 2008). This means that, in contrast to Butler, Benjamin proposes that we are not fundamentally constituted through loss, but through processes of separation that are tempered by the pleasures of mutual recognition and the possibilities of shared understanding made possible through surviving destruction. Difference can then be experienced as something that can be identified with, not just repudiated, negated or controlled. The infant can enjoy the fact that the mother has a life of her own to get on with, as it means that she is 'like me, with desires of her own'.

The bridging-across-differences element in Benjamin's writing works the terrain of a fundamentally relational theory of identities, albeit one which acknowledges the necessary robustness of both subject and other when faced with one another. In this respect, she is opposed to Levinas' (1991) prioritizing of the other over the subject: Benjamin is cautious about always making the other's needs primary, always taking responsibility in this way, because she wants to warn against a kind of self-abasement in which the subject gives up her or his agency and indeed her or his rights. That is, taking responsibility is not the same thing as always giving way; and indeed the analytic situation (characterized by 'analytic abstinence') is precisely one in which not giving way (too much) is seen as crucial both for the containment of a patient's anxiety and for the exploration of deep trauma. The analyst has to hold firm not only to maintain her or his sanity, but also in order to become 'real' for the patient; this must be tempered with an acknowledgement of errors and a readiness to participate in the intersubjective exchange, but not at the price of obliterating one's own subjectivity. The working out of this position can also be seen in Benjamin's more recent and highly productive concern with 'thirdness'. Whilst acknowledging the utility of Oedipal scenarios for understanding aspects of development, Benjamin has long been critical of the Oedipal framework as the overriding element in analytic theory, seeing it as fixing a bipolarity (father *versus* mother; reality *versus* narcissism) that is not only misogynist in its assumptions, but also misses the true 'overdeterminism' of psychic life. Benjamin's approach to

Goodbye to Identity?

this is to question the final authority of the Oedipus complex, which she sees as too easily accepting traditional bipolarizing notions such as that the father is the primary symbol of reality and maturity, while the mother's pull is always to fantasy and narcissism. As she notes in her major work on domination, *The Bonds of Love* (1988), versions of the Oedipus complex which draw on this 'Oedipus versus Narcissus' mentality, in which the father 'liberates' the child from the regressive pull of dependency and incest, produce misogynistic and lifeless accounts of the possible arrangements of masculinity and femininity, based firmly around idealization and denigration. What has to be achieved is a capacity to sustain identification with 'sameness in difference', a capacity to recognize the other yet also appreciate the other's subjectivity and 'authorship'. Benjamin implies that this is to be achieved neither by a regression to the pre-Oedipal mother, characteristic of object relations theory and involving a denial of the sexualized nature of gender differentiation, nor by the traditional Freudian or Lacanian adherence to the structuring power of the Oedipal situation, with its focus on lack and denial, but rather in the setting of a more mature, post-Oedipal complementarity which brings back together the various 'elements of identification, so that they become less threatening, less diametrically opposite, no longer cancelling out one's identity' (1998: 69–70). It is only through the achievement of this kind of integrative complementarity that the idealisation-denigration split so characteristic of Oedipal thinking can be overcome, hence facilitating an encounter between necessarily fragmentary subjects, relating to one another as agents rather than as threats. Multiple identifications forge the basis for identities which themselves are multiple and fluid, less defensive and hence less caricatured and stereotyped. *Connectedness* is emphasized here, recognizing difference but not discounting the other because of it.

   In developing the idea of the 'third' away from Oedipal structures, Benjamin formalizes her interest in connectedness and relationality through postulating a 'space' in which contact occurs. This space is a dynamic space; a principle, relationship or function which is constantly collapsing and needing to be repaired. It has two elements (Benjamin, 2004): the 'third in the one', which is the capacity (paradigmatically of the mother or the analyst) for a subject to hold in mind what subject and other can create together, a kind of reparative capacity to believe that it is possible to comprehend the other even when the other is destructive and alien; and the 'one in the third', a pattern of being that links subject and other and produces something new, a space (for example the projected space of the analytic encounter) for meeting, reflection and newness, owned by neither party but an aspect of them both. Whilst this is described as a kind of mechanism through which recognition can occur, particularly but not exclusively in therapy, it can also be seen to have implications for thinking on identities.

Not only are these now fluid, as they must be to allow for the kind of to-and-fro of agentic encounter that has displaced the apparent fixedness of the Oedipal scenario, they are also phantasmagorical in quite a specific sense: they draw on the capacity of all parties in an encounter to disperse their psychological boundaries temporarily to allow investment in a shared space of unconscious contact. Identities flow between people, at times seeming to provoke states of near-merger, at other times of separateness, but always, in this view, both real and imagined.

Conclusion

There is continued uncertainty over the utility of the notion of identity or identities, given that it now refers predominantly to something local, fluid, unstable and contingent, made up of momentary stabilities that are then instantly displaced. Under conditions of social instability there is little for identity to cohere around; the social nexus that has traditionally given it fixed points is itself too slippery and inconsistent. In addition, the humanist moment has long gone: it is completely clear that the human subject is not the centre of consciousness, that agency does not reside straightforwardly in the person, that the self and all its claims to fixedness (and hence to 'an' identity) is largely fictitious, retroactively constructed to cover over an unstable core. And yet ... amongst those whose sophistication in matters of theory and psychoanalytic understanding leaves nothing to be desired, there remains at least a tradition, and sometimes more, of reaching out for the vestiges of relational thought, in which identities are produced through a certain kind of wrestling with the demands and promises of the human other. Butler and Benjamin exemplify some of this, despite their very different trajectories and affiliations. Butler's focus is on how the status of the self is always *extrinsic*: to become a self, in her account, is to be outside oneself, or 'other' than oneself, and to have always already lost oneself through a relation to the other that returns one to oneself as different. Benjamin focuses on the capacity for transitional states that makes it possible for subjects to encounter one another in the space of the 'third', dissolving boundaries temporarily yet recovering them sufficiently to maintain agency and internality whilst recognizing the other as separate. These two approaches are at odds with one another in many respects – around what exactly constitutes recognition, for example, and the part played in this by destruction. Yet both give centrality to (different forms of) recognition and loss in their theories of subject formation, and this leads both of them towards a non-sentimental identity politics that insists on the significance of dependency and subjective depth even while it displaces the source of meaning away from the enclosed individual.

More generally, something is at work in many contemporary theoretical formulations, however widely they differ, that insists on the demise of classical 'identity' yet allows for a kind of contact between subjects that provides relational support, both physical and psychological, out of which identities can emerge. This is pretty fragile, it must be admitted, or 'precarious' in Butler's (2004) terms; there is still nothing stable about identities, nothing secure in them. Vulnerability is stressed, and the political focus is on the work involved in constructing and reconstructing identities in the face of forces that upend them, that write certain people out of existence, or subjugate particular voices to such a degree that they become silenced. It is perhaps this political use of identities that unites Benjamin, Butler and many others whose theoretical perspectives are different and even contradictory: they note the precariousness of contemporary lives, they see how infused they are with loss and violence, and they attend to the modes of stability and depth that remain viable, and to questions of how they can arise and be supported. If this is right, then the celebratory components of the postmodern assault on identity may be giving way, even though the key perception that identities are multiple and unstable remains crucial: the idea that identities are *nothing more than* fictions seems no longer as helpful as it was when the priority was to resist coercive normative identity formations. Identities, that is, may be precarious and unsettled, and may require constant analysis, deconstruction and reconfiguring; but it is perhaps too soon to wish them goodbye.

References

Altman, N., Benjamin, J., Jacobs, T. and Wachtel, P. (2006) 'Is politics the last taboo in psychoanalysis?', in L. Layton, N. Hollander and S. Gutwill (eds), *Psychoanalysis, Class and Politics*. London: Routledge, pp. 166–95.

Baraitser, L. (2008) 'Mum's the word: intersubjectivity, alterity and the maternal subject', *Studies in Gender and Sexuality*, 9: 86–110.

Benjamin, J. (1988) *The Bonds of Love*. London: Virago.

Benjamin, J. (1998) *Shadow of the Other: Intersubjectivity and Gender in Psychoanalysis*. New York: Routledge.

Benjamin, J. (2000) 'Response to commentaries by Mitchell and by Butler', *Studies in Gender and Sexuality*, 1: 291–308.

Benjamin, J. (2004) 'Beyond doer and done to: an intersubjective view of thirdness', *Psychoanalytic Quarterly*, 73: 5–46.

Braidotti, R. (1994) *Nomadic Subjects: Embodiment and Sexual Difference in Contemporary Feminist Theory*. New York: Columbia University Press.

Braidotti, R. (2006) *Transpositions*. Cambridge: Polity.

Butler, J. (1990) *Gender Trouble*. London: Routledge.

Butler, J. (1997) *The Psychic Life of Power*. Stanford, CA: Stanford University Press.

Butler, J. (2000) 'Longing for recognition: commentary on the work of Jessica Benjamin', *Studies in Gender and Sexuality*, 1: 271–90.

Butler, J. (2004) *Precarious Life*. London: Verso.

Butler, J. (2005) *Giving an Account of Oneself*. New York: Fordham University Press.

Deleuze, G. and Guattari, F. (1987) *A Thousand Plateaus: Capitalism and Schizophrenia*. London: Athlone.

Elliott, A. and Lemert, C. (2005) *The New Individualism: The Emotional Costs of Globalization*. London: Routledge.

Erikson, E. (1956) 'The problem of ego identity', *Journal of the American Psychoanalytic Association*, 4: 56–121.

Frosh, S. (2007) 'Disintegrating qualitative research', *Theory and Psychology*, 17: 635–53.

Frosh, S. (2008) 'Elementals and Affects, or On Making Contact with Others', *Subjectivity*, 24: 314–24.

Haraway, D. (1991) *Simians, Cyborgs and Women: The Reinvention of Nature*. New York: Routledge.

Laplanche, J. (1999) *Essays on Otherness*. London: Routledge.

Laplanche, J. (2003) 'Narrativity and hermeneutics: some propositions', *New Formations*, 48: 26–9.

Levinas, E. (1991) *Entre Nous: On Thinking of the Other*. London: Athlone.

Lingis, A. (1994) *The Community of Those Who Have Nothing in Common*. Indianapolis: Indiana University Press.

Segal, L. (2007) 'Identities: Who needs them? Possibilites for self-narration'. Paper presented to conference *After Butler*, University of Westminster, March.

Wetherell, M. and Mohanty, C. (forthcoming) 'Introduction', in M. Wetherell and C. Mohanty (eds), *The Sage Handbook of Identities*. London: Sage.

Winnicott, D.W. (1969) 'The use of an object', *International Journal of Psycho-Analysis*, 50: 711–16.

Žižek, S. (2005) 'Neighbors and other monsters: a plea for ethical violence', in S. Žižek, E. Santner and K. Reinhard (eds), *The Neighbor: Three Inquiries in Political Theology*. Chicago, IL: University of Chicago Press, pp. 134–90.

Žižek, S. (2006) *The Parallax View*. Cambridge, MA: MIT.

10

Cathected Identities: Governance and Community Activism

Jessica Evans

There is no list [...]. They said to me the list's all mental. I think then it did hit me what we were doing. (Jackie Rampton, Paulsgrove protester, quoted in Gillan, 2000: 5)

Introduction

There is an unceasing contact zone between private life and the domain of public policy, where a welter of not altogether coherent discourses circulate for citizens to make sense of – to take in, reject, act upon, reflect upon, as the case may be. It is the particular dynamic in the relationship between private and public that has, at any one time, consequences for the extent to which the moral ambivalence and social destructiveness of citizens are contained. Wilfred Bion (1962) referred to containment as the way in which individuals seek to find an other (whether a person, institution or group) which can be a temporary repository for experiences that cause anxiety or threaten to overwhelm us. This other has the function of providing a 'place for experience' that is 'safe, strong, benign and thoughtful' (Hoggett, 2005: 178) – roles that may be played by teachers, doctors, public officials, parents, postmen, local shopkeepers, friends and so on, and represent the 'holding' fabric of everyday life.

In recent years, neo-liberal programmes of governance have emerged that seek to make each of us 'responsible' for managing risk that is close to home – whether in our role as a parent, child-carer, or school teacher. When it comes to managing the safety of sexual offenders post-prison, information management involving forms of community input is in particular seen as the long-term solution. This managerialist strategy assumes, at least implicitly, a mature citizen who has the capacities to contain anxiety and their own destructive impulses. However, given the strains existing in the government's policies on sexual offenders, unintended consequences may easily follow, evidenced in campaigns aiming to cleanse a community of what is perceived as its bad objects. 'I fear' becomes 'I am frightened of X' (Hoggett, 2005: 181) and once the 'paedophile' becomes the object of a cathexis – an object of highly charged emotional investment – communities may revert to a more puritanical and moralising code that distinguishes absolutely between those who are good and those who are 'bad'.

Here, I give sociological consideration to the identities of the main protagonists of a particular episode of community activism, along the key axes of class and gender. But the questions raised cannot be answered fully if the chapter is limited to describing the social identities of the community members under discussion, crucial though these are. It is both true and certainly justifiable that there has been little interest in the concept of 'identity' in the classical psychoanalytic literature, given the psychoanalytic proposition that 'identity' is forged from an array of multiple and conflicting identifications, in part unconscious, that are often unpredictable and irrational. There is not, and cannot be, a neat 'fit' between 'society outside the head' and what goes on inside people's minds; the inner life of an individual and its particular history both intra-psychically and inter-personally make its own contribution to social relationships and to our social identities – as parents, teachers, sports fans and so on. Those social identities may be taken away, but we would not lose 'our identity' (Craib, 1998). In this sense there is psychic reality, which generates something in its own right: individuals unconsciously use aspects of the external world to represent aspects of their own internal world. If conditions are facilitating enough, we maintain some basic respect for external and internal reality and we manage pain and fear through toleration and containment. In the following case study, it is argued that there was an unhappy fusion between public discourses on sexual offenders and the collective state of mind of a group of protesters who made extreme investments of emotional energy in the idea of the persecutory 'paedophile'. We should use the term cathexis with caution, but it usefully conveys the psychosomatic aspect of the energy discharged by the protesters. In Freud's early hydraulic schema of the mind, he thought of frustration of desire as a blockage of energy that would build up and eventually require release. The release could occur by way of regression, an aspect of an episode that in more contemporary terms is called quasi-psychotic or borderline, and is described in detail in the following case study (see Cooper and Lousada, 2005). Borderline states are those in which a basic respect for external and internal reality is only precariously maintained and a realistic differentiation between self and other becomes difficult. In this way the 'identity' of a borderline patient is under constant threat as a result of the (con)fusion between self and other, a consequence of massive projection into others (Cooper and Lousada, 2005: 33).

Case Study

Paulsgrove is an estate built in the 1950s, as part of a policy of slum-clearance, on the edges of Portsmouth on the south-west coast of England. There is only one road in and out of Paulsgrove; one recent account (Silverman and Wilson, 2002) describes it as a 'beleaguered enclave' with a high degree of social problems.[1] On 23 July 2000, the national tabloid *News of the World* launched its campaign for 'Sarah's Law' in the wake of the murder of Sarah Payne. Its naming of convicted sex offenders and the printing of their police identity photographs was an indication of its objective: to provide open access to the location of all paedophiles and sex offenders in the UK. In the evenings of the first week of August 2000, about 100 adults and children, calling themselves 'Residents Against Paedophiles', marched through the Paulsgrove estate. They torched cars and firebombed flats and houses where suspected sex offenders and paedophiles were thought to live, including one Victor Burnett, who had the previous week been 'named and shamed' by the *News of the World*. Five families, all unconnected to sex offenders, fled the estate and one policeman was injured. At least 50 people were arrested according to newspaper reports (Hill, 2001). Similar events occurred in other areas of the UK such as the Southway area of Plymouth and Whitely in Berkshire, as well as in Manchester, London and Wales.

The Paulsgrove protests and their protagonists form the centrepiece for a psychoanalytic study that, I argue, demonstrates the existence of links between the vigilante state of mind and the 'mind of state' that places communities at the centre of crime management. It should be said straight away that the term vigilantism has unhelpful connotations: it is all too often understood by political and academic commentators as a simple expression of a latent moral authoritarianism in the popular 'masses' incurred through an admixture of endemic mental frailty and suggestibility – hence the key role attributed to populism's agent, the tabloid press (see Riddell, 2000, 2002). Expressions of outrage, aggression and anxiety abound as a response to 'crime' but it is facile to refer to the archaic, timeless responses of the prototypical 'mob', which is largely how the national press saw it. For example, more than one newspaper article used the archetype 'rough music' in relation to the Paulsgrove protesters (Ferguson, 2001), a reference to Grose's *Dictionary of the Vulgar Tongue* (1796), which describes women beating saucepans and pokers in procession in order to humiliate or scare a neighbour. Mentions of Salem, witches and the 'violent stupidity of the mob' in reporting were frequent (Ferguson, 2001). In this chapter, I analyse this specific case of 'vigilantism' as contextually specific – bounded by time and place – and propose that it is also contingent upon the contemporary politics of active citizenship in which the 'victim' (imaginary, actual or potential) is called upon to play an authoritative role.

My specific argument is that anti-paedophile 'vigilante' campaigns unconsciously manifest the strains existing in the New Labour government's dual approach to sexual offenders. These strains are consequent upon the government's deployment of the administrative techniques of neo-liberal governance and, at the same time, its continuing attachment to the rhetoric of contemporary punitive populism, reinforced by other agents in the public sphere such as the popular press. From the point of view of community actors, this distinction may not be as absolute as it is often assumed to be. One central outcome is the collapse of a meaningful distinction between vigilance and vigilantism, a collapse that can only be satisfactorily understood from within a psychoanalytic framework. It is certainly the avowed intention of the New Labour government in developing its policies on sexual offenders post-prison to inaugurate a renewal of vigilance in the minds of the populace. In its Latin derivation, vigilance means 'awake' or 'observant' (Johnson, 1996). However, in recent years it has become increasingly difficult to distinguish between vigilance and vigilantism, for the state of being vigilant implies non-action, which can 'bring us into contact with feelings which are very hard to bear' (Waddell, 1989: 14; see also Freud, 1984b: 38). Vigilantism, in contrast, occurs when the actual pressure of events promotes acting in order to provide a temporary sense of relief (see Bion, 1988).[2]

In conducting their protests, Paulsgrove residents made much of a 'list' of suspected paedophiles that had been drawn up and was used as the basis for their actions. However, there was no consensus between them as to the sources for this list. Neither has it ever been clear that such a list had a real existence; according to one account there is no firm evidence that anyone other than the protesters 'saw' it (Silverman and Wilson, 2002: 136–7). Other accounts suggest that what some of the protesters referred to as a 'mental list' was used as the basis for a list telephoned to police (Vasagar, 2000). Drawing from the accounts we have of this episode, including interviews conducted with the central protagonists, what is clear is that this list had a highly ambiguous status in the minds of the protesters (see Ferguson, 2001; Gillan, 2000; Silverman and Wilson, 2002: 136). The protesters resisted entreaties to have it verified by the council or the police; in fact they refused to make it public. But the protests became unsustainable after it became evident that 'innocent' individuals and their property were being attacked, and, more importantly for the purposes of this chapter, because the legitimacy of the list of sexual offenders became discredited among the protesters themselves. For it seemed that the list, seen and used as proof, and used in this way as a mechanism for binding the group together, had had a real existence only in their heads. A 'reality principle' set in (Freud, 1984b: 37; 1984a: 278), but only after considerable destruction had taken place. In offering a psychoanalytic view on these events, the case study indicates the arousal of paranoiac unconscious processes in a context where governance techniques of responsibilization inject (seemingly good and neutral) 'information' into communities as an innoculation against dangerous forces. My argument with respect to the case of the Paulsgrove vigilantes is that the list of paedophiles the protesters compiled played a central role in providing them with, in their eyes, legitimation for their actions. The list was a means of simultaneously creating and then acting upon a form of knowledge that was understood as normally belonging to office holders and therefore normally withheld from the public. It should be said that the idea that 'information' contains attractive potentiality was also underlined by key mediators in the public sphere who not only provided information on the whereabouts of particular 'paedophiles' but implicitly incited residents to use that information.[3]

In conducting a psychoanalytic approach, then, we are compelled to take these showy and often sadistic anti-paedophile demonstrations – of hatred, aggression and moral condemnation – wholly seriously as communicative utterances. In aiming to decipher the largely unconscious meaning of the paedophile for specific communities, there is no obligation to stick to social actors' perceptions of the problem and, indeed, every reason not to. For the particular perspective that psychoanalysis brings to the risk-fear problematic is one that refuses the assumption of 'a rational, risk-calculating individual whose fear of crime is a direct reflection of their risk' (Holloway and Jefferson, 2000a: 47). Paying attention to the life of events and objects as they form part of the internal world of social actors means that we allow them a relative affective autonomy. When it is said that a community 'fears' crime or a particular criminal protagonist, one has to interpret these phrases as if one were in a clinical situation, as a presenting symptom. Individuals, groups and 'community' organizations unconsciously and dynamically use aspects of the external world to represent aspects of their own internal worlds, and it is this relationship that forms my focus here.

Responsibilization, community and sexual offenders: the penal policy framework

As a number of criminologists have observed, community crime prevention has, since the late 1980s, metamorphosed into the discourse of 'community safety' (Crawford, 1998; Hughes and Edwards, 2002; Gilling and Barton, 1997). 'Building communities' is at least part of the community safety strategy itself, and, in part, this requires communities to be 'literate' (Garland, 1996) or 'intelligent' about crime by taking part in activities that will reduce crimogenic situations. As Nikolas Rose (1999a, 1999b) has argued, this mobilization of the community – the creation of initiatives to help people to help themselves – is a central plank of advanced liberal government, linking both the Thatcher and Major administrations with those of Blair and Brown. Political government is to be relieved of 'its powers and obligations to know, plan, calculate and steer from the centre' (Rose, 1999a: 476). In this reconfiguration of statecraft, a national government no longer guarantees security, rather it 'facilitates' and 'enables', through partnerships with independent agencies and powers – schools, hospitals, community organizations, parents, firms.[4] Thus its function is one of 'steering and regulating rather than rowing and providing' (Rose, 2000: 324; see also Donzelot, 1991).

This thesis, of a double movement of autonomization and 'responsibilization', originally advanced in the criminological context by O'Malley (1992) and Garland (1996) but drawn from the earlier work of Donzelot (1979), rests on a perception of a broader 'neo-liberal' shift that affects pensions, welfare, health care, and so on. The post-Keynesian state seeks to shift responsibility onto the private sector, the voluntary sector, communities and individuals (Donzelot, 1991; Rose, 1999a) to provide solutions to problems previously thought to be the exclusive responsibility of centralized authorities. Thus the strategies of neo-liberal governance, or what have been termed 'prudential techniques', act in situ rather than by the separation or exclusion of deviant cases; they 'act by manipulating the environment or the effects of problem behaviours, rather than attempting to correct errant individuals' (O'Malley, 1996: 191; see also Rose, 1999a: 488). In securing themselves against crime risk, 'the rational subject of risk takes on the capacity to become skilled and knowledgeable about crime prevention and crime risks' (O'Malley, 1996: 201). The control of crime is thus situated in the continuum of normal social interaction; it remains a risk that needs to be managed in order to predict future conduct (Castel, 1991). We are most able to see the displacement of the 'dependent' subject of welfare by these neo-liberal techniques of 'responsibilization' (Garland, 1996; O'Malley, 1992) in the new rhetoric of communitarian moralism that has made such inroads into New Labour policy in a variety of fields. Community is a means (and product) of government then, one that involves an intensification of detailed knowledge about the activities of its inhabitants and a promotion of its affiliations, ties and bonds (Rose, 2000: 329).

It is important for the argument of this chapter not to overlook the fact that this kind of governance does not involve a radical, democratic, communitarian version of totally self-governing communities. Steered politically from the centre 'at a distance', this is a state-sponsored rationality of rule in which the state will continue to 'monitor' and regulate the effects of its own 'governance mechanisms' (see du Gay, 2002). Therefore, what is perhaps not quite captured through the continuing distinction that is made between the terms 'communitarian' and 'neo-liberal governance' is the fact that contemporary punishment strategies are increasingly diversified and, at the same time, 'designed in' to the flows of everyday existence (Rose, 1999b) – witness the deployment of curfews, the removal of assets from those convicted of certain categories of crime, the imprisonment of parents of children who truant. In this way, the dividing line between the criminal and the previously non-criminal is mutating, as the net catching those 'responsible' for anti-social acts, and their regulation and prevention, widens. It is precisely within this diversified crime control environment that the still-developing policies towards sexual offenders need to be situated. These, as we will see, exemplify the tendency of the administrative strategy of the state to adapt its limitations in respect of crime control. However, and this is increasingly where the category of the sex offender (perhaps apart from child-to-child homicide – see Hay, 1995) stands alone, the political arm of the state operates in denial of this by resorting to exclusionary modes of populist punitiveness, normally involving moral authoritarianism and allied to an enlarged role for the media in determining individual sentencing and penal policy (see Bottoms, 1995; Garland, 1996). It may be that the state achieves this, too, 'at a distance'; the role of the popular press, as we will see, is given explicit as well as implicit legitimation by the government.

'Punitive segregation' (Garland, 2000: 349) is supplied by a harsh rhetoric of government law and order that is fundamentally 'expressive' and symbolic, seeking to show the strength of the state and its firmness in the face of crime. In a sense it absorbs the perceived sentiments of the public for a 'tough' approach to crime from the point of view of the 'victim'. As David Garland rightly says, this represents a climate of moral fundamentalism in which 'a zero-sum policy game is assumed wherein the offender's gain is the victim's loss' (2002: 351). When imputed to the community, the moral authoritarian response is predicated characteristically on the elimination of danger and dangerous social actors. It seeks to find, uproot and expel the Other, as if it were contaminated and contaminatory. The populist approach thus speaks the language of zero-tolerance in desiring the complete eliminination of crime and thus seeks a 'pure community' (Foucault, 1977: 198) that coheres around the expelling of foreign matter.

Discourses of populist punitiveness, preoccupied with dangerous individuals who threaten community normality from the outside, run ostensibly smoothly alongside an emerging neo-liberal strategy as applied to the management of sex offenders. The latter constructs high-risk populations, grading them into differentially risky categories (Simon, 1998). Offenders are reintegrated within 'the community' but with the proviso that their movements are tracked. This project is a managerial one, in that it seeks to classify and manage groups sorted by dangerousness, rather than seeking to respond to individual deviants with the purpose of rehabilitating and treating them. It looks to map out distributions of past conduct and calculations of future conduct across the sexual offender population as a whole, using incarceration for 'incurables' where risk cannot be managed through probation. This shift to 'risk thinking' (Rose, 1998) creates a space for different forms of community involvement: a different set of relationships between the individual patho-logical person, the community and an increasingly diverse range of profes-sionals. Central to this process is the anticipation of future conduct, in which the assumption is that in any reintegration into local communities re-offence is a realistic risk and therefore knowledge of the presence of sexual offend-ers is a realistic protection against such a risk.[5]

It is notable that the UK Crime and Disorder Act of 1998, following on from the Sex Offenders Act of 1997 (see Kemshall and Maguire, 2002) pur-sues this risk assessment strategy in seeking to manage more effectively the risks posed by sex offenders once they are relocated to the community (Ashenden, 2002). It is, fundamentally, an inclusive policy – although its 'effects', by which I mean the ways it comes to be appropriated by any par-ticular community, may not be. The Notes of Guidance that accompany the Act refer to the 'danger' of unmanaged publicity, and indicate a concern that the vigilance the Act is intended to bring about and reinforce in the life of the community should not turn into vigilantism (see Ashenden, 2002: 203). The much-used metaphor of paedophiles 'going underground', and becoming lost to the control mechanisms of managed visibility, is instruc-tive here.

So, what happens when communities are called upon to participate specif-ically in the management of sex offenders and the prevention of sex offences? The stated aim of the 1998 Crime and Disorder Act with respect to sex offender orders is to protect the public from future serious harm by a sex offender.[6] Based on an assessment of present behaviour in the commu-nity, police may apply to magistrates to take out an order against any sex offender, either already cautioned or convicted, to proscribe specific behav-iours as a preventative measure (see the Crime and Disorder Act (1998) *Introductory Guide, Anti-Social Behaviour Orders*: 2).[7] Moreover, there are further developments that exemplify the model of dispersed accountability put forward by Rose (2000) and others (Kemshall and Maguire, 2002). In June 2002, the government announced that members of the public were for the first time to be given a direct role in drawing up risk assessment plans and monitoring the thousands of paedophiles and other serious criminals released from prison each year by taking a place on Multi-Agency Public Protection Panels which were to be created in each of 42 police districts in England and Wales (see Bright and Hinsliff, 2002; Kemshall and Maguire, 2002).

These regulative developments are responses to the perceived threat posed by the 'paedophile', and the target is the stranger, unknown to his vic-tims (Levi, 2000: 589).[8] The number of children under 10 who are known to have been killed by strangers is small – in the UK, up to February 1996 fewer than six children under 14 had been killed by strangers each year since 1984. Three-quarters of the perpetrators of violence against children

Cathected Identities

are parents and other relatives (CSO, 1994, 1995). These facts have been widely reported. What requires further investigation are the reasons for the widespread desire to make these facts secret and/or unthinkable – and, moreover, the effects of so doing. Indeed, sexual offenders' registers and community notification laws are underpinned by the assumption that intrafamilial offences do not threaten the 'community' (by which is meant safety in the public domain) but only the private domain of offenders' families. But a number of research studies indicate a far more complex picture of victimization and offending that traverse distinctions between extrafamilial/intrafamilial categories of offender (Cossins, 1999; Hinds and Daly, 2001: 266). Furthermore, as my case study indicates, particular communities that share histories of family abuse may have an active collective fantasy life that invokes and aggressively targets one kind of offender in order to repress the existence of another closer to home.

All government announcements accompanying this parliamentary legislation have emphasized that:

> the construction and management of risk through sexual offender orders is thus figured as appropriate vigilance in the face of potential serious harm and is counterpoised to the danger of vigilante action. (Ashenden, 2002: 207)

The announcements in 2001 and 2002 of additions to the Act were accompanied by the statement that, in spite of the campaigns led by the parents of the murderered schoolgirl Sarah Payne, uncontrolled public access to the offenders register was not to be allowed. It remains the stated belief of the Home Office that improvements to the register will increase public trust that the system can protect communities from criminals. As Ashenden has argued (2002: 206–7), what we have in this governmental discourse is a discursive opposition between sex offenders being known and manageable to the authorities (which include those in responsible positions in the community, such as head teachers, doctors, youth leaders, sports club managers, doctors), and being widely and publicly known through unmanaged publicity which would lead to vigilante action and sex offenders going 'underground'. 'Information management' – the controlled disclosure of information (that would once have been confidential) – is seen as *the* way of allaying the fears of the public.

Three weeks after an 8-year-old girl, Sarah Payne, went missing and six days after her body was found, the *News of the World* published the names, photographs and whereabouts (but not the exact addresses) of 49 male and female 'convicted paedophiles' in its regular Sunday edition and on its website, as part of a 'name and shame' campaign (23 July 2000). In doing so, the aim was to put pressure on the government to implement 'Sarah's Law', closely modelled on 'Megan's Law' in the USA.[9] Private individuals cannot be expected unknowingly to bear the risk of living among sex offenders, argued the newspaper, and therefore their demand was that parents should be given direct access to information concerning the identities and where-abouts of child sex offenders.[10] As has been shown convincingly, the *News of the World's* declaration of a meaningful distinction between vigilantism and vigilance was undermined by its own rhetoric:

> ... When one combines the claims that police monitoring of sex offenders is insufficient, that the safety of children is more important than individual rights, that this safety can only be achieved by the public naming of sex offenders, and that such offenders are evil monsters, the political and legal disqualification of child sex offenders that follows carries with it the suggestion that the only way to achieve safety is by removing such individuals, purifying the community. (Ashenden, 2002: 215)

The *News of the World*, then, made its arguments for a community notification law on an open access basis the opportunity for punitive populism.[11] It is important to note that the government and the police were ambivalent in their response to the newspaper, whose demands were not, after all, congruent with government policy (see Kemshall and Maguire, 2002: 242; Silverman and Wilson, 2002: 152–8). Governed by its populist leanings, the government seemed to do everything possible to *appear* to support the *News of the World*: David Blunkett wrote an article expressing his view that 'local people should have a say' in the management of sex offenders,[12] and, subsequent to pressure from the Home Office and the Mental Health Unit (now the Dangerous Offenders Unit), the police decided not to prosecute for the illegal procurement of images.[13] Thus the national government's response was effectively to endorse and to encourage the purging mentality of the newspaper, stopping just short of actually supporting the specific demand for wholesale community notification as represented in Sarah's Law. Indeed, the paper's 'name and shame' campaign ended because the newspaper claimed the government had agreed to consider its proposals (*News of the World*, 6 August 2000: 6).

My argument so far, then, is that recent sex offender laws, following on from the community notification statutes in the USA, and combined with the rhetoric of government and the popular press, amount to an accommodation of the populist response while at the same time implementing managerialist neo-liberal policies (Simon, 1998) that involve the vertical delayering of responsibility. Where this is significant with respect to the life of 'communities' is that it creates a fundamental ambivalence about where authority lies. The community is to be the site of governmental strategies of risk management, but is also appealed to as the source of expressions of a popular will that creates an authentic moral order by expelling badness outside its bounds.

Cathected Identities

Psychoanalytic commentary: the Paulsgrove protesters

Although there was considerable press coverage of the week-long Paulsgrove protests in July and August 2000, only a few journalists sought to gain access to the actual residents involved in order to solicit their views (Ferguson, 2001; Gillan, 2000). No other descriptions of the attitudes and mental state of the protesters exist in the public domain except for those published a little later in a book by Jon Silverman and David Wilson, *Innocence Betrayed* (2002). The latter conducted interviews with members of the Paulsgrove 'Residents Against Paedophiles' group and other residents on the estate (see Silverman and Wilson, 2002: 125–45) and it is important for our trust in the accuracy of the verbatim accounts on which my analysis is based to note that these do not conflict with the reports of serious news journalists. However, Silverman and Wilson do produce a more nuanced account that draws attention to some of the inconsistencies and misunderstandings in the world of the protesters – even though from the point of view of this chapter they treat these only as cognitive discrepancies.

My hypothesis, therefore, was developed within the context of this currently available information, and I use quotations from these sources as if they were unproblematic and trustworthy. I presume that I can 'read through' these accounts in order to gain some access, however circumscribed, to something of the state of mind of the protesters. Refraining from an engagement with epistemological issues does mean taking some things for granted, but it would be an entirely different project to study the ways in which the media represented the protesters as if this constructed them in their entirety and, moreover, it would also be self-defeating to do both simultaneously. It should be said as a further qualifying point that this case study is deliberately not media-centric; and thus does not assume that the press simply has 'effects' on the public. An implication of my argument (one there is not the space to develop here) is that punitive wishes are not just shadowy effects of a relentless, rabble-rousing media campaign. It is the allocation of agency or the attribution of direct cause to the media that poses the problem here. Our understanding of the unconscious forces impinging on public life is impoverished if it assumes a simple fit between categories or concerns expressed in public discourse and internal states of mind of individuals and groups (see Evans, 2000).

That is not to say that the media should not be held responsible for helping to incite public order offences, for there is without doubt a strong relationship between the campaigns newspapers run and the subsequent actions of individuals in their community settings, both issues to which I have already alluded. What remains in need of explanation, however, is the question of what their actions mean to the particular 'communities' and individuals who do get involved; how these may be a consequence of unconscious projections and excitations depending on the prevailing anxieties and defences at the time, which are always contingent, and bounded in this case by class, gender and geography. As in the clinical context of psychoanalytic treatment itself, an external event is understood not so much as something that has 'effects' than as something that is used in relation to predisposing factors – 'a constellation of possible underlying dynamics' (Waddell, 2002: 191). The particular strength of the Kleinian tradition, which forms the basis for my account, is the evidence it garners for the claim that the 'internal objects' created from projections and introjections are not identical with the qualities of real, external others (Hinshelwood, 1994). Accordingly, there is a dynamic link between what is real and what is fantasized; from the point of view of psychoanalysis, there is no such thing as a purely 'external' event. Moreover, where one achieves a relationship with external events in order to confirm inner reality, the result as we will see can be an extreme difficulty in distinguishing between them, which leads me to suggest that the events at Paulsgrove amounted to a quasi-psychotic episode.

What was immediately striking about the Paulsgrove protest, according to all the available accounts (Ferguson, 2001; Gillan, 2000; Silverman and Wilson, 2002), was a conspicuous presence of working-class women. Moreover, there is ample evidence that children accompanied their mothers on the marches, carrying coffins and holding placards with slogans such as: 'Don't house them, hang them' and 'Kill the paedophiles' (Silverman and Wilson, 2002: 125). It is also important to take account of the fact that, as emerged in the course of some of the interviews, many of the leading women were single parents, undertaking the burden of care for their children with the help of extended families and networks on the estate (Ferguson, 2001; Gillan, 2000; Silverman and Wilson, 2002). Furthermore, as Silverman and Wilson (2002: 128) found out in the course of their research, many of the women active in 'Residents Against Paedophiles' (RAP) identified themselves as victims because of periods in their early life when they had been sexually abused. The self-styled, if unofficial, 'leader' of RAP, Katrina Kessell, had been sexually abused as a child by her paternal grandfather, and further sexually abused when she was sent into a care home by her mother: 'I was convinced I was just getting extra affection and attention. And no, I still haven't dealt with it, and I don't think I ever will ...' (Kessell, in Ferguson, 2001: 4). She had a history of chaotic sexual partnerships, with four children by three different partners (see Ferguson, 2001). In at least one press interview during that summer, she spoke of her abuse: 'My upbringing has made it very hard to accept paedophiles in society. The problems I've had have had a terrible effect on my family. It took

Cathected Identities

a long time before I could cuddle my children' (in Gillan, 2000: 5). Kessell herself was reported to the social services after her three year-old son was found wandering naked, having escaped from her garden, near a busy road half a mile from home (Milmo, 2000: 12). At the time, Kessell was being interviewed by a television station. A (harmless) stranger rescued her child. Another member of RAP, Sharon Mills, said in an interview: 'I've got people in my own family who were abused, and I know a woman of sixty on this estate who has only just admitted that she was abused as a child' (Silverman and Wilson, 2002: 129).

There was considerable confusion in the minds of the protesters about the real 'causes' and meaning of the protests. They produced accounts that were contradicted by others, such as witnesses and those holding official positions linked to the Paulsgrove estate. Katrina Kessell claimed in interviews (Silverman and Wilson, 2002: 125) that over a period of 18 months prior to the eruption of the protests, she and others had made concerted efforts, through petitions to Portsmouth City Council, to have convicted paedophile Victor Burnett removed from the estate. However, Kessell's account was contested by the local MP Syd Rapson, a witness to the nightly protests, and her own fellow protester Sharon Mills, both of whom independently claimed that Kessell had only found out about Burnett towards the end of July 2000, when the *News of the World* published his picture, and further claimed that his name had not been mentioned to the council (Silverman and Wilson, 2002: 127, 133). Rapson verified that the only person who did know about Burnett until the beginning of August was the Director of Social Services, because he was in close contact with the monitoring activities of the police (Silverman and Wilson, 2002: 133). Kessell, however, referred also to a more generalized and informal community-based knowledge of paedophile activity on the estate over the years: she hinted that there were quite a few paedophiles that residents 'knew of' (in Silverman and Wilson, 2002: 127). As Silverman and Wilson themselves comment, this is '"knew" as in taproom gossip and innuendo rather than incontrovertible fact ... ' (2002: 127; see also Vasagar, 2000). Rapson's own view (in Silverman and Wilson, 2002: 133 and endorsed by them) about the causes of the protests was that, in part:

> People were targeting paedophiles to distract attention from the sex abuse that goes on within families here. It was a way of assuaging their own guilt. One woman who joined the mob has a son who had been arrested for sexual assault. But she said: 'Oh that's different, he's not guilty – and he's not a paedophile'.

Silverman and Wilson's observations, combined with Rapson's interpretation, bring us closer to the argument that I want now to pursue (although the latter's formulation suggests the workings of a conscious conspiracy, a view that my account inevitably complicates). My argument follows from the observation that in the minds of many of the protesters under consideration, the distinction between abuser and victim, perpetrator and innocent bystander, was fairly permeable and therefore unconsciously blurred. This can be demonstrated by paying attention to the shifting and conflicting identifications made by key protesters, arising from their history as sexually abused women, which are fundamental to the defences employed by those who have endured trauma. Evidence for this is in part provided by the generally confused and endlessly contested interpretations of the 'truth' of the events. In particular, there is a general equivocation among the protesters concerning what was to be counted on as reliable 'knowledge'. What is of particular interest from a psychoanalytic viewpoint is the deep-seated ambivalence of the protesters towards the idea that truthful information should be the prerequisite for action.

However intense this drama, or rather because of its dramatalurgical colour, all the evidence points towards the fact that it remained oddly misdirected. It was not about exactly what it seemed to be about; the primary anxiety that is being acted upon is not simply about the fear of proximate paedophiles. For the actions of the women (seven nights of violent demonstrations, intense engagement with the media, and attacks on the property of suspected paedophiles) were excessive in relation to their aims and destructive in their results. They were 'sensational' in the visceral meaning of that term: acting on the senses. It seems likely that the protests exhibited an extreme quality of acting out. One protester, Jackie Rampton, was quoted as saying, 'I can't help it but this is how I felt. Walking the streets with all the noise, I got a buzz out of it. I know it sounds really childish' (in Gillan, 2000: 5). 'Acting out' is an action in which the subject, in the grip of unconscious wishes and fantasies, relives these in the present with a sensation of immediacy, which is heightened by his or her refusal to recognize its source. In clinical treatment, acting out is coupled with 'remembering', the two being contrasting ways of bringing the past into the present. What is typical in acting out is the replacement of thought by action, implying that the impulse being acted out has never acquired conversion to verbal representation and mental processing (see Rycroft, 1968). It was Lacan's inflection that recollection does not involve merely recalling something to consciousness but also requires communication to an 'Other' by means of speech (Evans, 1996). But when the other has become 'deaf' the subject cannot convey a message to him/her in words and is forced to express the message in actions. In this regard, Katrina Kessell's words are significant: 'How else do you get noticed? How else is anyone going to listen to a common person like me? [...] At least we were being listened to, and we got something done' (in Ferguson, 2001: 2).

What is evident is how pleasurably reckless these actions were for the protagonists, and how the mutual amplification shared by the media and the anti-paedophile protesters (for whom the enjoyment of minor celebrity status meant certain 'secondary gains') merely heightened their excited, narcissistic preoccupation with their own experience. At the same time, however, Kessell was suspicious of the trustworthiness of those sections of the media that appeared to support her cause (and, it could be argued, were inseparable from her cause). Of the *News of the World*'s campaign, she told one journalist that '... they shouldn't have done it that way. I think it was all too cynical. And I don't think they checked everyone properly, which allowed mistakes, and damaged all of us' (in Ferguson, 2001: 2; see also Silverman and Wilson, 2002: 136). This statement was typical: the facts that anyone else had were to be doubted and she was suspicious even of those who might appear to be 'on her side'. Moreover, not only were some of the protesters unimpressed by the fact that as a consequence of 'mistaken identity' 'innocent' people suffered as a result of their aggression, they also exhibited a lack of empathy with them (see Gillan, 2000: 5). It appears that these protesters were at one and the same time highly 'principled' and moralistic but also operating on the edge of illegality. It is relevant to refer at this point to the insight of psychoanalyst Arthur Hyatt Williams, who spent his career treating convicted murderers. Referring to the murderous intentions of his patients, many of whom had suffered early life-threatening experiences, he argued that where persecutory anxiety (a primitive response to threat, real or imagined) is all pervasive, 'aggrievement is rampant and responsibility muted'. He goes on, 'The victim or other people are felt to bear responsibility for the persecution' (Hyatt Williams, 1998: 31). Acute anxieties about psychic survival are thus managed by projecting aspects of the self into an object that is then felt to be entrapping or suffocating.

How should we proceed to interpret the meaning of this particular acting out? Well, the overt threat as the women perceived and expressed it came from unknown men. In the specific case of Katrina Kessell and some of the other women interviewed (see Silverman and Wilson, 2002: 129) the focus on the image of unknown men was likely to be based on the disavowal of the existence of real men they had known who had abused and asserted power over them. It was more bearable to locate in an external object the bad, persecutory, internal objects than to face the conflict that occurs when one has an attachment to the person who shames and humiliates. This is a defence based on a profound splitting and projecting out of painful and disturbing aspects of themselves. Kessell did know she had been abused by someone close to her and had not consciously forgotten this; in fact she draws attention to it in the many interviews she gave to the press (see Ferguson, 2001: 2; Gillan, 2000). But it is in the nature of disavowal – a split between belief and knowledge where the former predominates – that the real danger is perceived as external nonetheless.

It is worth reflecting here on the well established literature from those who have experience of working clinically with adults sexually abused as children (see Balbernie, 1994; Summit, 1983). Where the abuser is an attachment figure, then internal disunity is a survival strategy. Common to all experiences of abuse is the feeling of being used by another person as a thing existing purely for their benefit: 'identity thus receives its ultimate disconfirmation' (Balbernie, 1994: 25). In situations where the abuser does not have his/her experience validated by a saner adult, which we can infer was the case from what was said by Kessell and her colleagues, many have argued that child victims of sexual abuse face a 'secondary trauma' in which their attempts to 'reconcile their private experiences with the realities of the outer world are assaulted by the disbelief, blame and rejection they experience from adults' (Summit, 1983: 177). It is clear, then, that those who have experienced sexual abuse are highly sensitive to claims about beliefs and accusations of lying, and therefore have a troubled attitude to the very status of knowledge.

We can now arrive at my central hypothesis concerning the protesters' state of mind and their relationship to the external world. Quite consistently, across all the interviews and accounts of her that we have, Kessell proved to be evasive and contradictory about the external origins of the 'list' of 20 'known' paedophiles that was used as the basis and justification for the protest. She told journalist Audrey Gillan that she did not personally have the alleged list of 20 paedophiles used by the protesters to find their targets, but that she kept a lot of the details of these alleged offenders 'in her head' (in Gillan, 2000: 5; see also Ferguson, 2001). She went on to say that the list was made up from the number of people who had come to her and said 'I was abused by so and so' – but she also claimed that she had seen documentary proof of the offences (Gillan, 2000: 5). She said, 'We checked them all out properly, we had people down the library looking back through the newspapers' (Hill, 2001: 3) and, more importantly, that:

> Nine times out of ten, what is brought to us is official. The stuff is read by me and other people, then we go and check with the neighbours and then we check the electoral roll and confirm the details before we go to the houses. It didn't come from the Internet. People have told me their stories and I have come away in tears a few times. (Katrina Kessell, in Gillan, 2000: 5)

However, she would later tell Silverman and Wilson that the list had been drawn up from 'word of mouth and facts gleaned from the Internet' (2002: 136). We can surmise then, that the 'list' was for Kessell and her fellow protesters an object in fantasy – functioning in a way that echoes the expectations placed on the offenders register by the government. Like a talisman, it would arm her with good, powerful knowledge that would enhance her capacity to expel the paedophile persecutor. It is significant that her fellow protester, Jackie Rampton, resigned from the protest only when she discovered that the list of paedophiles did not 'exist' (that is, had a dubious connection to reality). Of this moment of disillusionment, which she presents as something of a revelation, she said to one reporter: 'There is no list [...]. They said to me the list's all mental. I think then it did hit me what we were doing' (in Gillan, 2000: 5). The list was in their heads; it was all mental: this is a very precise image of something that has an existence only in an imaginary space, in the mind.[14] It draws attention to the existence of an internal pressure that brought about the extreme grievance they expressed. In Rampton's statement we see an acknowledgement of her shift away from her earlier position that what is perceived and thus presented in her mind must conform to that which is agreeable, to one in which she accepts the truth of what is perceived even if it is disagreeable. This is what Freud referred to as the institution of the reality principle (Freud, 1984a: 278; 1984b: 36–7).

Taking up my earlier suggestion, we could refer to many of the women's actions and their own interpretations of them in terms of splitting and paranoia. The paranoid person is significantly aggressive and provocative. In paranoia, an extensive rationalization of aggression goes together with a strong predominance of projective mechanisms, as well as attitudes of alertness towards the external environment and justified indignation (Kernberg, 1998: 87). It is reasonably certain that these women, led by the galvanizing presence of Kessell, disowned the aggressive and destructive anxieties about their own incapacities and bad inner objects from their pasts (their primary anxieties), projecting them onto the figure of the paedophile. In terms of their attitude towards the present, these incapacities, I shall go on to suggest, lie in the area of not feeling able to provide adequately for one's children or to protect them. The women made definite secondary gains (Winnicott, 1986) from putting themselves in the position of the persecuted, once they had projected all the destructiveness onto the paedophile other. It therefore involved an attempt to establish one's own innocence. Strengthened by the group, individuals achieved a position of moral rectitude that left them feeling omnipotent, arrogant and in control, thus conferring a degree of power. The secondary gain therefore provided great relief because one could feel morally superior and cleansed of guilt or self-blame.[15] What I am implying then, is that there is a set of multiple identifications that allowed the women to feel at one and the same time persecuted and aggrieved – and powerful, aggressive, even sadistic.

If we take the world of unconscious defences seriously, we will not accept at face value the presenting symptom of the acted-out drama – the drama that is designed to attract our attention. For the presented symptom – the conscious message – announces a chasmic difference between the women and the paedophile. But this may cloak the existence of an identification with the aggressor. What might the women have shared unconsciously with the paedophile that was so terrible to acknowledge that it must be cast out as belonging to the paedophile alone?

In 'Group Psychology and the Analysis of the Ego', Freud (1985 [1921]) offered some thoughts on the reasons for the hostility connected with 'details of differentiation' – what he elsewhere termed the 'narcissism of minor differences'. Vamik Volkan takes up Freud's observations to draw attention to the connection, or recognition of similarity, that forms the basis of the relationship between the projector and the particular object of that projection:

> Because the enemy, whatever realistic considerations may be involved, is a reservoir of our unwanted self- and object representations with which elements of our projections are condensed, there should be some unconscious perception of a likeness, a reverse correspondence that binds us together while alienating us. However, these externalizations and projections we have given our enemy are repugnant to us, so we disavow them and do not want to acknowledge this connection consciously. (Volkan, 1994: 99)

It seems logical therefore that our best reservoir for phenomena that are originally our own would be those things and people who resemble us or are at least familiar to us (Volkan, 1994: 105). This defence mechanism is particularly pertinent as a way of thinking about individuals who have suffered physical and sexual abuse, perhaps through generations. Identifying with or even impersonating the aggressor is a common feature of the psychic makeup of sexually abused individuals, as was pointed out very early on by Freud (Freud, 1968; see also Ferenczi, 1980 [1933]). By assuming the attributes of the aggressor or imitating his aggression, the subject may transform herself from the person threatened into the person who makes the threat (Garland, 2005). It was Ferenczi (1980 [1933]) who first showed how the aggressor, who has the 'overpowering force and authority of the adult', takes up a powerful place in the inner world of the child. The vulnerable child's assumption, in the face of betrayal by a loved adult, that s/he is being punished for being 'bad' leads to the feeling that an obvious way to be 'good' is to copy the person who terrifies him/her. Compliance – the only way the child can make sense of what is going on when the abuser is also an attachment figure – is a phenomenon often referred to in sexual abuse literature (Balbernie, 1994: 21).

Kessell acknowledged her difficulties in managing her feelings towards her children but did not link this consciously to the paedophile figure, which on a conscious level is perceived as a threat simply emanating from the external world. The fact that the women involved their (in some cases, very young) children on the marches may be regarded as an example of this, and may be analysed in terms of the concept of introjective identification. Here, the women are unconsciously identifying with the paedophile, internalizing the aggressive and sadistic attributes of the paedophile other and subsequently projecting them onto their children. In injecting their children with knowledge of the sexual aggression of men they paradoxically pass on, or redistribute, toxic knowledge to the very people they feel are most in need of protecting – their young, the 'innocent'. It is an acknowledged pattern in abusive families that children are instilled with a sense of the external world as being a dangerous place, thus projecting the danger and viciousness that lies within the home and within adult carers outwards (see Walker, 1997: 109). This means the group would be predisposed to anxiety about additional 'matter' that intrudes, that is dirty and becomes associated with them by close proximity (Douglas, 1966). In a context where chief child-carers do not feel they have the capacity or the support to bear their young children's dependency on them and difference from them, they resort, in this case, to the perverted strategy of innoculating them with a detailed knowledge of all possible harms that could come to them. There is a strong possibility that the mainly single parents comprising the protesters felt unprotected and uncertain as to how they were managing parenthood. There is evidence from the interviews that they felt inadequate to the task (Gillan, 2000) and we have seen how they were destructive in a number of ways towards their own dependants. They were struggling, too, with a public culture that, as they perceived it, was asking them to 'accept paedophiles in society' (Kessell's phrase).

In psychoanalytic terms, the individual who is prey to primitive anxieties seeks relief by projecting these anxieties into another – the earliest experience of this is of course the mother–baby dyad (see Bion, 1962, 1967). Wilfred Bion argued that if all goes well enough, the mother helps the baby to find the capacity to think by 'processing' or taking in its unbearable emotions and handing them back in a way that makes them manageable; otherwise the baby introjects dread and the terror of complete helplessness (Bion, 1988: 182). Thus the baby, through a process of projective identification, splits off and projects its intolerable experiences onto the mother, who in turn, and through a capacity for 'reverie', is able to identify with the baby's feelings. She gives significance to the infant's somatic and sensory experiences, transforming them through thinking into something that can be processed and helping the baby to integrate destructive impulses with creativity. In this way the baby can 'learn from experience' as Bion (1962) put it and can sustain her/himself in the event of a parental absence. A felt or real incapacity on behalf of the main carer, then, can leave the infant struggling with his or her feelings in an unmodified form. This leads us to the question: who will support mothers – the heads of their families – who have received failed parenting, and who are therefore unable to protect their children against their own failures and anxieties, to contain their destructive impulses?

This is a social problem, but the solutions must make sense on a psychical level. Although Winnicott's (1964) writings on the need for the mother to be contained imply a gendered division of labour, he makes it perfectly clear throughout his writings that what is most important is the *structural* condition for containment. It therefore does not follow from his theory that these positions should be dictated by gender and so any relationship might potentially be able to provide maternal containment. When Winnicott spoke of the mother and the child being encircled by the father he was referring to the need for this structure, a set of circles of containment for child-carers:

> ... the father is needed to give mother moral support, to be the backing for her authority, to be the human being who stands for the law and order which mother plants in the life of the child. [...] Indeed every woman has to speak and act with authority; but if she has to be the whole thing, and has to provide the whole of the strong or strict element in her children's lives as well as the love, she carries a big burden indeed. (Winnicott, 1964: 115)

Where there is no literal or symbolic 'father', no substitute 'Other' for the mother in conditions of single parenthood and chaotic inter-generational family histories, a healthy projective identification process is inhibited. There is in this case, therefore, no containment for single mothers' dreads, whose aggressive ideas and impulses become unsafe. On the contrary, these particular mothers are vulnerable to experiencing in a visceral way the direct impingement of a very powerful 'Other'. The 'other' in this case comprises a number of 'authorities' in the public sphere that, as we have seen, offer quite contradictory messages (managing sexual offenders via social integration or purification via expelling) about what to do with the knowledge that there are imminent threats impinging upon the capacity to conduct everyday life. This, combined with the persistence of economic, geographic and social marginalization that already makes the lives of single mothers materially precarious, merely exacerbates their mental vulnerability to extreme ways of thinking. Thus these women in this case study may well feel they have nothing to lose and much to gain (unconsciously) in forming an 'autistic' group enclosed in its own circle of defensive moral righteousness (see Ignatieff, 1994: 8).

Conclusion

The issue this chapter has sought to address is the extent to which a particular language of empowerment, responsibility and active citizenship may be mentally burdensome for, and perversely used by, particular individuals in order to form a particular community. Empowerment, along with its sister concepts such as 'responsibility', 'active citizenship' and 'initiative', has the quality of an idealization that unconsciously sets itself against a bad object that must be denigrated – in this case, 'dependency', passivity and a lack of initiative to harness knowledge in the steering of oneself. However, it may well be that these policy initiatives based on the production and exchange of information (Pratt, 1995), and which aim to allay 'fear' and involve citizens directly in the regulation of risk, have unintended consequences. In an atmosphere where the disclosure of information to 'local communities' is seen as a moral right and where the government refuses a role as the representative of external reality, the more individuals will cohere into groups which absorb government into their closed system.[16] As Michael Ignatieff has argued, in seeking to put forward the case for toleration from a liberal perspective, intolerant people are uninterested in the individuals who compose despised groups, since what they are really interested in is a more primal opposition between 'us' and 'them' (1994: 11). He makes the point that threatened or anxious individuals take a leap into collective fantasy in order to 'avoid the burden of thinking for themselves or even thinking of themselves as individuals'. The perpetrators of intolerant acts are involved in procedures of abstraction in which there is an unconsidered fusion of personal and group identity (1994: 11) – an abstraction which of course they also project onto individual paedophiles who become the members of a despised and hounded group. Those susceptible to collective fantasy are often individuals, such as those in Paulsgrove, who may feel that the boundaries of their private existence are too permeable and will not withstand violent disruption and change coming from their own internal pressures and conflicts, let alone from without. Knowledge presented as 'empowering' to a community, even if presented as dry and neutral, can easily become the object of a cathexis by that community. But what are communities supposed to do with knowledge that is presented to them in the spirit of the co-production of community safety?

No one discusses the state of mind that is required to deal with this knowledge, or the quality of the emotional resources that will be brought to bear upon it, or the ways in which it might turn out to be impractical.

Those taking a psychoanalytic approach will be bound to point out that this question cannot be satisfactorily answered without paying attention to the internal relationship they create with that knowledge and therefore what community members feel about this knowledge. Responsibilization desires a politics of presence that seeks to make everything transparent. From the perspective of neo-liberal programmes of governance that seek to responsibilize, information management involving community input is seen as the long-term key to managing the safety of communities with respect to sexual offenders post-prison. At the same time, the 'community' is pressured – both by government and the media – into manifesting idealizing norms based on expelling dangerous matter, matter that originates from outside the community. What results is something of an illusion. In the hands of one particularly vulnerable and ill-resourced community, lacking both the social capital and psychical resources for containment, 'knowledge', in this case in the form of a 'list', may assume a talismanic quality that becomes the justification for instantaneous cathartic action, providing those in the know with a sense of omnipotent preparedness.

For the Paulsgrove 'list' was, as we have seen, invented by a community in the grip of a quasi-psychotic episode. Although it was based almost entirely on unsubstantiated rumour, it incited feelings of curiosity, self-righteousness and perverse forms of identification (see Bion, 1967). The imaginary list mimicked the real, official, sexual offenders' register, one that is perceived – by the government, police, and other authorities – as having the potential to offer a literal index of the location of dangerous, unknown men. But whereas the former could be used to satisfy a desire for action, the knowledge contained in the official register was regarded as frustratingly providing only half-knowledge because access to it was restricted; hence the support by most of the protesters for 'Sarah's Law'.[17] As a self-styled anti-paedophile campaigner in Los Angeles put it, when justifying his creation of an open access website on which he posted the names of his county's most dangerous sex offenders: 'When they [the authorities] keep that information under lock and key in police stations, thousands of men will be getting closer to children' (in Riccardi and Leeds, 1997: 14). The Paulsgrove events thus represent one manifestation of a community mobilizing itself in the name of a strategy to govern at a distance.

From the perspective of the group life of a particular community, it may be impossible to recognize that the intention of the authorities (whether they go so far as to implement unrestricted access or not) is to use information as a way of defending against the toxic potential of dangerous individuals. But information does not always function, as it is intended to, as administration without emotion. As we have seen, access to information does not necessarily have the effect of containing adults in such a way that enhances their capacity to act as good-enough parents. Instead, through a number of complex identifications, it can become a passport to an impulsive acting-out of unacknowledged bad objects.

An idea – in this case, that individuals should take on responsibility for the safety of their communities – inevitably will become appropriated by a particular community and infused with unpredictable kinds of projected meaning. The distinction between vigilance and vigilantism, then, is highly amenable to elision or confusion in the circumstances under consideration in this chapter. The particular (adult) community under consideration here was, for a number of reasons to do with the pasts of its individual members, vulnerable to collective fantasy, fearful of its own dependency needs, and in

Cathected Identities

need of social containment. In response to the protesters, Portsmouth City Council has run a 'keep safe' programme in local schools, and has launched council-funded child protection awareness sessions (Hill, 2001) as well as a neighbourhood civilian warden scheme (Bennetto, 2000: 11). Although no doubt well intentioned and perhaps effectual in the short term, this kind of policy response seems only to endorse the massive projections born of collective paranoia and a group assumption that the 'problem' is indeed what everyone consciously deems it to be.

Psychoanalysis uniquely, I think, offers another picture, one that indicates how the regulative methods now being used may exacerbate rather than allay public anxiety about the management of sexual offenders for particular parts of the population. 'Responsibilization' strategies are predicated on the assumptions that trust is increased when the differences between officials and laypersons are diminished and that particular communities have the emotional and cognitive capacities to be responsible. The broader implication is to draw attention to the deleterious consequences that follow when government colludes with the disowned, unwanted and often persecutory feeling states of distressed citizens instead of taking on some of the responsibility for containing and modifying them.

Notes

1   Silverman and Wilson usefully compare the working-class protests at Paulsgrove with the methods a middle-class group in London used to conduct a campaign against paedophiles (2002: 137–45).
2   In the late nineteenth century, Gustav le Bon made one of the first links between the group (for him 'the crowd') and the need to act, born of a sense of unreflecting moral rectitude: 'We have shown that crowds do not reason, that they accept or reject ideas as a whole, that they tolerate neither discussion nor contradiction, and that the suggestions brought to bear on them invade the entire field of their understanding and tend at once to transform themselves into acts' (cited in Freud, 1985: 103).
3   Namely, *The News of the World*, whose editor Rebekah Wade headlined its name-and-shame campaign 'Everyone in Britain has a child sex offender living within one mile of their home' (23 July 2000: 1).
4   A paper issued to accompany the Guidance Notes for the Crime and Disorder Act 1998 (Ekblom, 1998: 5), setting out a conceptual role for the development of professional discipline within the context of community safety, states: 'The professional preventer may directly intervene in the chain of cause and effect leading to the criminal event ... But more often, the professional's role is to *act at a distance* – to motivate, inform and assist other, more informal, preventers (such as families, teachers or site managers) to implement it (emphasis added).
5   As a recent analysis by Ron Levi indicates courts in the USA that have upheld the constitutionality of community notification statutes modelled on Megan's Law have assumed that 'any harm that community notification may cause to an individual registrant is generally said not to be attributable to ... the state'

(2000: 585). These actions are regarded as 'private harms' since they stem from the actions of private individuals (who have acted on the information released to them) and the state is therefore not held to be responsible for the 'misuse' of information released.

6   This should be understood in the context of the lack of political will in meeting what are in any case low targets for therapeutic treatment programmes in prisons (see Kemshall and Maguire, 2002: 241; Vallely, 2002).

7   For a detailed analysis of the orders from a governance perspective, see Ashenden, 2002.

8   In the USA, sexual predator laws attempt to target those who are likely to pose a threat to community safety, which therefore discursively excludes those whose victims are their own children or intimates. Sexual predator designates both a type of law and a type of person. Whereas 'psychopath' is a psychological term and thus describes mental disease diagnosable and potentially treatable by medical experts, the concept of the 'sexual predator' that emerged in the 1990s has no medical definition and refers to someone who is believed to suffer from a disorder that is untreatable. As Simon (1998) suggests, sexual predators are monsters conjured up from images of evil and thus are an embodiment of the 'limits of science to know or to change people' (Simon, 1998: 467).

9   The populist tone of Sarah's Law, like Megan's Law in the USA, is readily apparent in its timing and nomenclature. Personalizing a law in this way is metonymic. One is forced to confront Sarah's presence: it stands in for her and as such seems to bear the weight of public outrage. Being against the law is to be 'against Sarah', an attack on her being. See Simon (1998: 463).

10 The *News of the World* also asked for unlimited sentences for the worst cases of what it terms 'sexual predators', based on its opinion that child sex offenders cannot be cured and that incapacitation is the only way to prevent re-offending.

11 The reproduction of criminal photographic portraits was probably the most potent weapon the newspaper had and was a central contributing element to the elision in the media between vigilance and vigilantism. When police identity photographs appear in a national newspaper the reader is confronted with an image of individual dangerousness; the sexual offender is interpolated as an individual threat to them and their loved ones, one whose dangerousness is an immanent property of his person. However, in the context of the police database, the extent to which each portrait signifies dangerousness is merely contingent upon a distribution of categories of riskiness across a whole population.

12 *News of the World* (16 December 2001: 6).

13 A series of confidential e-mails seen by the BBC's Home Affairs correspondent Jon Silverman (discussed subsequently in Silverman and Wilson, 2002: 152–8) indicated that the government was so alarmed about the violence that it considered applying for an injunction against the *News of the World* on the grounds that it had made unauthorized use of information culled from files held by the Scout Association. Evidence had been collated by Acpo and Acops in August 2000 of concrete evidence that the work of the probation service was being impeded by the publications and that sex offenders were going underground and breaking their licence conditions – evidence that would be required for a court case to proceed. However, concerned about the political dimensions, in short an expected outcry about attempts to 'gag the press', the Home Office decided not to follow this path.

14 Freud says, paraphrasing le Bon, that 'groups have never thirsted after truth. They demand illusions and cannot do without them. They constantly give what

is unreal precedence over what is real; they are almost as strongly influenced by what is untrue as by what is true. They have an evident tendency not to distinguish between the two' (1985 [1921]: 107).

15 This is largely how the *News of the World*'s campaign worked – through a dictatorial assertion of its own righteousness and a furious hatred of anyone in doubt as to what constitutes truth. For instance, a headline the day after Roy Whiting was convicted (16 December 2000: 11), reads:

> Q: *Would you want to be told if a predatory paedophile lived next door to you?*
> A: *If you say Yes then you back Sarah's Law. If you say No then you are a LIAR.*

16 See David Levine's illuminating (2000) discussion of the psychical relationships between communities, citizens and government.

17 It is quite simply wishful thinking that the provision of knowledge, quite specific knowledge of individually named sexual offenders whose address is known, will be enough to protect a child. But it is this idea that is used to justify responsibilization strategies in general and community notification laws in particular (see Levi, 2000: 582).

References

Ashenden, S. (2002) 'The contemporary governance of paedophilia', *Cultural Values: Journal for Cultural Research*, 6(1/2): 197–222.

Balbernie, R. (1994) 'There is no such thing as an abused child – but there is a phantom hybrid of the mind', *British Journal of Psychotherapy*, 11(1): 20–31.

Bennetto, J. (2000) 'Wardens to patrol Paulsgrove Estate', *Independent*, 19 September, p. 11.

Bion, W.R. (1962) *Learning From Experience*. London: Heinemann. (Reprinted London: Karnac Books, 1984.)

Bion, W.R. (1967) 'On arrogance', in *Second Thoughts*. London: Heinemann, pp. 93–100.

Bion, W.R. (1988) 'A theory of thinking', in E. Bott Spillius (ed.), *Melanie Klein Today*. London: Routledge, pp. 178–86.

Bottoms, A. (1995) 'The philosophy and politics of punishment and sentencing', in C. Clarkson and R. Morgan (eds), *The Politics of Sentencing Reform*. Oxford: Oxford University Press, pp. 17–49.

Bright, M. and Hinsliff, G. (2002) 'Public to help with paedophile checks', *Observer*, 18 August, p. 8.

Castel, R. (1991) 'From dangerousness to risk', in G. Burchell, C. Gordon and P. Miller (eds), *The Foucault Effect: Studies in Governmentality*. Hemel Hempstead: Harvester Wheatsheaf, pp. 281–98

Cooper, A. and Lousada, J. (2005) *Borderline Welfare: Feeling and Fear of Feeling in Modern Welfare*. London: Karnac.

Cossins, A. (1999) 'A reply to the NSW Royal Commission Inquiry into paedophilia: victim report studies and child sex offender profiles – a bad match?', *Australian and New Zealand Journal of Criminology*, 32(1): 42–60.

Craib, I. (1998) *Experiencing Identity*. London: Sage.

Crawford, A. (1998) 'Community safety and the question for security: holding back the dynamics of social exclusion', *Policy Studies*, 19(3/4): 237–53.

Crime and Disorder Act (1998) 'Anti-Social Behaviour Orders and Sex Offenders Orders – Guidance', pp. 1–22. Available at http://www.homeoffice.gov.uk/ cdact/soo.htm

CSO (1994) *Social Focus on Children*. London: HMSO.

CSO (1995) *Social Trends* 25. London: HMSO.

Donzelot, J. (1979) 'The poverty of political culture', *Ideology and Consciousness*, 5: 71–86.

Donzelot, J. (1991) 'The mobilization of society', in G. Burchell, C. Gordon and P. Miller (eds), *The Foucault Effect: Studies in Governmentality*. Hemel Hempstead: Harvester Wheatsheaf, pp. 169–80.

Douglas, M. (1966) *Purity and Danger*. London: Routledge & Kegan Paul.

Du Gay, P. (2002) 'A common power to keep them all in awe: a comment on governance', *Cultural Values: Journal for Cultural Research*, 6(1): 11–27.

Ekblom, P. (1998) 'Community safety and the reduction and prevention of crime – a conceptual framework for training and the development of a professional discipline', Home Office Offenders and Corrections Unit, pp. 1–14. Available at http://www.homeoffice.gov.uk/cdact/cstrng5.htm

Evans, D. (1996) *Introductory Dictionary of Lacanian Analysis*. London: Routledge.

Evans, J. (2000) 'Psychoanalysis and psychosocial relations: introduction', in P. du Gay, J. Evans and P. Redman (eds), *Identity: A Reader*. London: Sage, pp. 121–9.

Ferenczi, S. (1980 [1933]) 'Confusion of tongues between adults and the child: the language of tenderness and passion', in *Final Contributions to the Problems and Methods of Psycho-Analysis*. New York: Brunner/Mazel, pp. 117–67.

Ferguson, E. (2001) 'The unrepentant vigilante', *Observer*, 4 February. Available at http://www.society.guardian.co.uk/children/story/0,1074,536871,00.html

Foucault, M. (1977) *Discipline and Punish*. London: Penguin.

Freud, A. (1968) *The Ego and the Mechanisms of Defence*. London: The Hogarth Press and The Institute of Psycho-Analysis.

Freud, S. (1984a [1920]) 'Beyond the pleasure principle', in *On Metapsychology: The Theory of Psychoanalysis*. (Penguin Freud Volume 11). Harmondsworth: Penguin, pp. 275–338.

Freud, S. (1984b [1911]) 'Formulations on the two principles of mental functioning', in *On Metapsychology: The Theory of Psychoanalysis* (Penguin Freud Volume 11). Harmondsworth: Penguin, pp. 35–44.

Freud, S. (1985 [1921]) 'Group psychology and the analysis of the ego', in *Civilisation, Society and Religion* (Penguin Freud Volume 12). Harmondsworth: Penguin, pp. 95–178.

Garland, C. (2005) 'Trauma and the possibility of recovery', in S. Budd and R. Rusbridger (eds), *Introducing Psychoanalysis*. London: Routledge, pp. 246–62.

Garland, D. (1996) 'The limits of the sovereign state: strategies of crime control in contemporary society', *British Journal of Criminology*, 36(4): 445–71.

Garland, D. (2000) 'The culture of high crime societies: some preconditions of recent law and order policies', *British Journal of Criminology*, 40: 347–75.

Garland, D. (2002) *The Culture of Control: Crime and Social Order in Contemporary Society*. Oxford: Oxford University Press.

Gillan, A. (2000) 'Chorus of fear and loathing swells in the streets of a latterday salem', *Guardian*, 12 August, p. 5.

Gilling, D. and Barton, A. (1997) 'Crime prevention and community safety: a new home for social policy?', *Critical Social Policy*, 17(1): 63–83.

Grose, Captain Francis (1796) *A Classical Dictionary of the Vulgar Tongue*. London: C. Chappel. (Quotation from later version (1811), *A Dictionary of Buckish Slang, University Wit and Pickpocket Eloquence*. Available at: http://www.webroots.org/library/usamic/dotvt000.html, p. 30.)

Cathected Identities

Hay, C. (1995) 'Mobilization through interpellation: James Bulger, juvenile crime and the construction of a moral panic', *Social and Legal Studies*, 4(2): 197–223.

Hill, D. (2001) 'After the purge', *Guardian*, 6 February. Available at http://www.society.guardian.co.uk/Archive/Article/0,4273,4131392.00.html

Hinds, L. and K. Daly (2001) 'The war on sex offenders: community notification in perspective', *Australian and New Zealand Journal of Criminology*, 34(3): 256–76.

Hinshelwood, R.D. (1994) *Clinical Klein*. London: Free Association.

Hoggett, P. (2005) 'A service to the public', in P. du Gay (ed.), *The Values of Bureacracy*. Oxford: OUP, pp. 167–91.

Hollway, W. and Jefferson, T. (2000a) 'The role of anxiety in fear of crime', in T. Hope and R. Sparks (eds), *Crime, Risk and Insecurity: Law and Order in Everyday Life and Political Discourse*. London: Routledge, pp. 31–49.

Hollway, W. and Jefferson, T. (2000b) *Doing Qualitative Research Differently: Free Association, Narrative and the Interview Method*. London: Sage.

Hughes, G. and Edwards, A. (eds) (2002) *Crime Control and Community: The New Politics of Public Safety*. London: Willan.

Hyatt Williams, A. (1998) *Cruelty, Violence, and Murder: Understanding the Criminal Mind*. London: Karnac.

Ignatieff, M. (1994) 'Nationalism and the narcissism of minor differences'. Text of a lecture given at The Open University to inaugurate the Pavis Centre for Sociological and Social Anthropological Studies, October, pp. 1–14.

Johnson, L. (1996) 'What is vigilantism?', *British Journal of Criminology*, 36(2): 220–35.

Kemshall, H. and Maguire, M. (2002) 'Public Protection, partnership and risk penality: the multi-agency risk management of sexual and violent offenders', *Punishment and Society*, 3(2): 237–64.

Kernberg, O. (1998) 'Paranoid social developments as a consequence of ideological and bureaucratic regression', in J.H. Berke, S. Pierides, A. Sabbatini and S. Schneider (eds), *Even Paranoids Have Enemies: New Perspectives on Paranoia and Persecution*. London: Routledge, pp. 87–99.

Levi, R. (2000) 'The mutuality of risk and community: the adjudication of community notification statutes', *Economy and Society*, 29(4): 578–601.

Levine, D.P. (2000) 'Closed systems, social symptoms, and social change', *JPCS Journal for the Psychoanalysis of Culture and Society*, 5(1): 28–40.

Milmo, C. (2000) 'Anti-paedophile leader is reported for child neglect', *Independent*, 12 August, p. 12.

News of the World (2000) 'Named Shamed; NOW campaign; For Sarah Campaign against paedophiles', *News of the World*, 23 July.

New of the World (2000) 'You spoke, now they are all listening; For Sarah Campaign against paedophiles', *News of the World*, 6 August.

O'Malley, P. (1992) 'Risk, power, and crime prevention', *Economy and Society*, 25(2): 252–75.

O'Malley, P. (1996) 'Risk and responsibility', in A. Barry, T. Osborne and N. Rose (eds), *Foucault and Political Reason*. London: UCL Press, pp. 189–207.

Pratt, J. (1995) 'Dangerousness, risk and technologies of power', *Australian and New Zealand Journal of Criminology*, 29(3): 236–54.

Riccardi, N. and Leeds, J. (1997) 'Inside America: "Megan's Law" goes on-Line as abusers' names posted on Internet', *Guardian*, 19 August, p. 14.

Riddell, M. (2000) 'Salem comes to Portsmouth', *Observer*, 13 August. Available at: http://www.observer.co.uk/comment/story/0,6903,353728,00. html

Riddell, M. (2002) 'Shun this mob of pariahs', *Observer*, 25 August, p. 24.

Rose, N. (1998) 'Governing risky individuals: The role of psychiatry in new regimes of control', *Psychiatry, Psychology and Law*, 5(2): 1–19.

Rose, N. (1999a) 'Inventiveness in politics', *Economy and Society*, 28(3): 467–93.

Rose, N. (1999b) *Powers of Freedom: Reframing Political Thought*. Cambridge: CUP.

Rose, N. (2000) 'Government and control', *British Journal of Criminology*, 40(2): 321–39.

Rycroft, C. (1968) *A Critical Dictionary of Psychoanalysis*. Harmondsworth: Penguin Books.

Silverman, J. and Wilson, D. (2002) *Innocence Betrayed: Paedophilia, the Media and Society*. Oxford: Polity.

Simon, J. (1998) 'Managing the monstrous: sex offenders and the new penology', *Psychology, Public Policy and Law*, 4(1/2): 455–67.

Summit, R.C. (1983) 'The Child Sexual Abuse Accommodation Syndrome', *Child Abuse and Neglect*, 7: 177–93.

Sunday Herald (2000) 'The shame and danger of publicity-stunt journalism', 6 August.

Vallely, P. (2002) 'Child sex offenders: how one clinic managed to curb the deviance of paedophiles', *Independent*, 5 July, p. 5.

Vasagar, J. (2000) 'Paedophile list used to settle scores', *Guardian*, 15 August. Available at http://www.guardian.co.uk/Archive/Article

Volkan, V.D. (1994) *The Need to Have Enemies and Allies: From Clinical Practice to International Relations*. New Jersey: Jason Aronson.

Waddell, M. (1989) 'Living in two worlds: psychodynamic theory and social work practice', *Free Associations*, 15: 11–35.

Waddell, M. (2002) 'The psychodynamics of bullying', *Free Associations*, 9(2) (No. 50): 189–210.

Walker, M. (1997) 'Working with abused clients', in E. Smith (ed.), *Integrity and Change: Mental Health in the Marketplace*. London: Routledge, pp. 99–113.

Winnicott, D.W. (1964) 'What about father?' in *The Child, the Family and the Outside World*. Harmondsworth: Penguin, pp. 113–18.

Winnicott, D.W. (1986) 'Delinquency as a sign of hope', in *Home is Where We Start From*. Harmondsworth: Penguin.

11

Psy-Art: Re-Imagining Identity

Janet Sayers

'Men make their own history, but not of their own free will; not under circumstances they themselves have chosen but under the given and inherited circumstances with which they are directly confronted' (Marx, 1973[1852]: 146). Women and men, and children too, are likewise makers of their own identities, but not in circumstances of their own choosing. We can use psychoanalysis and art, or 'psy-art', as Jacques Lacan did, to conceptualize this process of identity-formation as effect of imposition on us of the past and present social order – Lacan called it 'patriarchy' – so that, to use Marx's words again, '[t]he tradition of the dead generations weighs like a nightmare on the minds of the living' (Marx, 1973[1852]: 146). Or we can use psy-art, as I will in the second part of this chapter, to re-imagine identity-formation as a two-way process between others and ourselves. We could call it a work of genius which, says Kristeva, 'culminates in the birth of a subject' (Kristeva, 2001a[1999]: x).

Imposing identities

How did Lacan use psy-art to theorize identity formation? In doing so he was undoubtedly influenced in his account of it being structured by the imposition of patriarchy, mediated to us by others, by Salvador Dali's celebration of artists imposing their interpretation of reality on their public. Identity-formation examples include his self-portrait, *The Great Masturbator* (1929), making us see his profile, a horse, a woman, a man's torso, and a host of other things that he interprets and imposes on the viewer to see. Interpretation, particularly self-interpretation, was his driving ambition. After reading Freud's *The Interpretation of Dreams* in Madrid in the early 1920s, he confessed to becoming 'obsessed with the vice of self-interpretation – not just of my dreams but of everything that happened to me, however accidental it might at first seem' (in Martínez-Herrera et al., 2003: 855). In 1924 the surrealist artist, André Breton, recommended his fellow-artists to adopt Freud's free association method as a means of inspiring their art in a rebellion against the tradition of the art of their time. Dali advocated also using the freedom afforded by the ambiguous meanings or 'double image' of visual imagery. 'I believe the moment is at hand when', he declared, 'by a paranoiac and active advance of the mind, it will be possible (simultaneously with automatism and other passive states) to systematize confusion and thus help to discredit completely the world of reality' (in Lippard, 1970: 97). 'Paranoia', he explained, 'uses the external world in order to assert its dominating idea and has the disturbing characteristic of making others accept this idea's reality'. It uses the external world for 'illustration and proof', he said, 'and so comes to serve the reality of our mind' (in Lippard, 1970: 98).

Dali illustrated his 'double image' and 'paranoia-criticism' method with his painting, *Invisible Sleeping Woman* (1930), in which he makes the viewer see a horse, a woman, a lion, or other figures, 'limited', he said, 'only by the mind's degree of paranoiac capacity' (in Lippard, 1970: 98). Another example was his painting, *The Stinking Ass* (1928), which can be seen, he said, 'covered with thousands of flies and ants' or as 'the hard and blinding flash of new gems'. Artists can thus shape and determine our wishes and desires, make us 'desire ideal objects', he said, and thus bring about 'the imminent crisis of consciousness' (in Lippard, 1970: 99,100).

Lacan was impressed. After reading Dali's 'stinking ass' article, published in July 1930, he phoned him to arrange a meeting. He too was studying paranoid impositions on reality. His translation of Freud's (1922) essay on paranoia was published in 1931. The same year he defended his dissertation on the case of a 38-year-old paranoid patient, Marguerite Pantaine-Anzieu, whom he called Aimée in his dissertation, and who he first examined on 18 June 1931, following her hospitalization in Sainte-Anne after stabbing an actress, Huguette Duflos. Her paranoia was the effect of imposing and displacing hatred of her mother onto one of her sisters, onto a close woman friend whose mother knew the actress, Sarah Bernhardt, and then onto Bernhardt's actress friend, Duflos. Questioned by the police after stabbing Duflos, Marguerite explained that Duflos had been spreading malicious rumours about her. She had to look her in the eye, she said. Otherwise Duflos might think ill of her for not defending Marguerite's 7-year-old son from her. That was why she had gone to the theatre where Duflos worked. That was why she had stabbed her. After writing up this case, and its resolution through the intervention of the law in punishing Marguerite, after which her delusional imposition and identification of her hateful image of her mother with Duflos waned, Lacan went on to write more about paranoia, including two articles published in the 1934 volume of the surrealist journal, *Le Minotaure*: 'The problem of style and the psychiatric conception of paranoiac forms of experience' and 'Motivations of paranoid crime: the crime of the Papin sisters'.

Why is it, though, that an actress, in the case of Marguerite's paranoid obsession with Duflos, and celebrities more generally, can cause us to misidentify and impose what we feel for others – hatred in the case of

Marguerite – on what is given to us to identify with by external social reality? Describing the developmental origins of just such outwardly-determined mis-identification, Lacan pointed out (as follows) examples of this occurring in early childhood:

> One need but listen to the stories and games made up by two to five year olds, alone or together, to know that pulling off heads and cutting open bellies are spontaneous themes of their imagination, which the experience of a busted-up doll merely fulfills. (Lacan, 2006a[1948]: 85)

Bosch, with interest in his paintings having been revived by surrealist artists in the 1920s, shows us similar images. 'One must leaf through a book of Hieronymus Bosch's work, including views of whole works as well as details, to see an atlas of all the aggressive images that torment mankind', Lacan noted, adding:

> The prevalence that psychoanalysis has discovered among them of images based on a primitive autoscopy of the oral organs and organs derived from the cloaca is what gives rise to the shapes of the demons in Bosch's work. Even the ogee of the *angustiae* of birth can be found in the gates to the abyss through which they thrust the damned; and even narcissistic structure may be glimpsed in the glass spheres in which the exhausted partners of the "Garden of Delights" are held captive. (Lacan, 2006a: 85–6)

The same phantasmagorias occur in the dreams of analysands when their analysis, wrote Lacan, 'appears to reflect off the backdrop of the most archaic fixations'. An example was a patient who saw himself in a dream in a car with a woman with whom he was having a difficult love affair. They were pursued, said Lacan, 'by a flying-fish, whose balloon-like body was so transparent that one could see the horizontal level of liquid it contained: an image of vesical persecution of great anatomical clarity' (Lacan, 2006a[1948]: 86).

'After the repeated failures encountered by classical psychology in its attempt to account for the mental phenomena known as "images"', he argued, 'psychoanalysis proved itself capable of accounting for the concrete reality they represent … because it began with their formative function in the subject' (Lacan, 1948: 85). Particularly important in this respect, he maintained, were the child analysis findings of Melanie Klein. Referring to an article in which she depicted a 10-year-old analysand Richard's drawings of the advance of the German empire across Europe during the Second World as representing his and his father's and brother's advance into his mother's body (Klein, 1975b[1945]), Lacan said:

> through her [Klein] we have the mapping, drawn by children's own hands, of the mother's inner empire, and the historical atlas of the internal divisions in which the images of the father and siblings – whether real or virtual – and the subject's own voracious aggression dispute their deleterious hold over her sacred regions. (Lacan, 1948:)

Klein, he added, enables us to see the outward, inverse image – '*Urbild*' – of the self in bits and pieces which makes so attractive the identification of ourselves with others as ideal and whole (Lacan, 2006a[1948]: 93–4).

In mistakenly identifying with bits and pieces of the mother's body, the latter may serve as images of ourselves as 'a mosaic structure like that of a stained-glass window' (1953: 13), said Lacan. It may resemble 'a jig-saw puzzle, with the separate parts of the body of a man or an animal in disorderly array' (1953: 13). Bosch makes us see this too with his paintings featuring

> the incongruous images in which disjointed limbs are rearranged as strange trophies; trunks cut up in slices and stuffed with the most unlikely fillings, strange appendages in eccentric positions, reduplications of the penis, images of the cloaca represented as a surgical excision, often accompanied in male patients by fantasies of pregnancy. (Lacan, 1953: 13)

If these are the images through which our identity is first formed then no wonder, Lacan observed, 'the jubilant interest shown by the infant over eight months at the sight of his own image in a mirror'. For it provides and imposes an image and identity which is whole and thus particularly seductive to the infant given the 'organic disturbance and discord', as Lacan put it, and 'the image of the "body in bits and pieces"' with which it begins (Lacan, 1953: 14,15).

'In comparison with the still very profound lack of coordination in his own motor functioning', Lacan explained, the image of another – like 'the visual gestalt of his own body' in the mirror – serves as 'an ideal unity, a salutary imago', its value, he added, 'heightened by all the early distress resulting from the child's intra-organic and relational discordance during the first six months of life, when he bears the neurological and humoral signs of a physiological prematurity at birth'. It is the toddler's confusion of its feelings with those reflected to it by others that accounts for the early appearance of in-feeling empathy, '*Einfühlung*', of the fact that, at this age, '[a] child who beats another child says that he himself was beaten', or, as Lacan also put it, 'a child who sees another child fall, cries' (Lacan, 2006a[1948]: 92). As further evidence he quoted St Augustine recalling in his *Confessions*: 'I myself have seen and known an infant to be jealous even though it could not speak. It became pale, and cast bitter looks on its foster-brother'. St Augustine thereby located, Lacan commented, 'spectacular absorption (the child absorbed), the emotional reaction (pale), and the reactivation of images of primordial frustration (with an envenomed look)' as 'psychical and somatic coordinates of the earliest aggressiveness' (Lacan, 2006a[1948]: 93).

Seduced into a mistaken identification with what is imposed on or given us by others to see is the pre-condition of our likewise mistakenly identifying ourselves with the first person pronoun, 'I', of the language into which we are born and live. We should call it the 'ideal-I', said Lacan. Equated by the infant with its mirror image, it appears, he states, 'as the contour of his stature that freezes it and in a symmetry that reverses it, in opposition to the turbulent movements with which the subject feels he animates it' (Lacan, 2006b[1949]: 76). Writing about the after-life in adults of the allure exercised on the infant of misidentifying itself with its mirror image as ego or I, Lacan wrote:

> the *I* formation is symbolized in dreams by a fortified camp, or even a stadium – distributing, between the arena within its walls and its outer border of gravel-pits and marshes, two opposed fields of battle where the subject bogs down in his quest for the proud, remote inner castle whose form (sometimes juxtaposed in the same scenario) strikingly symbolizes the id. (Lacan, 2006b[1949]: 78)

Lacan thereby sought to illuminate the split introduced into identity – between the id and ego – by the seductive and imposing allure of identifying with socially-given symbols and images.

Perhaps he intended to say this in his talk, 'The Mirror Phase', to the International Congress of Psychoanalysis in Marienbad in August 1936. But he left after Ernest Jones interrupted him ten minutes after his talk began, and it was never published. The following July, Salvador Dali showed Freud his painting, *The Metamorphosis of Narcissus* (1937). '[I]f one looks for some time, from a slight distance and with a certain "absent-minded intentness"', Dali explained, 'at the hypnotically motionless figure of Narcissus, it gradually disappears until it becomes absolutely invisible' (in Descharnes, 1962: 222). Freud was evidently impressed. Thanking Stefan Zweig for introducing Dali to him, he wrote:

> I had been tempted to regard the Surrealists, who have apparently chosen me as their patron saint, as complete madmen (let us say 95 percent, like "absolute" alcohol). The young Spaniard, with his candid fanatic's eyes and his undeniable technical mastery, has impelled me to reconsider my opinion. It would in fact be quite interesting to study the genesis of a painting of this kind analytically. (in Roudinesco, 1997[1993]: 34)

He had been puzzled by why – although the first objects attracting the infant's desire are, for instance, its mother's breast, its feces, and penis, so that, he said, 'a unity comparable to the ego cannot exist in the individual from the start' – as adults these 'love objects' can become unified into narcissistic self-love (Freud, 1914: 77, 87). How, Freud asked, does this come about?

How, furthermore, we might ask, do we become severed from what Dali called the 'death and fossilization' involved in narcissistically identifying with our mirrored reflection (in Descharnes, 1962: 166)? Marguerite was severed from paranoid identification with Duflos by the intervention of the law. More generally, Lacan argued, we are severed from paralyzing identification with what we is imposed on us to identify with by the others as mediators of the imposition on us of the patriarchal social order in which, according to the anthropologist, Claude Levi-Strauss, people have always and everywhere lived. A central image or symbol of this order is the phallus. 'The whole problem of the perversions', argued Lacan, combining Levi-Strauss's structuralist anthropology with his psy-art theorization of identity, 'consists in conceiving how the child, in its relationship with its mother … identifies with the imaginary object of her desire insofar as the mother herself symbolizes it in the phallus' (Lacan, 2006a[1955–56]: 462–3). The mother or father or others thus impose and determine, through the phallic imagery of their objects of desire, the desires of the toddler and infant. 'If the mother's desire is for the phallus', Lacan said of this determination of the child's desire by patriarchy, 'the child wants to be the phallus in order to satisfy her desire' (Lacan, 2006b[1958a]: 582). It only becomes severed from paralyzing and ossifying identification with the mother's phallic object of desire by the intervention of others, by the father, for instance, imposing his law, saying as it were 'No, you won't sleep with your mother' and to the mother 'No, the child is not your phallus, I have it' (Benvenuto and Kennedy, 1986: 134).

But it is not only parents who impose images and symbols ordained by patriarchy so as to determine our identities and desires. So too do artists. Lacan illustrated the point as regards the transformation from medieval feudalism to bourgeois individualism with Holbein's painting, *The Ambassadors* (1533). He pointed out the seductive wealth of the objects and the garments of the men Holbein depicts. Most of all he emphasized the painting's large enigmatic image which suggests, he said, 'that loaf composed of two books which Dali was once pleased to place on the head of an old woman' (Lacan, 1979[1973]: 88). Referring perhaps to Dali's painting, *The Persistence of Memory* (1931), Lacan added that the image suggested 'Dali's paintings of soft watches, whose signification is obviously less phallic', he added, 'than that of the object depicted in flying position in the foreground of this picture [*The Ambassadors*]' (Lacan, 1979[1973]: 88). If, however, we look at it from its extreme right-hand edge we can see that what was enigmatic due to distorting geometrical projection is a skull. 'All this shows that at the very heart of the period in which the subject emerged and geometral optics was an object of research, Holbein makes visible for us here something that is simply the subject as annihilated', commented Lacan, 'annihilated in the form that is, strictly speaking, the image embodiment of the *minus-phi* [(−?)] of castration, which for us, centres the whole organization of the desires through the framework of the fundamental drives' (Lacan, 1979[1973]: 88–9).

'This picture is', said Lacan, 'simply what any picture is, a trap for the gaze' (Lacan, 1979[1973]: 89). We lose ourselves in being seduced into identifying with what artists impose on us, and make us see in their art. 'In Holbein's picture', emphasized Lacan, 'we are literally called into the picture, and represented as caught'. We are represented as nothing. 'It reflects our own nothingness in the figure of the death's head' (Lacan, 1979[1973]: 92). The same is true of other paintings, and also of mirrors too; in so far as identifying with the images they reflect and impose on us we thereby disappear in oneness with what is not us. Something similar occurs, arguably, if we go along with the invitation of the figure in Caravaggio's painting, *St John the Baptist with a Ram*, to identify with we know not what. 'Join me', St. John seems to say, 'although where I am is somewhere between two realms of being, between my physical, individuated existence and my being as a disseminated connectedness throughout the universe', comment the art historians, Bersani and Dutoit. This 'between-ness', they point out, is 'concretely figured in the painting by a casual, poignant and haunting intimacy between two species' – human and animal, boy and ram (Bersani and Dutoit, 1998: 82).

Carvaggio's paintings nicely highlight and illustrate Laplanche's account of the social formation of our identities by messages imposed and implanted in us by others. Having previously written with Pontalis about the mediation by others of socially given imagery in shaping our identities, specifically the meanings and signifiers and fantasies constituting the unconscious (Laplanche and Pontalis, 1968), Laplanche writes of ways in which those who first look after us as infants seduce us into identifying with their repressed, and therefore unconscious, 'enigmatic traumatizing messages' (Laplanche, 1999: 165). The work of the analyst accordingly involves enabling the analysand to become conscious of these messages as they are manifested in the analysand's mistaken transference identification of them with the figure of the analyst and their work together. The analyst's task is to discern and put this mistaken identification into words. This depends, argues Laplanche, on the analyst operating as a quasi-mirror. We can illustrate this using the following diagram borrowed by Lacan from a 1934 book, *Optique et Photométrie dites géométriques*, by Henri Bouasse (Lacan, 2006a[1960]: 565). If we represent the analyst by the vertical mirror 'A', and the unconscious meaning or fantasy in the analysand, '$', by the vase containing the flowers on the right-hand side of the diagram, then this can only become conscious in $ by virtue of the flowers and the inverted vase on the left-hand side of the diagram being inverted and brought together by the convex mirror, 'xy', as reflected and mediated by the analyst as mirror, 'A'.

The analytic situation – like the actress, Duflos, in the case of Marguerite – seduces the analysand into mistakenly identifying their more or less unconscious fantasy images, meanings, and intentions with the analyst. The latter's ability to discern and put these meanings or signifiers into words depends on analysts following Lacan's prescription that, as he put it, 'we

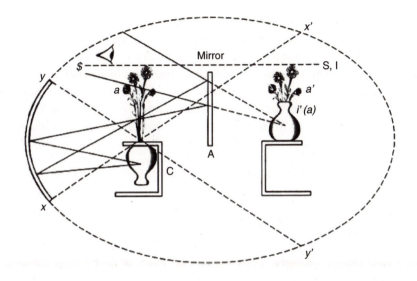

avoid all expression of personal taste, we conceal whatever might betray them, we become depersonalized, and try to represent for the other an ideal of impassability'. Or so he claimed. The slightest pretext, he said, is enough to arouse the analysand's aggressive intent, thereby re-actualizing the unconscious meanings and fantasies bringing them into analysis. These are revealed only to the extent that the analyst becomes 'as devoid as possible of individual characteristics', he maintained, and 'offers the subject the pure mirror of a smooth surface' (Lacan, 2006a[1948]: 87, 89). These meanings, fantasies, and images are first imposed on and determined in us by others mediating the patriarchal social order, the 'Other' with a big 'O', into which we are born and live. It is through analysis inviting the analysand into mistakenly identifying their unconscious fantasies and meanings with their image of the analyst and their work together, and through the analyst putting this into words, that the analysand discovers who, said Lacan, 'he is truly addressing, without knowing it' (Lacan, 1988[1954–55]: 246). But surely, as I indicated at the outset, although 'the given and inherited circumstances with which [we] are directly confronted' (Marx, 1973[1852]: 146) impose themselves in shaping our identity, we are also makers of our own histories, identities, and subjectivities. How can psy-art illuminate this?

Re-imagining subjectivity

To answer this question we might do well, I suggest, to replace Lacan's psy-art account of the imposition of identities on us by others as mediators of the patriarchal social order in which we live with an account of the re-imagining of subjectivity based in developments in psychoanalysis from Freud to today. Despite his celebrated 'return' to Freud, Lacan overlooked one aspect of Freud's (e.g., 1901) method, namely his suggestion that, where necessary, the analyst might usefully supplement the analysand's free associations to their symptoms and dreams with their already existing knowledge of dream-symbolism. Jung immensely expanded this suggestion with his techniques of amplification, personification, individuation, and active imagination in which the analyst supplements and thereby enables the analysand to become conscious of their unconscious subjectivity through the analyst linking the imagery of the analysand's fantasies and dreams with their knowledge of archetypes gleaned from cultural, religious, and philosophical systems of meaning bequeathed us by our ancestors.

Influenced perhaps by Jung's as well as by Freud's insights, and also by his paediatric clinical practice in which he saw mothers and babies together, Winnicott argued, in effect, that subjective imagery begins with the baby's readiness to imagine and hallucinate meeting the mother's readiness to give it the breast, this giving shape and form to its imagination in terms of details of what is actually available. Soon after, Bion, on the basis of working with analysands who complained of their inability to imagine and dream, speculated that what we might now call our capacity to realize our subjective experience in imaginative shape and form depends on our mothers transforming into meaningful responses the impressions made on them by our self-sensations as infants through the preconceptions and fantasies these impressions evoke in them. Armed with these developments in psychoanalytic theory, we can think of the birth of subjectivity in infants an effect of the baby's pre-figurative or precursory signs of meaning being elaborated in terms of the 'phantasies' or 'signifiers' (to use Klein's and Lacan's terminology) they evoke in the mother. (For further details of these developments, from Freud through Bion, see Sayers n.d.)

Understood in these terms, the psychoanalytic work of enabling analysands to recover subjective meanings unconsciously fixated and repressed into the unconscious, or projected and identified with others, lies in analysts supplementing the manifestations of these meanings in the impressions of what the analysand does and says in analysis with the images, fantasies, and symbols these impressions evoke in them. To highlight the coming together of the two worlds of self and other in this process of imagining and re-imagining the birth and re-birth of subjectivity in infants and others, as theorized by psychoanalysts from Freud to the present, we can use examples of paintings described by Kristeva.

She begins her first major article about psychoanalysis and art by quoting Freud's account of ways in which our subjective experience can become unconscious through our over-valuing symbols, words, and specifically thoughts severed from their embodied origin in talk with others. As a result, he said, 'thought proceeds in systems so far remote from the original perceptual residues that they have no longer retained anything of the qualities of those residues, and, in order to become conscious, need to be reinforced by new qualities' (Freud, 1915: 202). Colours readily serve as just such 'new qualities'. For, at least in painting, they are less rigidly restricted by abstract rules – such as those governing perspective – dictated by the community in which the artist works. 'In a painting, color is pulled from the unconscious into a symbolic order', argues Kristeva (1980a[1972]: 220). Hence Matisse's observation:

> When the means of expression have become so refined, so attenuated that their power of expression wears thin, it is necessary to return to the essential principles which made human language. They are, after all, the principles which "go back to the source," which relive, which give us life. Pictures which have become refinements, subtle gradations, dissolutions without energy, call for beautiful blues, reds, yellows – matters to stir the sensual depths in men. (Kristeva, 1980a[1972]: 221)

To illuminate the contrast between the two worlds of the artist's prefigurative signs of subjective experience and their realization through the prevailing systems of symbolization they evoke we can use Kristeva's account of the contrast between Giotto's frescoes, depicting familiar Bible stories, and his fresco of *The Last Judgement* (1306) on the end wall of the Arena Chapel in Padua, of which she writes, 'the contours of the characters are blurred, some colors disappear, others weaken, and still others darken: phosphorescent blue, black, dark red' (Kristeva, 1980a[1972]: 213). By contrast, Giotto depicts in clear shapes and forms scenes of life and death on the chapel's side walls – '*The Lamentation*', for instance – by using Christian symbols and figures, enlivened by his radical use of colour which, says Kristeva, 'tears these figures away from the wall's plane, giving them a depth related to, but also distinct from, a search for perspective ... masses of color become spherical through their own self-differentiation; set within an angular space of blocks and squares, they serve as transition between clashing surfaces'. She also illustrates the point with side wall frescoes of *The Annunciation to Anna*, *The Meeting at the Golden Gate*, and *The Betrothal of the Virgin*. 'Colour thus succeeds in shaping a space of conflicts', she says of these frescoes, 'a space of noncentered, unbordered and unfixed transitions, but a space turned inward' (Kristeva, 1980a[1972]: 226, 230).

Other examples of artists realizing precursory signs of subjective meaning through using the socially-given symbolic systems and language of art of their day include Giovanni Bellini. Whether or not he consciously intended it, Bellini evidently used the Byzantine and Roman Catholic Christian symbolism and art of the Venice in which he lived to realize in his art his more or less unconscious subjective fantasies about mothering. Examples include the aggressive hands of the Virgin Mary grasping at the infant Jesus depicted in his *Madonna and Child* painting, now in Amsterdam. It shows, says Kristeva, 'a shiver of anguish and fear in the child's hand, which grips the mother's thumb'. We can also see something of Bellini's fantasies about mothering in his *Madonna and Child* painting in Bergamo, in which the mother's 'aggressive hands', as described by Kristeva, 'prod the stomach and penis of the frightened baby'. After he became a father, however, his fantasies about mothering seem to have changed as is evident in their seeming realization in his *Madonna and Child* painting, now in São Paolo, in which, Kristeva observes, 'eluding the hands of the henceforth weary mother, he [the baby] grabs her by the neck as if to strangle her' (Kristeva, 1980b[1975]: 254, 260).

Kristeva adds to this example the realization by Piero della Francesca of more or less unconscious fantasies about mothering in terms of social conflicts regarding the use of the symbolism of Mariolotry. 'Mary's function as guardian of power, later checked when the Church became wary of it', Kristeva reports, 'nevertheless persisted in popular and pictorial representation, witness Piero della Francesca's impressive painting, *Madonna della Misericordia*, which was disavowed by Catholic authorities at the time' (Kristeva, 1987a[1976]: 244). The realization of subjective fantasy through the use of socially-given, albeit conflict-ridden, systems of symbolism and meaning is also evident in Piero's *Nativity* which, says Kristeva, 'replaces the high spirituality that assimilated the Virgin to Christ with an earthly conception of a wholly human mother' (Kristeva, 1987a[1976]: 246).

But what about the seeming death of meaning and animated subjectivity occurring in melancholia? Freud argued, in a sense, that this collapse is due to the melancholic evading of the task of facing and grieving the loss of those they hate as well as love by identifying with them as ideal figures in their ego. Healing the melancholic collapse of subjective life and meaning involved in thus falsely identifying with what is lost and gone entails grieving their absence. It entails doing what Freud called 'the work of mourning' (Freud, 1917: 245). Winnicott added, in effect, that this entails the analyst subjectively knowing their own capacity for depression so as to enable the analysand to have the image needed to reanimate this capacity in themselves. 'The depressed patient requires of his analyst the understanding that the analyst's work is to some extent his effort to cope with his own (the analyst's) depression', he maintained, 'or shall I say guilt and grief resultant from the destructive elements in his own (the analyst's) love … [he] needs his analyst to be able to see the analyst's un-displaced and co-incident love and hate of him' (Winnicott, 1958[1945]: 146–7).

Similarly, we could argue, artists, in realizing their subjective feelings in painting through using, even if only to rebel against, the conventions and language of art of their time, enable us to see and re-imagine what we are otherwise unconscious of. An example from the Northern renaissance is Holbein's painting, *The Dead Christ in the Tomb* (1521). 'It is true, it is the face of a man who has only just been taken from the cross – that is, still retaining a great deal of warmth and life', wrote Dostoyevsky, in describing this paintings impact on his fictional character, Ippolit, 'rigor mortis had not yet set in, so that there is still a look of suffering on the face of the dead man, as though he were still feeling it' (Dostoyevsky, 1868–9: 446). Holbein conveys this by looking and making us look at what is dead not as a symbol, as in the skull of his 1533 painting, *The Ambassadors*, detailed by Lacan. In *The Dead Christ* he makes us see the subjective experience of death realized in the flesh and blood of a body like ours. He does this by showing us the dead body of Christ 'stretched out alone', says Kristeva, without any mourners to offset the subjective isolation of death as in Mantegna's painting, *The Dead Christ* (c.1470–80). Isolation is further conveyed by Holbein designing the painting to be placed in a recess above those looking at it. The subjective experience of death is further realized by Holbein depicting Christ's 'head bent backwards, the contortion of the right hand bearing the stigmata, the position of the feet', notes Kristeva, 'the whole being bonded by means of a dark palette of grays, greens, and browns'. We are also drawn into Christ's suffering by the body's hair and hand falling over the base holding it, 'as if they might slide over toward us', she adds, and by Holbein using as a model an ordinary person, probably a corpse recovered from the Rhine (Kristeva, 1989a[1987]: 113, 114).

While Holbein's *Dead Christ* realizes in paint the subjective experience of facing death by using the Christian symbolism of his time, other artists realize other experiences through using classical symbolism and mythology. Examples include the use by artists of the classical myth of Medusa to realize the prevalent misogynist horror of women's sexuality, not least as embodying men's fear of castration. 'Ferenczi', wrote Freud approvingly, 'traced back the mythological symbol of horror – Medusa's head – to the impression of the female genitals devoid of a penis' (Freud, 1923: 144). Or we could see Medusa, as Kristeva sees the seventeenth century drawing, *Tête de Méduse*, from the studio of Giacinto Calandrucci in the Louvre, as the realized image of the 'teeth-filled primitive mother of that archaic undifferentiated state in which there is neither subject nor object, nothing but the gluey and viscous stuff of abjection' (Kristeva, 1998: 37).

Benvenuto Cellini's statue, *Perseus with the head of Medusa* (1545–54), can be seen as a realization of subjective triumph over woman as enveloping mother. Perseus is depicted in this statue with his phallic sword in one hand, his other hand holding Medusa's head aloft as he treads down her decapitated, writhing corpse. One mirrors the other, 'lying-standing, severed-erect, man-woman, young-old', writes Kristeva, 'more masterful than other representations of the Medusa myth, Benvenuto Cellini's *Perseus* shows us that it is in the two-way mirror that the triumph over the mother lodges' (Kristeva, 1998: 41). To this she adds Poussin's drawing, *The Birth of Coral* (1630s), in the Royal Library, Windsor, showing us the transformation of the beheaded Medusa's slimy, serpentine tresses into coral, as metaphor of the transformation of fluid subjective semiotic signs into the realized meaning conveyed by dried and hard paint in painting. 'Medusa has to be beheaded for it [subjective signs of meaning] to take form', Kristeva comments, 'for menacing lack of form to become the visible coral, for what is slimy-soft-menacing-invisible to take shape' (Kristeva, 1998: 40).

But womanhood does not only evoke horror. It also evokes sex, joy, and pleasure. The subjective marks or semiotic signs of this can also be realized, as other aspects of our subjectivity can be re-imagined and thus realized, through the artist's use of prevailing, socially-given systems of symbolism and meaning. An example here is Georgia O'Keeffe. Telling Sherwood Anderson what she sought to realize in her paintings, she wrote, with rebellious or scant regard for orthodox grammar and punctuation:

> I feel that a real living form is the natural result of the individuals effort to create the living thing out of the adventure of his spirit into the unknown – where it has experienced something – felt something – it has not understood – and from that experience comes the desire to make the unknown – known – By unknown – I mean the thing that means so much to the person that he wants to put it down – clarify something he feels but does not clearly understand – something he partially knows why – sometimes he doesn't – sometimes it is all working in the dark – but a working that must be done – Making the unknown – known – in terms of ones medium is all absorbing. (O'Keeffe, 1987a[1923?]: 174)

O'Keeffe contrasted her art – gearing it to realizing her feminine subjectivity – to that of her photographer lover, later her husband, Alfred Stieglitz. 'My work this year is very much on the ground – There will be only two abstract things – or three at the most – all the rest is objective – as objective as I can make it', she told Anderson. 'He has done with the sky something similar to what I had done with color before – as he says – proving my case – He has done consciously something that I did mostly unconsciously' (O'Keeffe, 1987b[1924]: 176). In doing this she used the desert landscapes near where she lived in New Mexico, just as Salvador Dali and other surrealists had used deserts in their dream-like paintings. In using their language of art she realized her feminine subjectivity in paintings revealing, asks Kristeva, 'an oneiric world: dream landscapes? volcanic craters? crust of earth tormented in canyons? or, more prosaically and intimately, burning membranes of feminine hollows, feminine sexuality, seen close up, enlarged, leaf-like sensitive folds on folds?' (Kristeva, 1989b: 12). She dubs O'Keeffe a high priestess of colour and female eroticism. She invites us into her paintings as in the following example

Let us then see *Black Iris III* [1926] ... You see "the humid entrance to the obscure val-
ley," as the Chinese thinker puts it? Georgia O'Keeffe is the painter of feminine eroticism: present, blinding, but invisible under its natural and offered appearance; no
transgression, no perversion – the pleasure is permanent, continual flourishing which
dilutes itself in appeasement, neutrality, quietism. Not to be seen with coldness, but simply with neutral and interiorized distance which knows to wait its instant of flourishing.
Passion filtered by ebbing. (Kristeva, 1989b: 13)

In thus realizing her feminine subjectivity by using the sexual licence and
language of the surrealist art of her time, O'Keeffe's paintings are in striking contrast to those who abject any such experience.

Examples of just such abjection include Freud's 5-year-old patient, Little
Hans, who, horrified on seeing his mother's blood just after she had given
birth to his sister, Hanna, and, having been threatened with castration by his
mother for touching his penis, displaced the horror by parroting men's words,
the words he overheard his friend's father saying to her, 'Don't put your fin-
ger to the white horse or it'll bite you' (Freud, 1909: 29). Soon after he
became agoraphobic. 'I am afraid of horses', he told his mother. 'I am afraid of
being bitten' (Kristeva, 1982[1980]: 39). In thus displacing subjective experience into a phobic or obsessive echoing of the words of fathers and others
as mediators of patriarchal society, we can become subjectively lifeless, this
leading to the analysand's plea to the analyst, says Kristeva, 'I displace, therefore you must associate and condense for me'. In such cases the analysand asks
the analyst, she adds, 'to build up an imagination for him ... to be saved like
Moses, to be born like Christ', for 'a rebirth that ... will result from a speech
that is recovered, rediscovered as belonging to him' (Kristeva, 1980: 50).

This entails the analyst formulating constructions and interpretations
which are 'true', Kristeva claims, to the extent that they trigger associations
which can help bring about the re-birth of the analysand's subjectivity
(Kristeva, 1986[1982]: 309). Unlike Freud who argued that the analyst's
attitude should be one of 'emotional coldness' (Freud, 1912: 115), unlike
Laplanche (1999) who, following Lacan (e.g. 1948), emphasizes that analysts should efface themselves to maximize their function as mirrors of the
unconscious meanings implanted in them by others as mediators of the
social order in which we live, Kristeva urges her fellow-analysts to shed this
'benevolent neutrality' and 'indifference'. For it is 'by implicating ourselves',
she explains to her fellow-analysts, '[that] we bring to life, to meaning, the
dead discourses of patients which summon us' (Kristeva, 1986[1982]: 319).

Winnicott wrote of psychoanalysis, or at least psychotherapy, as taking
place 'in the overlap of the two areas, that of the patient and that of the
therapist' (Winnicott, 1974[1971]: 63). Just as art arguably involves the
overlap of the artist's subjective experience with the social conventions and
language of art of their day, Kristeva writes that analysis involves 'a broad-
ening of the rhetorical or sublimatory capacities of the analyst and the

analysand' (Kristeva, 2000[1996]: 61), 'interaction between the two imaginaries' (Kristeva, 2001[2000]: 148). She illustrates the point with the case of an artist patient, Didier, obsessed with masturbating and painting in whom the subjective *élan vital* seemed lifeless and dead. His talk in analysis was mechanical, unanimated, dull. Kristeva conveys this by telling in the third person, as follows, one of his dreams:

> Didier is leaning out of a window in his family home. He feels ill, or someone pushes him. He falls into an open space. He experiences a moment of intense anxiety that makes him scream, though he is unsure about this. In any event, the dream is a silent one. He suddenly finds himself in front of mirror and sees a reflection of his sister's face. This agitates him quite a bit and makes him wake up. (Kristeva, 1995[1993]: 15)

As for his art, he described it in such technical detail Kristeva could not imagine it. So she asked him to bring examples for her to see. '[He] worked with various entities – docile objects that were fractured, cracked, and broken up as if slaughtered', she tells us, 'not a single face espoused the fragments of these mutilated persons, who were primarily female, and who were shown to have a derisive nature and an unsuspected ugliness' (Kristeva, 1995[1993]: 19).

He had regretted his mother's death only because it deprived him of her as spectator of his art. She was, said Kristeva, 'kind enough to accept her son's artwork even though she never showed any reaction to it'. By contrast Kristeva gave words to the images of woman-hating mayhem that it evoked in her. Writing of her adding to the images of his art the images it prompted in her, she says, 'I dissociated myself from the maternal position and performed a veritable "phantasmatic graft" on this patient' (Kristeva, 1995[1993]: 19). This led to his variously accepting, adjusting, altering, or rejecting her resulting interpretations, with this involving him becoming more animated in free associating and telling her his dreams, including one in which he imagined he was both his parents making love with each other. He also told her dreams in which he imagined extreme violence towards his father for having passively let his mother dress him as a girl when he was a child. He worried lest Kristeva might be similarly passive, or reduce him to passivity. At the end of his analysis he made a picture of her from a photo in which she was holding a cigarette. But he had cut out the cigarette. 'Nothing between the hands, no penis, no fetish', he said. 'I did well, didn't I?' (Kristeva, 1995[1993]: 19).

Conclusion

Tradition can weigh as fetish or nightmare on the minds of the living, to quote Marx again. Its impositions can make us vulnerable to trauma, defined by Freud as 'any excitations from outside which are powerful enough to break through the protective shield' (Freud, 1920: 29). Arguably this shield of the ego is formed and fixed by the traditions, including its fetishes, which first constrain the ego in bringing it into being. Louise Bourgeois's mixed-media art-work, *Sublimation* (2002), provides an illuminating, psychoanalytically-minded illustration of the traumas to which the ego is vulnerable. *Sublimation* tells a story, in pictures and words, beginning with people working silently in a foundry, concentrating on what they are doing, when suddenly, says Bourgeois, 'there was a clash of voices' resulting from a woman violently attacking her husband. Bourgeois shows us, with a pair of eyes, their 14-year-old son seeing the chaos. His parents go on fighting. He does not disintegrate, says Bourgeois. Instead he gets a broom and starts cleaning. For Bourgeois this is the trauma. It breaches the conventions of everyday working life. She starts crying at his controlling the chaos thus. This calls for 'symbolic action', she says. Faced with chaos disrupting convention, one can mend one's ego, identity, or subjective sense of oneself by becoming a perfectionist, by writing a story, by working on the house, or, Bourgeois adds, by beginning work, as she does, on making a sculpture. 'We are talking about sublimation', she concludes, 'and the gift of sublimation' (see also Jones, 2005).

In this chapter I have used psychoanalysis and art – or 'psy-art' – to contrast two accounts of the formation of the ego, identity, and subjectivity: first, I used Lacan's account of the ego as the mistaken effect of identifying with the images imposed on us by others in mediating to us the patriarchal social order in which we live; second, I used developments in psychoanalysis from Freud to the present, as well as Kristeva's accounts of various art from Giotto through to O'Keeffe, to which I have just added the recent example of Louise Bourgeois's *Sublimation*, to highlight the generation and regeneration of subjectivity (or the 'life of the mind', as Hannah Arendt (1978[1971]) called it) through the transformation into meaning of prefigurative signs of subjectivity *via* their being completed with images and fantasies evoked in others – mothers, analysts, artists, and others – informed not least by the social conventions and languages of representation prevailing in the culture in which we live. This is what I mean by psy-art as a way of re-imagining identity or subjectivity in place of the psy-art theory of imposed identities that with Lacan became something of a dogma in academic theorizing about identity. By contrast re-imagining identity or subjectivity in the psy-art terms I used in the second section of this chapter tells us much more about making our own histories, albeit in circumstances not of our own choosing, with which I began.

References

Arendt, H. (1978[1971]) *The Life of the Mind*. London: Secker & Warburg.
Benvenuto, B. and Kennedy, R. (1986) *The Works of Jacques Lacan*. London: Free Association Books.

Bersani, L. and Dutoit, U. (1998) *Caravaggio's Secrets*. Cambridge, MA: MIT.

Descharnes, R. (1962) *The World of Salvador Dali*. London: Macmillan.

Dostoyevsky, F. (1868–9) *The Idiot*. Harmondsworth: Penguin.

Freud, S. (1901) 'On Dreams'. *SE5*: 633–86.

Freud, S. (1909) 'Analysis of a phobia in a five-year-old boy'. *SE10*: 5–147.

Freud, S. (1912) 'Recommendations to physicians practising psycho-analysis'. *SE12*: 109–20.

Freud, S. (1914) 'On narcissism: An introduction'. *SE14*: 73–102.

Freud, S. (1915) 'The unconscious'. *SE14*: 166–215.

Freud, S. (1917) 'Mourning and melancholia'. *SE14*: 243–58.

Freud, S. (1920) 'Beyond the Pleasure Principle'. *SE18*: 7–64.

Freud, S. (1922) 'Some neurotic mechanisms in jealousy, paranoia and homosexuality'. *SE18*: 221–32.

Freud, S. (1923) 'The infantile genital organization'. *SE19*: 141–5.

Jones, J. (2005) 'Louise Bourgeois', *The Guardian*, 31 January.

Klein, M. (1975a[1928]) 'Early stages of the Oedipus complex', in *Love, Guilt & Reparation*. London: Hogarth, pp. 186–98.

Klein, M. (1975b[1945]) 'The Oedipus complex in the light of early anxieties', *Love, Guilt & Reparation*, pp. 370–419.

Kristeva, J. (1980a[1972]) 'Giotto's joy', in L. S. Roudiez (ed.), *Desire in Language*. New York: Columbia University Press, pp. 210–36.

Kristeva, J. (1980b[1975]) 'Motherhood according to Bellini', in L. S. Roudiez (ed.), *Desire in Language*. New York: Columbia University Press, pp. 237–70.

Kristeva, J. (1982[1980]) *Powers of Horror*. New York: Columbia University Press.

Kristeva, J. (1986[1982]) 'Psychoanalysis and the polis', in T. Moi (ed.), *The Kristeva Reader*. Oxford: Blackwell, pp. 301–19.

Kristeva, J. (1987a[1976]) *Stabat mater. Tales of Love*. New York: Columbia University Press, pp. 234–63.

Kristeva, J. (1989a[1987]) *Black Sun*. New York: Columbia University Press.

Kristeva, J. (1989b) 'Georgia O'Keeffe: la forme inévitable', in S. Greenough (ed.), *Georgia O'Keeffe*. Paris: Adam Biro, pp. 7–16.

Kristeva, J. (1995[1993]) *New Maladies of the Soul*. New York: Columbia University Press.

Kristeva, J. (1998) *Visions capitales*. Paris: Editions de la Réunion des musées nationaux.

Kristeva, J. (2001a[1996]) *The Sense and Non-Sense of Revolt: The Powers and Limits of Psychoanalysis*. New York: Columbia University Press.

Kristeva, J. (2000[1999]) *Hannah Arendt*. New York: Columbia University Press.

Kristeva, J. (2001 [2000]) *Melanie Klein*. New York: Columbia University Press.

Lacan, J. (2006a[1948]) Aggressiveness in psychoanalysis. *Écrits*. New York: Norton, pp. 82–101.

Lacan, J. (2006b[1949]) 'The mirror stage as formative of the *I* function as revealed in psychoanalytic experience', New York: Norton, pp. 75–81.

Lacan, J. (1953) 'Some reflections on the ego', *International Journal of Psycho-Analysis*, 34 (1): 11–17.

Lacan, J. (1979[1973]) *Four Fundamental Concepts of Psycho-Analysis*. London: Penguin.

Lacan, J. (1988[1954–55]) *The Seminar of Jacques Lacan, Book II*. Cambridge: Cambridge University Press.

Lacan, J. (2006a[1955–56]) 'On a question prior to any possible treatment of psychosis', *Écrits*, pp. 445–88.

Lacan, J. (2006b[1958a]) 'The signification of the phallus', *Écrits*, pp. 575–84.

Lacan, J. (2006c[1958b]) 'The direction of the treatment and the principles of its power', *Écrits*, pp. 489–542.

Lacan, J. (2006d[1960]) 'Remarks on Daniel Lagache's presentation: "Psychoanalysis and Personality Structure"', *Écrits*, pp. 543–74.

Laplanche, J. (1999) *Essays on Otherness*. London: Routledge.

Laplanche, J. and Pontalis, J.-B. (1968) 'Fantasy and the origins of sexuality', *International Journal of Psycho-Analysis*, 49 (1): 1–18.

Lippard, L. (1970) *Surrealists on Art*. Englewood Cliffs, NJ: Prentice-Hall.

Martínez-Herrera, J., Alcántara, G., García-Fernández, L. (2003) 'Dalí (1904–1989): psychoanalysis and pictorial surrealism', *American Journal of Psychiatry*, 160 (5): 855–6.

Marx, K. (1973[1852]) 'The Eighteenth Brumaire of Louis Bonaparte', in D. Ferenbach (ed.), *Surveys from Exile*. Harmondsworth: Penguin, pp. 146–249.

O'Keeffe, G. (1987a[1923?]) 'Letter to Sherwood Anderson', in S. Greenough (ed.), *Georgia O'Keeffe: Life and Letters*. New York: Little Brown, pp. 173–5.

O'Keeffe, G. (1987b[1924]) *Letter to Sherwood Anderson*. New York: Little Brown, pp. 175–6.

Roudinesco, E. (1997[1993]) *Jacques Lacan*. New York: Columbia University Press.

Sayers, J. (n.d.) *Psy-Art: Re-Imagining Psychoanalysis*. Available as e-mail attachment.

Spector, J. (1997) *Surrealist Art & Writing 1919/39*. Cambridge: Cambridge University Press.

Winnicott, D. W. (1958[1945]) 'Primitive emotional development', *Collected Papers*. London: Tavistock, pp. 145–56.

Winnicott, D. W. (1974[1971]) *Playing and Reality*. Harmondsworth: Penguin.

Index

consumerism 9–10, 42–3, 55, 56, 92–3, 94
    see also mass media/communications
        technology
containment 170, 188–9, 191–2
Cornell, D. 70, 75, 127–8, 136
    and Thurschwell, A. 76, 77
Crimp, Douglas 147, 148–51, 153–4
critical theory 49–50, 120–1, 123
    Frankfurt School 39–40, 42
    see also specific theorists
Crompton, Rosemary 90
cultural transformation, politics of 106–11
Cunningham, M. 17, 19

Dali, Salvador 198–9, 202, 203
de-routinization of the mundane 18–21
The Dead Christ in the Tomb (Holbein) 209
decisions/choice 7, 8, 17, 18, 19–20, 49
'disembeddedness' 5, 6
displaced subject 158–61
do-it-yourself biography (DIY identities)
    15, 20, 29–30, 48, 49, 58–9
Donzelot, J. 175
Dostoyevsky, Fyodor 209
'double consciousness' 65–6
'double image' 198–9
dream interpretation/symbolism 198, 200,
    202, 206, 212
Durkheim, E. 20, 52, 99

economic inequalities 62–3
education, women's 87–9
emotional costs of isolated privatism 51–6
employment 57
    women's 90–1, 92–5
Eng, D.
    and Han, S. 146–7
    and Kazanjian, D. 146
enigmatic messages 126–7, 163, 204
Enzensberger, Hans Magnus 27–8, 30
Erikson, E.H. 7, 142, 158
ethical feminism 70–1
ethnicity 32–3, 141
    and melancholia 145–6, 146–7
    women's re-identification 75

fantasy
    'acting out' 183–4
    collective 190, 191–2
    see also imagination; primary repression
father(s)
    containment role 189
    imaginary (phallus) 125–6, 127–8, 133–4,
        135–6, 203
    see also Oedipal identity/pre-Oedipal
        phase; patriarchies

fear see anxiety/fear
feminine imaginary 74, 75
feminine subjectivity and eroticism 210–11
feminist perspective 65–6, 70–8
    gender relations 45
    post-feminist masquerade 82–6, 93–4
    psychoanalytic theory 127–8, 133–4
    sites of capacity 86–91
Ferenczi, S. 187
Ferguson, E. 172, 180, 181, 183, 184
Foucault, Michel 79
Francesca, Piero della 208
Frankfurt School 39–40, 42
Fraser, Nancy 90–1
'free agents' 102–3
freedom
    fear of 20
    'precarious freedoms' 13, 14, 19
    women's 80
    see also liberty
Freud, Sigmund 99, 121–2, 123, 125, 127,
    130, 131, 132, 135, 142–3, 145, 147,
    148–50, 152–3, 154, 161, 162, 173,
    186, 187, 198, 202, 206–7, 208, 209,
    211, 212–13
Friedman, J. 10–11

Garland, David 175, 176, 187
gender relations 45
gendered and heterosexual identity 153
German Civil Code 23
German Federal Republic 27–8, 31
Germany
    National Socialist/Nazi era 23–4, 49–51,
        200–1
    post-war society 144–5, 146
Gillan, Audrey 180, 181–2, 183, 185, 188
Gillis, J.R. 141
Gilroy, Paul 145–6
Giotto (Renaissance artist) 207
globalization 8–9, 10–11, 45–7, 48–9
    and new individualism 58–63
    and technology 159

Habermas, Jürgen 40–1, 42, 50–1
Hill, D. 172, 185
Hirschman, Albert 100–1, 102, 103, 116
Hirst, Paul and Woolley, Penny 102–3, 115
Hobbes, Thomas 103–4, 106–15, 116–17
Hobsbaum, E. 10
Hochschild, Arlie 45
Hoggett, P. 170, 171
Holbein, Hans 203–4, 209
Holloway, W. and Jefferson, T. 174
Holmes, S. 101, 102, 103, 104, 105,
    107, 117

Index

Index